tramps like us

tramps like us

Music & Meaning among Springsteen Fans

DANIEL CAVICCHI

New York   Oxford

Oxford University Press

1998

Oxford University Press

Oxford   New York

Athens   Auckland   Bangkok   Bogotá   Buenos Aires   Calcutta
Cape Town   Chennai   Dar es Salaam   Delhi   Florence   Hong Kong   Istanbul
Karachi   Kuala Lumpur   Madrid   Melbourne   Mexico City   Mumbai
Nairobi   Paris   São Paulo   Singapore   Taipei   Tokyo   Toronto   Warsaw

and associated companies in
Berlin   Ibadan

Published by Oxford University Press, Inc.
198 Madison Avenue, New York, New York 10016

Oxford is a registered trademark of Oxford University Press.

Library of Congress Cataloging-in-Publication Data
Cavicchi, Daniel.
    Tramps like us : music and meaning among
Springsteen fans / Daniel   Cavicchi.
        p.   cm.
    Includes bibliographical references and index.
    ISBN 0-19-511833-2; 0-19-512564-9 (pbk.)
        1. Rock music fans.   2. Springsteen, Bruce—Appreciation.
    I. Title.
    ML3534.C38   1998
    782.42166'092—dc21   97-32610

The author gratefully acknowledges permission to reprint lyrics from the following songs by
Bruce Springsteen: "Factory" © 1978 by Bruce Springsteen (ASCAP); "Trapped" © 1985 by
Bruce Springsteen (ASCAP); "Brilliant Disguise" © 1987 by Bruce Springsteen (ASCAP);
"Better Days" and "My Beautiful Reward" © 1992 by Bruce Springsteen (ASCAP). All rights
reserved.

9 8 7 6 5 4 3 2 1

Printed in the United States of America
on acid-free paper

For Lynn and Noah

Preface

This is a study of music fandom, of the ways in which people form special, sustained attachments to musical performers or genres. In particular, my focus is on one of the most sustained and devoted groups of fans in contemporary popular music, Bruce Springsteen fans, and on their activities and experiences—what they do; how they talk about what they do; and, finally, why they do it. I use the word "they" hesitantly, for my knowledge of Springsteen fans is based not only on my ethnographic fieldwork with various Springsteen fans over a period of three years, but also, since I am a Springsteen fan, on my own experiences and interpretations. This work presents an "insider's narrative" of music fandom which, rather than relying on a distant, objective analysis of fans' public behavior, instead examines the intersection of others' experiences and my own. The text moves constantly back and forth between fans' stories and ideas about their experiences and my own stories, commentary, and analysis.

This book began as my Ph.D. dissertation in American Civilization at Brown University. I conducted the bulk of my fieldwork with Bruce Springsteen fans from spring 1993 to spring 1995, while I was a graduate student. There are few dissertations on music in the field of American civilization (or American studies, as it is known elsewhere) if only because people who are interested in studying music usually do so in music departments. But I learned early on that my interest in popular music and my reluctance to learn a symphonic instrument made me unwelcome at most American university music departments. Instead, I drifted into American studies, which, by encouraging a broad interdisciplinary study of the culture and history of a geographical area, allowed me the flexibility to study musical life as I pleased. This is not to say that I abandoned any notion of working in the field of music; I spent much of my time at Brown in the music department, taking courses on ethnomusicology, attending recitals and lectures, reading musicology journals, and teaching courses about American music. But at the same time, I was doing a lot of thinking about ideas from my other classes in anthropology, history, and literary studies. This book is clearly a product of my eclectic studies at Brown.

I also see this book as a continuation of the work I did as an interviewer and editor in the Music in Daily Life Project at the State University of New York at Buffalo, while I was a master's degree student in the late eighties. The project was a six-year-long investigation of the ways music worked in the day-to-day existence of ordinary people. Along with thirty or so other interviewers, I asked relatives, friends, and others the simple question, "What is music about for you?" and listened carefully to their answers. The project was the first one of its kind—no one had explored the ways in which ordinary people used and understood music in the United States before—and it opened my eyes to new ways of studying music based not on aesthetics and history but rather on ethnography and culture. In this book I have continued the exploration of music in daily life. Instead of talking to people in general about their musical experiences, I have focused on a particular group of people who have made participating in the world of popular music a central part of their lives.

Overall, I hope this book will find a place among the growing number of works about music audiences. I am still shocked when I go into major bookstores and find plenty of books about musical performers but none about music listeners. One can always find a biography of Beethoven but rarely an engaging account of what it was like to attend the performance of one of his symphonies. One can always find all sorts of analyses about the Beatles' lives and recordings but very little about all the people who used the music to get through the day, week after week, year after year. Indeed, the academic field of music seems to be one of the last of the arts disciplines in the humanities to experience a revolution akin to the rise of reader-response criticism in literary studies, where the prevailing paradigms about the importance of authorship and the structures of a work have been challenged by new concerns regarding how people use and undestand those works. In music, it is still the creation of music that reigns supreme; everyone is expected to be a musician or composer and be concerned with musicianship and composition.

In both the Music in Daily Life Project and my research with fans, the people to whom I spoke were often taken aback when I approached them; several were astounded that I would even be interested in their musical activities. Yet when they decided to tell me about music in their lives, they spoke with enthusiasm and clarity, recounting experiences that were rich in emotion, memory, and complexity, sharing with me whole realms of meaning about which no one in the modern university seemed to care. On the whole, I hope this work will further the idea that studying music must include the exploration of not only musical performances and performers but also those who are *performed to.* I hope it will show that we need more studies of audience in order to achieve a better understanding of the ways in which cultural production is useful and important, not only in abstract aesthetic terms like "truth" or "beauty" but also in everyday life, as a means of education, communication, pleasure, memory, identity, and community. I hope that this work will show that seriously engaging the cultural experiences and activities of a majority of people in modern society has value and can move scholarship into a better position for the purpose of aiding and intervening in the problems and concerns of those people.

Acknowledgments

Because I see this work as a collaboration with fellow Springsteen fans, I am wary about simply listing their names. The thoughts, words, and insights of the fans I met have shaped this entire book. Whenever I found myself mired in the frustratingly endless complexities of culture and identity, trying to make sense of theories and hypotheses and concepts, my solution was always the same: I would ask myself, "Well, what do the fans say?" And again and again, they led me out, provided a map, and strengthened my resolve. I will list the fans' names here as convention dictates, but I hope that readers will recognize how much such fans' participation contributed to the tenor and very existence of this work.

First, I would like to thank those who talked with me in extended and sometimes multiple interviews, as well as offered advice and commentary throughout the process of writing; I am indebted to their openness, friendship, and good conversation: Kirk Anderson, Alan Chitlik, Gene Chyzowych, Michael Condouris, Russ Curley, Zach Everson, Paul Fischer, Carrie Gabriel, Jackie Gillis, Timothy Henrion, Judi Johnson, Lowell Kern, Al Khorasani, Mary Krause, Andrew Laurence, Alan Levine, Louis Lucullo, Laurie McLain, David Merrill, David Mocko, John O'Brien, LeAnne Olderman, Roy Opochinski, Lisa Pantano, Eric Raskin, J. D. Rummel, Anna Selden, Monica Shareshian, Andrew Sirk, Monty Smith, Alan Stein, Amy Thom, Mark Van Atten, Linda Warner, Susan West, and Mary Beth Wilson.

In addition, many fans responded to an advertisement I placed in *Backstreets* asking for people to complete a questionnaire; many sent the questionnaires back with long, detailed letters and requests to be interviewed. Unfortunately, I did not have the time or the money to respond to everyone. Nevertheless, the responses were integral to my thinking in this book, and I hope, someday, to meet the people who gave them so generously. Thanks to Brent Albala, Kenneth

A. Baum, Michael Bournazian, Jeffery P. Butcher, Donna d'Amico, Dave from St. Catharines, Adam Dietz, Greg Dollak, Janet L. Fickeissen, Jerry Floyd, Bill Freeswick, Jami Gelfand, Melissa Gray, Scott Griffith, Leannah Harding, Terri Hopkins, Norma Infusino, Jersey Joe, Adam Kaye, Faith King, Barbara Kornexl, Mike Kruzel, Stuart Kohn, Alicè Long, Eric Lubitz, Ali Lux, Robert MacNeil, Gwen Tyra May, Bill Normyle, Carmen A. Palograto, Denise Pastor, Bruno Pelletier, Jon Poklop, Chris Riccardi, Mark Riendeau, Phil Robinson, Tony Solari, David Stamberg, Michael Stanford, Brenda Trump, Steve Venditti, Doreen Wood, and several others who preferred to remain anonymous.

Of course, this work has been significantly shaped by my mentors over the years. I wouldn't be writing about music at all if Charles Keil hadn't welcomed me to the American Studies Department at SUNY Buffalo in the late eighties; he was the first to teach me about ethnomusicology, ethnography, and the joys of participation, groove, and community. Jeff Titon introduced me to the history of ethnomusicological thought in a graduate seminar in the Department of Music at Brown University in the fall of 1990; his interdisciplinary approach to the study of music in the United States inspired me not to worry about disciplinary boundaries and led me to discover the place where anthropology, history, literature, and music intersect, and his advice and good humor have deeply affected the way I think about fieldwork, ethics, and knowing others. William Beeman, of Brown's Department of Anthropology, taught me all I know about performance theory and has guided my study of anthropology; his probing questions, stories, and occasional admonitions to "just do it" have been vital to my fieldwork and to the arguments I make in this book. Finally, Barton St. Armand, of Brown's Department of English, has been an important source of encouragement and support ever since he served as an advisor for my Ph.D. oral exam in the history of the book; his breadth of knowledge and keen eye have led me to places I would not have otherwise gone.

In 1993, while I was beginning fieldwork for this project, a group of graduate students in the Department of American Civilization at Brown decided to form a dissertation group; I was honored to have been able to share portions of this work with Crista Deluzio, Kristen Farmelant, Joanne Melish, and Mari Yoshihara. They pored over many of these chapters, enthusiastically discussed my topic and approach, and sometimes challenged my ideas. Their advice and friendship was immeasurable during the crucial initial stages of this book, and I owe them my gratitude.

I have delivered lectures based on the fieldwork for this book over the years; for their encouragement and debate, I am grateful to the students in my seminars on music and popular culture at Brown University and Rhode Island School of Design as well as to the participants of the Annual Conference of the New England American Studies Association in 1994, the musical community panel at the American Folklore Society Annual Meeting in 1996, and the Conference on

Music Fan Cultures at the Centre for Youth Media Studies at the University of Copenhagen, Denmark, in 1997.

Several anonymous readers for Oxford University Press read an earlier draft of this book; I would like to thank them for their constructive and insightful criticism. Soo Mee Kwon, my editor at Oxford University Press, also deserves much praise for her guidance, perceptive comments, and enthusiasm. And I am indebted to music editor Maribeth Payne and associate music editor Jonathan Weiner for their kind and expert assistance with administrative matters.

Finally, I would like to thank the friends, family, and colleagues who discussed this project with me at various stages and whose interested questions and comments led me to reevaluate my ideas and articulate my aims more clearly. In particular, a heartfelt thanks to my wife, not only the person who—along with Mary Krause—introduced me to Bruce fandom but also the person who endured several years of my queries, tangents, frustrations, sudden insights, abandoned theories, bouts of writer's block, moments of intellectual joy, late nights writing, and repeated demands like: "Listen to this paragraph and tell me what you think." She saw what I was trying to do even when I did not, and she consistently kept my eyes on the horizon and my feet on the ground. She deserves a long vacation.

Contents

tramps like us

Introduction

Studying Fandom

*L*ocating Fandom

Early in the morning of April 30, 1976, after playing a two-and-a-half hour concert in Memphis, Tennessee, Bruce Springsteen took a cab to Elvis Presley's Graceland Mansion and jumped the gate in an attempt to meet his boyhood idol. At the time Springsteen was a star; his album *Born to Run* (1975) was a hit, and he had been on the covers of both *Time* and *Newsweek*. But the guard who emerged from the bushes to remove the intruder didn't know him. "He thought I was just another crazy fan," Springsteen said. "Which I was" (Marsh 1979, 193).

Springsteen's identification with Elvis, even after becoming a national rock star, represents the extent to which fandom is basic to participation in rock-'n'roll. Fandom has always been part of rock'n'roll's myth, appeal, and strength. Over the years, hundreds of teenagers like Springsteen, stuck in dead-end towns without much hope for the future, have found meaning and escape by identifying with a rock performer. Especially today, when rock music has achieved massive popularity and established success, fandom has become a vital element of rock'n'roll culture. In the sixties and seventies, rock was the anthem of youth; now younger and older generations *share* the music. The music business used to market "teen idols" specifically to youth audiences; today, the business markets all sorts of music stars as a basic strategy, from securing magazine interviews to sponsoring syndicated radio shows that give people a chance to call their favorite musicians and ask questions. In addition to the hundreds of official fan clubs for music artists set up by their management and record companies, there are, at any given time, hundreds of unofficial clubs run by a few interested fans out of their homes (see Trinajstick 1993). Fanzines, newsletters, or computer networks exist for practically every star in the business, old and new, from Tony Bennett to Baby Face.[1]

3

While music fandom is most notably associated with rock music, it has long been a part of audience behavior for a variety of musical cultures. From opera fans who worship divas and scour flea markets for rare recordings to rap fans memorizing and performing rhymes from the latest songs, from polka fans who travel to distant polka parties in search of their favorite bands to punk rockers who publish 'zines about underground culture, fandom provides a ready framework with which to understand and use music. Traditionally, there have been few formal studies conducted about the nature of music audiences, but recent studies in the sociology of music have suggested that fandom is far more pervasive in contemporary musical life than anyone ever suspected. For instance, Ruth Finnegan (1989) has pointed out the importance of people's devotion to certain musical "worlds," in which they play in or follow a local musical group or listen to a certain musical genre, as a way to shape personal and communal identity. Susan D. Crafts, Daniel Cavicchi, Charles Keil, and other researchers in the Music in Daily Life Project at the State University of New York at Buffalo (1993) likewise have outlined ordinary people's deep and lasting attachments to various musical stars and genres, ranging from Lawrence Welk to punk, which they use to manage their emotions, sense of self, and social relationships with others.

Some scholars have traced the beginnings of music fandom to nineteenth-century tours of the United States by European opera and classical music performers, who were regularly mobbed by enthusiastic crowds and spawned the sale of various items—from boots to champagne—bearing their names (see Levine 1988, pp. 108–109). Others have located the emergence of fan behaviors like "fantasy" and "hysteria" in the tango, jitterbug, and other dance crazes of the early twentieth century (Vermorel and Vermorel 1989, p. 24). Still other scholars have situated fandom in the development of mass-produced music before and after World War II. Most notably, in the 1930s, cultural critic Theodor Adorno ([1941] 1990, pp. 311–313) identified two different types of popular music listeners with fanlike relationships toward music: the "rhythmically-obedient type," who participated in the "cult of the machine" and had enthusiasm for dancing; and the "emotional type," who sentimentally identified with characters in Tin Pan Alley songs. In the late forties, David Riesman ([1950] 1990) interviewed teenage popular music listeners on the south side of Chicago, identifying two groups: those who had an uncritical attitude toward mainstream culture and identified with music "personalities" and "hot jazz lovers" who were more rebellious and unconventional, using jazz in different ways to establish a specific, new, social identity.

In fact, while I focus on music fans in this book, "fan" is actually a much wider social category, referring to a mode of participation with a long history in a variety of cultural activities, including literature, sports, theater, film, and television. Some of the earliest fans were readers in eighteenth-century Europe who, with an enthusiastic interest in authors spawned by the advent of commercial publishing, began sending letters to them, making pilgrimages to actual places mentioned in their books, and developing intense identification with the characters and settings of their various stories (Darnton 1984; Bakhtin 1986, pp. 46–47; Braudy 1986, pp. 380–389). In the United States, the earliest examples of fans were "kranks," or the members of early fraternal baseball clubs in the mid-1800s who saw baseball games as central to their lives rather than a leisurely diversion and were utterly committed to their teams to the point of fighting and disrupting a game if things were not going their way (Riess 1980, pp. 13–47; Rader 1983, p. 122).

Fan behavior also arose in nineteenth-century American theater, where use of a "star system" to promote touring acting companies drew new audience members, particularly young women, who scandalized conservative male theater critics by caring more about the leading man than about the play (Auster 1984, p. 40; McConachie 1990). Such attitudes were even further elaborated in film-going before 1950, when Hollywood studios purposely promoted every aspect of stars' lives to attract audiences to films (Staiger 1991; Fowles 1992) and women formed cultures around the adulation of stars as a way to negotiate gender relations (Ewen 1980; Peiss 1986).

The differences between such fans are significant; each occurs in different historical moments and derives meaning from specific cultural contexts. However, they all do point to similar, broad social and economic factors which, together, set some limits about what fandom is and where it originated.

First, fandom is a phenomenon of public performance. Historians consistently talk about fandom with reference to the audiences for organized, public performances like sporting events, published literature, dramatic productions, cinematic productions, recorded music, and concerts. While this may seem obvious, it is important to understand that fandom is not generally attributed to other kinds of cultural behavior like religious devotion, intellectual study, or personal relations.

Second, fandom is a phenomenon of Western industrial capitalism since the late 1700s. Some historians claim that social changes created by capitalism introduced to performances new audience members who had different ideas about how to act and how to understand the event. Thus publishing, for instance, introduced new bourgeois classes into what was previously an elite literary culture, and increasing industrialization moved women out of the domestic sphere, into the public workplace, and into the previously male domains of theater and film. Other historians locate the origins of fandom in the developing technology of capitalism itself, in the ways in which mass production created new kinds of philosophical problems for understanding performance. Thus, for instance, mass publishing, because it quickly produced and disseminated facsimiles of an author's work, raised questions about an author's "reality" as well as the "reality" of his text; the microphone, because it favored a relaxed and more personal style of singing, opened up new ways of understanding and interpreting old songs.

On the whole, fandom is not an obscure and insignificant realm of culture. It deals with fundamental questions about who we are and how we understand ourselves and our relationships to others in this modern, mediated world.

*A*pproaches to Fandom

Unfortunately, fandom's origin in the reorganization of public performance by capitalism and technology has meant that fandom has often come to epitomize those changes, particularly for critics. For many people, fans represent the negative effects of modern media and are often stereotyped as unhealthy and dangerous. From the negative connotation of the word "groupie" to an episode of the *Oprah Winfrey Show* examining the *problem* of "husbands with wives who are in love with pop stars,"[2] common discourse conflates the word "fan" with "fanatic." At worst, fans are characterized as pathological and deviant. They are portrayed as nymphomaniacal groupies participating in seamy escapades backstage (e.g., DesBarres 1988) or mentally ill loners who stalk and sometimes murder their idols, as did Mark Chapman and John Hinckley Jr. (e.g., Wallace 1974; Munson 1993; Abrahams 1995).[3] At best, they are amusing and quaint, suitable for a three-minute spot on *Entertainment Tonight*. The obsessive activities of fandom—collecting artifacts and photographs, imitating a star's dress and manners, camping overnight for concert tickets, creating fanzines, joining fan clubs—are accepted only as the temporary behavior of hormone-driven (usually female) teenagers who, when reaching adulthood, are expected to settle into the more mature behavior of work or motherhood.

Media critics, in particular, have located fandom's meaning in the alleged corrupting power of the media and characterized fans as living in fantasy worlds based on "artificial social relations" with media figures (Caughey 1984), or as one step away from pathological delusion (Schickel 1985). In fact, critics frequently link fandom—if only through juxtaposition on the page—to more dangerous kinds of social deviance. As film critic Richard Schickel writes:

> We are dealing here with something unprecedented prior to recent years, the most appalling working out, acting out, of the habit of false intimacy with well-known people into which so many of us have fallen of late. John E. Hinckley, Jr., is assuredly a psychopath, and there is a difference of degree, therefore perhaps in kind, between his behavior and that of a middle-aged, middle-class woman first-naming talk show hosts in the beauty parlor, but there is an obvious analogy between the two types of self-deceptions, or, if you will, self creations, and it grows increasingly clear that we live now in an age rife with such falsities. (1985, p. 7)

The most significant challenge to such negative fan stereotypes has come from the interdisciplinary field of cultural studies. While Marxist theorists of the

Frankfurt School in the thirties and forties first characterized popular culture as a "consciousness industry" imposed on a passive and powerless public, contemporary cultural studies theorists, using new interpretations of Marxist theory, portray audiences and consumers as active negotiators of their own power, using mass products in ways not intended by producers. Developed in the seventies by those working out of the School for Contemporary Cultural Studies at the University of Birmingham, England, cultural studies theorists see popular culture as a site of ideological struggle between those in power and those without power; instead of denigrating participation in popular culture, they see participation as contributing to action for social change.[4] For such scholars, fandom represents a particularly important form of this resistant consumerism. Most recent work has focused on television; for instance, Henry Jenkins (1992) has characterized television science fiction fans' creation of their own stories out of the plots, characters, and materials given them in certain programs as a kind of "textual poaching" that resists commercial producers' values. Along the same lines, Constance Penley (1992) has argued that female *Star Trek* fans who create and share homoerotic stories involving *Star Trek* characters are resisting both commercial producers' values and contemporary feminists' rejection of pornography.

A second challenge to fan stereotypes has come from those trained in the more traditional disciplinary approaches of folklore, anthropology, and sociology. Emphasizing research based on human interaction—interviewing, participant-observation—social scientists have a long history of studying the varying aspects of social life, including popular culture (Mukerji and Schudson 1991, pp. 18–37). Several scholars, following this tradition, have used ethnographic methods to locate the meaning of fandom not in specific theories of resistance but in fans' own valuing of their activities. For example, Judy and Fred Vermorel (1985) collected letters and interview responses that detailed how rock fans across England used fantasy relationships with stars to manage their daily lives. Camille Bacon-Smith (1992) spent time with women in the *Star Trek* fan community and carefully outlined how their fandom allowed them to form an expressive, communal culture not generally fostered in everyday life. And Helen Taylor (1989) used correspondence and interviews to show the ways in which people have used *Gone with the Wind* as a vehicle for nostalgia, identification, a sense of community, escape, and inspiration.

Of course, I do not mean to imply that cultural studies works have no empirical grounding or that ethnographic works do not employ theory; Jenkins, for instance, draws on years of ethnographic research to make his arguments, and Bacon-Smith clearly addresses current feminist thought in her ethnographic analysis. But cultural studies and ethnographic works do come from different directions when considering their subject: the former is concerned more with fandom as a concept or social force, locating its meaning in institutions and ideologies; the latter is concerned more with fandom as a practice or experience, locating its meaning in fans' own accounting of their activities. In fact, scholars who have attempted to combine these two approaches, like Janice Radway (1984) and Ien Ang (1985), have been unable to reconcile scholarly accounts of what is happening with participants' own accounts of what is happening and, in the end, have juxtaposed the two.

This study uses an ethnographic strategy. As a fan of several music stars since my teenage years, I am concerned about views of music fandom promoted by media critics and cultural studies scholars that seem to have little to do with my own experience. Many media critics consider fans abnormal or dangerous; however, I have found that my fandom for various musical performers has, instead, gotten me through many tough times over the years and has been the source of many friendships, including my relationship with my wife. Many cultural studies scholars portray fans as rebels fighting against the tyranny of a "consciousness industry." However, I do not spend a lot of time thinking about record companies or how to "resist" them; my fandom feels to me far more like religion than politics.

As a scholar trained in the social sciences and someone who, in the words of anthropologist Clifford Geertz, "grows uncomfortable when I get too far away from the immediacies of social life" (1973, p. vii), I am also concerned about the prescriptive use of theory underlying these portrayals. Most media critics' characterizations of fans do not stem from any prolonged study of fan beliefs and behavior; rather, as Joli Jensen has pointed out, their portrayals of fans are often based on elitist and negative views about the character of modern life (1992; see also 1990). Likewise, few cultural studies scholars have ventured out to speak to fans and ask them about their fandom; rather, to revise notions of consumption as a form of passive degradation, many have interpreted fandom according to a different theory of culture and power. In fact, fans often end up in cultural studies works as something other than individual, thinking people. Any ideas fans might have about their lives are often read as part of a larger social ideology, and fans are often homogenized as an abstract element of "popular culture" or the "star system."

Joli Jensen has called for studies that "explore fandom as a normal, everyday cultural or social phenomenon" and, rather than defining people according to abstractions like "psychic needs" or class position, illuminate "the experiences of others in their own terms" (1992, pp. 13, 26). This project addresses Jensen's challenge. While I would not reject existing views of music fans as "untrue"—certainly one could argue their merits—I do think that such views ignore the pragmatic effects of music fandom and rely *absolutely* on values other than those of fans for their orientation. Rather than thinking about music fandom as pathology or as resistance, to me it might be more interesting to think about music fandom as the creation of much-needed meaning in the daily lives of otherwise ordinary people, a way in which members of this modern media-driven society make sense of their selves and their relations to others. It might be more useful to think about the *work*, rather than *worth*, of fandom, what it *does*, not what it *is*, for various people in particular historical and social moments. To find out the significance of fandom, one must ask fans themselves about their activities, not simply look at them from afar and make judgments.

The Work of Ethnography

As it has been developed in cultural anthropology, ethnographic research involves participation in and observation of a certain culture. Unlike literary criticism, where knowledge is based on historical position and theoretical conventions of interpretation, and unlike historical or scientific research, where knowledge is based on inference from primary documents or controlled experiment, in ethnography, knowledge is based on uncontrolled, interactive experience with other people. In the words of John Van Maanen, "It rests on the peculiar practice of representing the social reality of others through the analysis of one's own experience in the world of these others" (1988, p. ix). Ethnography is detailed and personal, yet it serves as the basis for broader cultural and social understanding.

Traditionally, ethnographic research was used by Western cultural anthropologists to study the rites and customs of non-Western, tribal cultures. Often, an ethnographer would approach such a culture as a scientist might approach any natural phenomenon: it was treated as a general collection of institutions that could be assessed and analyzed scientifically. Recently, however, cultural anthropologists have begun to question this traditional focus on an exotic "other" and on science. Instead of searching for the static laws, rites, and customs of a non-Western culture, many scholars today see ethnography as means for appreciating the complexities and ambiguities of life in a variety of group contexts, including Western and non-Western, urban and rural, and permanent and temporary. As part of this shift in focus, many have begun to give greater attention to the potential abuses of power involved in ethnographers' interactions with their subjects and to the biases involved in ethnographers' analyses of their own experiences (Marcus and Fischer 1986; Tyler 1987; Clifford 1988; Rosaldo 1989). My research for this project addresses many of these concerns.

First, my project challenges traditional ethnography by focusing on the experiences and everyday lives of fans rather than on abstract laws or models of behavior and thought. In particular, I draw heavily from the work of many contemporary anthropologists who collectively practice what has been labeled "processual anthropology." As formulated by the late Victor Turner (especially 1974), this type of anthropology interprets culture not as a collection of timeless institutions and fixed rules for behavior but rather as a disorganized, varied, and never-finished process of creating behavior and values. For example, instead of outlining an abstract and generalized "fan culture" by describing how a "typical fan" goes to concerts, listens to CDs, trades tapes, and reads fanzines, I have tried to show how a group of specific fans have used, variously and at different times in their lives, concert going, listening, tape trading, and reading to release tension, reaffirm values, create a sense of self, and meet others.

Of course, such a focus on the complexities of experience and the everyday, in an effort to escape the inaccuracies of scientific generalization, is nothing new. Existential sociology, borrowing from postwar French existentialism, has long advocated a focus on how people deal with the disorder and uncertainty of everyday life (Douglas and Johnson 1977; Kotarba and Fontana 1984). Ethnomethodology, a sociological school that precedes the current critiques of traditional ethnography by several decades (see Watson 1991), has provided an alternative to the abstractions of traditional sociology by focusing on the rules and methods of common, everyday activities like standing in line or buying a cup of coffee. However, while these movements have been concerned with the mundane, they have been generally dependent on esoteric methods: existential sociology is based on arguments from obscure texts of Western philosophy, and ethnomethodology embraces statistical analysis.

I am concerned with the everyday not only as a topic of study but also as a means of understanding. It is generally expected in the Western university that ordinary people should learn about the world from the intellectual theories of academics, but I believe that academics, in turn, can learn much about the world from the folk explanations of ordinary people. In particular, I have been significantly influenced by the work of anthropologist Unni Wikan (1990, 1991), who has argued for an "experience-near anthropology," meaning one that tries to understand the experiences of people in their own terms rather than in the terms of outsiders. I have been careful to focus on fans' daily thinking about what is important in fandom, rather than what academics or journalists or critics think is important, and to introduce only those academic interpretations that complement or highlight fans' views. Indeed, I have made every effort to avoid "silencing" fans with complex interpretive models that explain what they are "really" saying or what is "really" happening. In this book, fans are not problems or theories or data but real people trying to make sense of their lives in the late twentieth century; I have tried to present the sum of what they do—fandom—in those terms.

Second, my project challenges traditional ethnography by focusing on members of my own culture rather than exotic "others." While I do not know all Springsteen fans personally, they are people with whom I share an identity and toward whom I feel a strong sympathy. In fact, in many ways, I have acted as a native anthropologist in this project. Stemming from the use of indigenous informants by early Western ethnographers, native anthropologists are those who study their own society, presumably having some sort of authentic, insider knowledge of their culture.[5] While the category of "native anthropologist" is often based purely on geographical origin, I use the term to refer not so much to one's nation or home as one's relationship to the people with whom one is working. American anthropologists have long studied American culture, but many have still focused on communities removed from the mainstream or alien to them (Ortner 1991). Native anthropology means studying people of your own community, who share your values and experiences.

My own activities as a "Bruce" fan gave me extensive background knowledge about Springsteen fan culture and allowed me access to people and to realms of fandom to which I would not ordinarily have had access. Fandom is an intensely personal thing; that I practiced similar activities and had knowledge similar to the people I studied helped me to ask intelligent questions and to better understand their points of view. Whereas I would have felt out of place and uncomfortable with a group of Madonna fans and would have felt odd about sharing my inevitably distanced observations of them with the academic community, I had something to offer and share with Springsteen fans and was in a better position not only to enter their world of fandom but also to respect their right to privacy.

Of course, such an insider status is problematic. Critics of anthropology have raised new ideas about space and called for a stronger recognition of the increasingly global nature of social life in which, for instance, Aborigines sell their native artwork in New York City galleries. Culture is no longer always bounded by nation-states or by face-to-face community with an "inside" and an "outside" but rather exists across traditional boundaries and shifts relative to one's perspective (Ardner 1986; Appadurai 1991; Myers 1991; Wallerstein 1991). And as native anthropologists have attested, being a native or insider depends on a mutually accepted definition of what constitutes "native" or "inside," often in the face of other social categories like gender, age, class, and race, which are only heightened by the peculiar situation of fieldwork (Jones 1982; Hastrup 1986; Kondo 1990; Limon 1991; Narayan 1993).

During the course of my own fieldwork, I found that my insider status was not always as clear as I envisioned. In fact, fandom tends to enhance problems of being a native, since most people are not wholly defined by being a fan, and their identities are always shaped by various other social connections and relationships. In particular, simply being able to think about fandom as part of my profession has separated me from other fans; by doing this project, I have come to understand fandom in ways that most fans would not—according to three years of fieldwork and my linking fan experience to various academic theories of community, performance, and popular culture. Many fans think about fandom, of course, but few have written Ph.D. dissertations about it, and the accompanying stamps of class and power are considerable.

I discovered this difference when I first asked fans to participate in my project.

One person answered an advertisement I had placed on the Springsteen fan computer network by remarking, "Since when can you get a Ph.D. from Brown for writing about Bruce fans?!?! If I'd have known an advanced degree could be so easy, I might still be in school." Another, declining to participate, remarked that at least he now knew what "ethnomusicology" was. While I don't think such comments were intended as anything more than friendly jests, they made me painfully aware of my academic identity and challenged me to justify that what I was doing was worthwhile. Other fans were less direct in relating their feelings about my academic connections. Nevertheless, I was not quite prepared for some of their assumptions about who I was and what I was doing. For example, several resisted conversation and thought it necessary to be "scientific," sending me unsolicited "data" about themselves, including birthdate, religion, ethnic identification, and the like. Others, assuming that as an academic I must not participate in popular culture, offered to help me by sending me information about when Springsteen's works were going to be released, his latest activities, and how to subscribe to various fanzines.

Not only my class status as an academic but also my age complicated my insider status. I met and talked with fans of a wide range of ages, from fifteen to fifty-seven. On the one hand, that I was only seven years old when Springsteen's first album came out certainly affected the ways in which older fans interacted with me; several, for instance, were initially quite self-conscious about the differences in our ages and felt it necessary to justify their participation in fandom, while others explained nostalgically what it was like to be a fan before the days of ticket wristbands, computers, and CDs. On the other hand, younger fans who had just discovered Springsteen's work initially viewed me as quite knowledgeable and hesitated to completely open up about their fandom, thinking that I already had been through their experiences or had had even better ones and wouldn't be interested.

Gender was another factor complicating my insider status. While it was not always as clear to me as age, my gender seemed to limit some of my conversations with women; indeed, some women were hesitant to discuss with me their romantic interest in Springsteen, perhaps for fear that I might find it too stereotypical, too "teenybopper," as teenage girl fans were called in the fifties. In one case, I learned of one woman's infatuation with Springsteen only from her friend.

I did my best to be conscious of such differences and to address them when possible by giving people different media for expression, including letters, e-mail, telephone conversations, and face-to-face meetings; by trying to get people to talk about such issues directly, if necessary and where possible; and also by interrogating my own experiences in relation to those of others and presenting that interrogation in the text. I did not adopt Stella Mascarenhas-Keyes's (1986) "multiple native" strategy during her fieldwork in India, which consisted of dressing up in different consumes and acting differently for various informants. I tried simply to "be myself," to interact with fans with sensitivity and respect, and, through a reflexive consideration of my presence in the different contexts of fieldwork, carefully interpret what fans were (and were not) telling me.

Third, in addition to focusing on everyday understanding and problematizing the distance between ethnographer and those studied, this project also addresses current critiques of ethnography by raising questions about evidence and representation. I chose to focus my research on a single group of fans in order to discuss the meaning of fandom with adequate depth and complexity. Although fans for several different music performers would have been appropriate for research, Bruce Springsteen fans represented a well-organized following for one of the major stars in rock'n'roll.

Bruce Springsteen has had a surprisingly steady career in a field where musicians tend to remain popular for only a few years before disappearing into obscurity. Born on September 23, 1949, to a working-class family living in Freehold, New Jersey, Springsteen turned to music early in his life, playing in his first professional rock band while in high school. After leading several local bands in the New Jersey Shore area during the late sixties, he signed with Columbia Records in 1972. His first recordings included two albums of densely lyrical, streetwise songs in the vein of Bob Dylan: *Greetings from Asbury Park, New Jersey* (1973) and *The Wild, the Innocent, and the E Street Shuffle* (1973). After meeting writer and record producer Jon Landau, he recorded his breakthrough record, *Born to Run* (1975), a highly romantic album with dramatic, "wall-of-sound" arrangements and songs of youthful idealism and escape. He followed up *Born to Run* with several albums of darker material: *Darkness on the Edge of Town* (1978), arguably his hardest and angriest album; *The River* (1980), which sandwiched feel-good rock songs and ballads about the plight of the working class; and *Nebraska* (1982), a stark, sometimes nihilistic collection of songs about gambling, murder, and despair.

In the mideighties, he gained international fame with *Born in the USA* (1984), which used catchy rock arrangements to probe the lives of hard-luck characters and detail the downside of the American dream, and he continued his ride to commercial success with *Live 1975–85* (1986), a compilation of live performances of many of his songs to that point. After *Live 1975–85*, Springsteen shifted his focus to more personal themes. *Tunnel of Love* (1987) was a quiet, personal exploration of marriage and commitment, and *Human Touch* (1992) and *Lucky Town* (1992), released simultaneously, contained a wide range of songs about family life. He released a *Greatest Hits* CD in 1995, but by the midnineties he had generally returned to his earlier social realism, first releasing a song about a man with AIDS for the movie *Philadelphia,* in 1993 and then making *The Ghost of Tom Joad* (1995), a folk protest album in the tradition of Woody Guthrie.

Over this continually productive career, Springsteen has spanned the gamut of popularity, moving from an unknown cult figure in the early seventies to his current status as a megastar. His fans have grown from a small, devoted, East

Coast following to an international group of people of all ages and various backgrounds, who share a devotion to his music and his message. Today, polls and critical retrospectives often cite Bruce Springsteen as one of the most important performers in rock music in the past twenty-five years. He has sold millions of records, won numerous awards (including an Academy Award, five Grammy Awards, and the Swedish Polar Music Prize), and is expected to be inducted into the Rock and Roll Hall of Fame when he becomes eligible in 1998. Overall, his music has become a regular part of American social discourse, from political speeches to poetry textbooks.

While Springsteen and his fans are clearly appropriate for a study of fandom, one could argue that they are an anomaly in the world of popular music and not representative of fandom as a whole. In particular, Springsteen's relationship with his audience tends to collapse the performer-audience boundaries and corporate-consumer divisions that have been prevalent in much of rock music history. He is more like a folk singer than a pop star: unlike most stars, who offer fans glamor and escape, Springsteen shuns stardom and emphatically identifies with his fans. In the words of Merle Ginsberg (1985): "Bruce's legions don't try to dress like him; in fact, they believe he tries to dress like them." This stance makes Springsteen's stardom quite ironic; as Simon Frith (1988) has written: "It is his very disdain for success that makes Springsteen so successful."

I do not deny that Springsteen fans may not be representative of most popular music fans; however, I want to make clear that I have not attempted to create a universal model of music fandom, if such a thing exists. In fact, I intend this study of particular fans and their fandom to *challenge* the whole idea of universal fan stereotypes. People are fans of Springsteen, and I believe that alone makes Springsteen fans legitimate objects of study. Of course, some of the themes I present in this text about listening, collecting, or concert going, for instance, apply to other kinds of music fans and may describe widespread aspects of musical life in the late-twentieth-century United States, but I suspect that the details about the meaning or significance of such activities vary across different fan communities. In the end, my hope is that this project will provide other scholars with the solid ground from which to conduct further research about other stars and other fans and that, in the future, we will be able to make careful comparisons that may lead to more general theories of fandom.

*M*ethods of Inquiry and Interpretation

In *Passing the Time in Ballymenone*, folklorist Henry Glassie set out to investigate an Irish community, not concerned so much with speaking to every member or creating complex models of its social structure but rather discovering the community's "wise speakers" by letting people direct him to one other and allowing such people to "turn interviews into conversations" and "present [the community's] significant texts." His goal was to view people's lives as formed wholes, not as parts to be compared, and only then, after understanding culture in practice, to make comparisons. As he explained, "Culture as a whole must come out looking like a human product. Then it can be compared with others to scientific ends, and it can be compared with our own to keep us from drowning in vanity" (1982, pp. 11–34). Glassie's work was an inspiration for this project. While the community to be investigated was fundamentally different in familiarity, composition and cohesiveness, I shared his goals.

My primary concern in my research was what Charles Keil has called "idioculture" or an understanding of the world not in terms of universal laws but in terms of singular experiences (Crafts, Cavicchi, and Keil 1993, p. 2).[6] I did not attempt to contact a particular cross section of "types" of fans to fulfill the definitions of an abstract sample but, instead, allowed myself to follow the paths fans opened up to me and to move from fan to fan, one by one, learning how different people build meaning from their values, triumphs, dilemmas, and choices. Only from those encounters did I then carefully try to build a greater, more general understanding of what it means to be a Springsteen fan.

I used several different sources to contact fans. In the first phase of my fieldwork, I asked friends, students, and colleagues, who I knew were fans, to talk to me about their fandom. I asked those who replied if they knew anyone else who might be interested in talking with me, and my research branched out from there. In addition, during this initial phase of fieldwork, I placed two advertisements—which outlined the purpose of my project and asked fans to contact me—on the Springsteen fan Internet discussion group, *Backstreets Digest* (or *Luckytown Digest*, as it was renamed in 1994). An electronic mailing list to which people with computers subscribe and on which they may post messages about Springsteen or his work, *Backstreets Digest* was started in 1986 and by the early nineties had become one of the larger computer discussion groups centered around Bruce Springsteen. It proved to be a good additional source of contacts.

A second phase of fieldwork began after about six months of interviewing, when, to reach some of the fans whom I hadn't addressed yet—especially those without access to computers—I placed an advertisement in the classified section of the American Springsteen fanzine, *Backstreets*. It was an obvious place to go next; while *Backstreets* started out as a free newsletter in 1980, it had become, by the early nineties, a professional, glossy-looking publication and the main source of Bruce news for most fans. During this second phase, I asked people to fill out a questionnaire; fifty-six people responded to the ad and, remarkably, forty-eight sent the questionnaire back. The questionnaire was not meant as a systematic survey; I wanted to use it instead as a form of contact, a way to introduce myself and meet others. Unfortunately, while I had intended to speak further with all those who sent me a questionnaire, the sheer number of people who responded and my dwindling funds prevented me from speaking to everyone. I did, however, meet and correspond with several more people. In total, I communicated with approximately one hundred fans and kept in frequent contact with about thirty-five.

My interaction with fans took several different forms. The primary form of contact was the face-to-face interview; if at all possible, I met fans in places where they would feel comfortable—a restaurant or bar, the Brown student union, their homes—and, with their permission, recorded our conversations. Meeting face-to-face a stranger at an appointed time and talking about one's personal life produced anxiety in some people. It did, however, allow a maximum amount of communication and best helped other fans and me to get to know one another. Not only could we simply hear and see one another but also we could learn about the changing subtleties of each other's expressions, body language, manners, humor, and general demeanor.

Many fans, however, lived too far away for me to be able to meet with them in person, or they simply didn't feel comfortable meeting with me; instead, I arranged to talk with them over the telephone. Phone interviews are decidedly different than face-to-face interviews in that the focus is on spoken language. Although silence in a face-to-face conversation often simply represents a harmless pause in the flow of talk in which the speakers may interact in other ways, in a telephone conversation silence represents a breach of contact and is commonly associated with anger or rudeness. Speaking on the telephone pushes most people into being more articulate than they might be ordinarily, but it can backfire if they are uncomfortable in expressing themselves verbally. In one instance, a fan with whom I had fine conversations over e-mail became silent and rather withdrawn when we continued our discussion over the telephone. On the whole, however, many fans preferred the telephone because it allowed them to remain in familiar surroundings and refer to relevant materials such as Springsteen CDs, books, or posters, as they talked.

Finally, I contacted many fans personally over electronic mail.[7] Basically, electronic mail allows one computer user to type a message on the computer screen and, with the stroke of a key, "send" it to the screens of selected other computer users. It a very flexible form of contact; messages sent by one person to another sit in the recipient's "mailbox" until he or she chooses to read them, reply to them, or forward them to others. Mailbox entries often have the senders' names as well as "subject headers," which allow the recipient to pick and choose which messages to read first. The text of the message itself is marked by several unique features. Since the subject heading already introduces the sender and the topic, the message usually starts without any formal introduction. Indeed, over the years, electronic mail has developed a language which privileges speed; it includes much abbreviated jargon like "IMHO" ("In my humble opinion") or "BTW" ("By the way"). In addition, to account for the absence of physical expression and vocal intonation, the text also often includes symbols, created with parentheses and colons, called "emoticons," which provide cues to various forms of expression such as happiness [:)], sadness [: ( ], or sarcasm [;)].

Electronic mail has several benefits. Because of its lack of physical or vocal elements, it is less anxiety producing and tends to create a welcoming informality. The lack of face-to-face interaction over electronic mail also tends to remove elements of sexism and racism and, as Judith Perrolle (1991) has explained, "democratizes otherwise awkward conversation." I would add, from my own experience, that e-mail tends to give people time to digest what is said in a conversation and to think about their own responses. Over e-mail people tend to be quite articulate and direct. However, electronic mail also has several drawbacks. For one, the lack of physical cues can easily lead to misunderstandings. As many scholars point out, there is a weakening of self-awareness and context on electronic mail, which can lead to more aggressive or antisocial behavior than would be otherwise acceptable (Dunlop and Kling 1991; Kiesler, Siegal, and McGuire 1991). Being "flamed," or thoroughly castigated for voicing an unpopular opinion, is quite common on many electronic mail discussion groups. The informality and flexibility of electronic mail also makes it quite easy for people to drop out of a conversation without any social consequences. I "lost" several people, for instance, simply because they became tired or bored. Finally, the lack of physical contact over electronic mail allows the easy creation of false identities and other kinds of deception (Van Gelder 1985).[8]

My sources of contact naturally led me toward some fans and away from others. My status as a graduate student and professor during my research led me toward college students; several were enrolled in classes that I taught. *Backstreets Digest* led me toward people with enough personal or family income to own a computer and maintain an electronic mail account or to attend a university with such resources; most of the fans with whom I corresponded over electronic mail either had full-time professional jobs or were college students—all were well-educated. Finally, because most of my contacts were through either local or national sources, members of Springsteen's international audience were largely inaccessible, and most of the fans I met were American citizens.

In the end, the people found in this book are American citizens, between eighteen and forty years of age, white, heterosexual, college-educated, and either currently or soon-to-be full-time professionals who earn between $30,000 and $45,000 a year. Most fans said they were practicing some form of religion, though which religion was equally split among Roman Catholicism, Judaism, and various Protestant denominations. I contacted more men than women. The same number were married and unmarried; a few were divorced, and several had children. There were many exceptions, of course; for example, in addition to talking to lawyers, accountants, professors, engineers, and managers, I also corresponded with a dog groomer, a grocery store clerk, a cook, and several full-time mothers.

In addition to meeting with mostly American citizens, I also talked with a fan from Germany and a fan from the Netherlands. But on the whole, the fans I met shared a fairly similar American, white, straight, middle-class background.

The fact that African American, gay, or poor Springsteen fans did not come forward in the research process does not mean that they do not exist. Reasons for the absence of such fans may have had to do with my sources of contact (I did not put an ad in a gay or lesbian publication, for instance) or with my own background as a white, middle-class, Ivy League–educated graduate student, which may have made some people uncomfortable. However, the absence of minorities among Springsteen fans has been echoed informally by other fans and more formally in other polls; it does seem to indicate, at least, that various minorities do not form a visible presence in the American Springsteen fan community.

That minority fans did not come forward in the research process does, however, limit the scope of this text. Because I have tried to privilege the voices of the people to whom I spoke, and because I have followed their lead in determining what kind of theories I introduce, certain issues are not given the time they might be given in other contexts. In particular, while there were periodic discussions among fans on the Internet about the racial composition of Springsteen's audience or gay characters in Springsteen's songs, the fans to whom I spoke did not tend to focus on issues of race or sexual orientation much in discussing their own lives but instead focused on age, gender, and regional differences, which tapped more directly into their own experiences. Overall, the text reflects these interests.

In any case, whenever I contacted someone in the research process, I tried to be informal and leave our interaction relatively open-ended. I often started out with a few "interview" questions to ease our awkwardness and get things started but always tried to steer the talk toward conversation, toward a situation in which the fans would feel comfortable to share, not simply tell, their personal stories and in which I, too, could share my own experiences. Initially, our conversations tended to focus on topics such as becoming a fan, attending concerts, listening habits, collecting Springsteen materials, knowing other fans, or encountering nonfans. Later, when we forgot that we were strangers, we moved from the details of fan practice into more intractable issues of meaning and value, of interpreting why we do what we do.

While I have learned about people through formal interviews, I have also learned that interviews have limited use, that they are often not based on friendship and collaboration but rather on distance and exchange. Fandom is not a bounded entity to be discovered and commented on, or a problem to be questioned and answered; it is a complex, private yet shared, ongoing experience. The things fans said in interviews were not data, specimens to be captured and put in a jar, but rather openings for further exploration, interpretations kindly but hesitantly offered at a particular time about the complexities of their experience.

Of course, one of the problems with studying experience is that one can never truly move beyond one's own; another person's experience can be shared only through the artifice of expression. Performance studies—a burgeoning field that combines anthropology, folklore, and linguistics to explore the nature of various forms of expression, including language, stories, drama, music, rituals, and art—has been especially important to me in thinking about such problems. Over the years, several performance studies scholars have focused on ways people share their experiences through forms of performance and the ways in which such forms influence experience itself (e.g., Bauman 1986; Fernandez 1986; Schechner 1988; Turner 1988).

Throughout this work, I argue that sharing experience through performance is one of the keys to understanding the connections not only between fans and Bruce Springsteen in the phenomenon of fandom but also between fans and me in the course of fieldwork. The interesting aspect of Springsteen fans is that they have a significant relationship with a performer and also *themselves* perform in various contexts. In particular, Bruce Springsteen fans are storytellers; they are constantly shaping their experiences through narrative and sharing those narratives when they meet. I paid particular attention to their oral styles, thinking about how features of fans' speech (shifts in point of view, uses of metaphor, metonymy, meta-language and reported speech, etc.), as well as paralinguistic features of delivery (changes of vocal tone, pauses, laughter, sighs, etc.), influenced the meaning of what they told me.

I nevertheless resisted treating fans' stories and analyses as texts to be interpreted after the fact; their meaning was created in the context of their utterance, and I viewed them primarily as representations of our meetings, guides to our discussions about certain issues, always open-ended and able to be amended, changed, or clarified in future discussions. In fact, although I was limited by time, I tried to arrange to meet with people several times, continuing conversations by clarifying points and raising new issues. In particular, I used a form of "dialogic editing," or sharing one's scholarly writing with those written about and incorporating their comments and corrections into the text (Feld 1982, 1987; Tedlock 1983). Dialogic editing is a reaction to the traditional, analogical form of ethnographic writing, which precludes any process of dialogue between the anthropologist and those he or she meets in fieldwork. It is an effort to open up the politics of writing ethnography and to control (or expose) the authority of the critic.

Dialogic editing was particularly useful for this project, since fandom has been particularly distorted by the authority of critics. As I completed drafts of chapters, I sent them to fans so that they might have an opportunity to respond and make comments about my views. Of course, not every fan had the time or interest to respond, yet several appreciated the opportunity and sent me pages of comments and clarifications. If they did not respond to my ideas about fandom, then at least they responded to my specific representations of them in the text.

In the end, through this dialogue with fans about their fandom, patiently, over time, I believe I learned more deeply about fandom's meaning than if I had simply conducted formal interviews with fans and then left to analyze their detached words on a page.

*O*rganization of the Text

Much of the critique of the discipline of anthropology and its theoretical perspectives has focused on the writing of ethnography and the ways anthropologists use language to represent those they have studied. In response, a number of experimental ethnographies have appeared in recent years, all with the purpose of using style and form to better represent the politics and the practice of fieldwork. They range from critical readings of texts to novelistic narratives to postmodern bricolage to dialogues to a mixture of any of these. To be honest, the very number of different types of ethnographic writing is somewhat daunting. I will be happy enough if I simply have been able to, in Glassie's words, "probe and write and learn without harming anyone." Nevertheless, the text employs particular strategies to that end.

I am a scholar, and I have selected and represented what I have learned in the form of a text that stands as a testament to my abilities as a professional academic. However, in an approach that attempts to humanize fandom, it seemed unethical to me to simply translate fans' voices into academic jargon or to absolutely impose my worldview on those people who have trusted me enough to give their time and open up their lives to me. Instead, in the text, I have presented my experience as a fan, other people's experiences as fans, and how those come together in fieldwork. My own experience as a fan has required a certain amount of autobiography; as I met fans and learned about their lives, I learned more about fandom in my own life. In order to present the meaning of fandom in the daily lives of specific fans, I have used fans' own words and stories; all quotations in the text are verbatim transcriptions from tape recordings or excerpts from electronic mail messages and letters. All fans are mentioned by their real and full names, except where anonymity was preferred or prudent. In addition, I have drawn on academic theories which have helped me to interpret their experience. Such theories are not necessarily the latest or the best known—they are simply tools that I found useful as I thought about what fans said to me. Finally, to present the context of my interpretations, I have sparingly used what John Van Maanen (1988) calls the "confessional tale," meaning a close attention to my own experiences as I met and came to know specific people in different situations. My overriding goal was to present a view of fandom that is grounded in the expressed experiences of a particular group of people and that represents the meaningful collaboration between a scholar and those he or she meets in the process of fieldwork.

I begin the book, in chapter 1, with a narrative description of my experience at a Bruce Springsteen concert as I was beginning my research. The concert, for me, represents all the important elements of fandom: the music business, audience, meaning, identity, and community. This chapter, at least, shows where my thinking about fandom began. In chapter 2, I attempt to define fandom, discussing how fans see it as a process of conversion, a turning to the music with intense and personal feelings of connection. Chapters 3 and 4 then deepen and problematize that definition by placing it into the larger social context of modern popular music practices. In chapter 3, I look at fans' dependence on, but disregard for, the music business; in chapter 4, I present their complex and ambiguous relationship with nonfan audience members.

The last three chapters of the book focus on the various ways in which fans use and value fandom in their daily lives. In chapter 5, I show how fans use the music to make sense of the world, interpreting both sound and experience in a circular process of listening. In chapter 6, I probe the relationship between fandom and personal identity, particularly the ways in which fans shape ideas of themselves over time through various kinds of collecting and listening. Finally, in chapter 7, I describe the power of fans' sense of community, especially the ways it fosters and strengthens their social relationships. In the end, I argue that a view of fandom in fans' own terms looks quite different than it does in the terms of critics or scholars and that such a difference matters. It raises important issues about the relevancy of popular culture scholarship for society in general.

Does Anybody Have Any Faith Out There Tonight?

1

Seeing Bruce in Concert

*G*etting Tickets, October 31, 1992

When my wife and I first heard on the radio that Bruce Springsteen would be doing two shows at the Boston Garden, we flew into action. It was a Wednesday; the DJ said that ticket wristbands—which would assure us a place in line when tickets went on sale Saturday morning—would be available at all Ticketpro outlets at 5 P.M. We had just moved to a new area of Massachusetts and had no idea where any Ticketpro outlets were. After calling around, we discovered that the closest was at a video rental store in a local bus station. I picked up my wife from work at 5:30, and we drove directly to the outlet.

We knew from experience that tickets to Springsteen shows were not easy to come by. My wife was a long-time fan who had stood in many lines, camped out, and driven hundreds of miles just to get tickets for shows during Springsteen's highly successful *Born in the USA* tour in the mideighties. And we had failed to get tickets for either of Springsteen's two previous appearances in the Boston area. So, we drove to the ticket outlet with both excitement and trepidation, envisioning enormous crowds and the general mayhem that accompanies an announcement of a Springsteen show. However, when we arrived, we were the only people there, and the clerk at the video counter seemed a bit amused at the whole thing. He said only about five others before us had come to get wristbands, and they had been equally anxious.

Wristbands are similar to those worn by hospital patients. They are plastic and fastened permanently to the wrist, not to be taken off until tickets are bought. Each has a number printed on it, which assures the wearer of a place in line the morning tickets go on sale. Their use was first instituted sometime in the late eighties to alleviate problems with unruly crowds and people camping out at ticket agencies. With wristbands, camping out becomes moot; at a certain time, everyone shows up, a random number is called, and people line up behind that number appropriately.

My wife and I both got wristbands to better our chances of getting a good place in line—she had number 64 and I had number 82. If they called number 82, I would be first in line; if they called 83, I would be last. We wore the wristbands for two days, being careful not to damage them or risk being disqualified. It became a badge, a symbol of fandom for me; people often asked me what it was, and I proudly explained to them that I was going to try to get tickets for a Springsteen concert. Of course, most people did not understand the importance of the wristband and simply smiled at me patronizingly. But those who understood nodded thoughtfully and wished me luck.

We arrived at the bus station early Saturday morning. It was a crisp and cold day and, like many others who arrived soon after we did, we waited in the warmth of our car for the terminal to open. It was fun to know that other people were as eager as we were to get tickets, though I wondered anxiously whether we actually would. What number would be called? What number did all these other people have? What if we're last in line and tickets sell out right as we get to the counter? Eventually, at 8:30, one person got out of her car, went into the station, and didn't come back out. Suddenly all who were waiting got out of their cars and gathered in the station waiting room.

The bus station was like most other small-town bus stations: a barren, square room with a newsstand and ticket windows on either end and two small rows of plastic bucket seats in the middle. The tiny video store occupied one corner of the station, adjacent to the door. As people entered, those who knew each other stood in groups; others, including my wife and I, sat at the seats alone and waited. As people entered the station, those of us who were already inside looked up and smiled at them knowingly. Some of the people who were sitting behind us started up a conversation about getting tickets and about how close they'd gotten to the stage at other shows. Another group of people chatted repeatedly about the whole process of wristbands and speculated on what would happen when the video store opened.

While we were waiting, a man sitting across from me got up to greet the video store clerk, who had finally arrived. They disappeared inside the store, and the crowd mumbled things like "There he is" and "Here we go." The man who had been sitting across from me, apparently a security guard or a Ticketpro official, reemerged a minute later to explain the process to us. In a commanding voice, he announced that the line would begin with "01." People immediately began to ask each other about their numbers and line up appropriately around the video store and out the door of the station. "I've got three!" someone called. "Are you forty or forty-one?" With my wife's number of sixty-four, we ended up toward the rear of the line, standing in the unheated foyer to the station.

People were slightly miffed that the number chosen was 01; it seemed not very random and therefore a defeat of the wristband process. In the back of the line, people joked about how far they were. There was a little confusion about the order of certain people; the security guard eventually made his way to the rear of the line and straightened out the line, saying that when tickets went on sale at 9:00 all late people, regardless of wristband number, would go to the end of the line and that people without wristbands would not be allowed even to get in line. Everyone seemed to agree that that was a good system—obviously we all wanted to be as close to the front of the line as possible.

Unfortunately, at 9:00 the ticket computer crashed. With groans of disgust, many people said that it was typical and that you can never get tickets without *something* happening. A woman in front of us told us of the time that she stood in line in the cold for hours with her son in a baby carriage in order to get *Born in the USA* tickets. Other people asked each other questions to which they already knew the answers in order to pass the time and reassure themselves that all was okay. A couple behind us asked if the dates really were the thirteenth and the fourteenth of December, I asked if anyone knew the size of Boston Garden, and others asked how much the tickets were. The tension created by the downed computer system was the source of many jokes about the competency of the video store clerk, and people frequently tried to peer past movie advertisements taped to the windows of the store to see what was going on. Some people went to the head of the line to ask questions and then reported back to those of us too far away to hear official announcements. "Still broken," they would say, or "They're on the phone talking to someone." After ten minutes or so, someone announced that the whole computer system for the state had failed, which, ironically, brought great sighs of relief from everyone in the rear of the line. "Thank God!" someone exclaimed. "That's good, that's good," another thought aloud. They still had a chance to get good seats.

Eventually, conversation groups began to develop. Like links in a chain, people formed tiny circles while in line and started talking about past concerts they'd been to, how they got tickets, where they sat, and what songs Bruce played. Someone who had brought a portable stereo started playing a tape of Springsteen's new album, *Lucky Town*. No names were exchanged, yet people laughed with each other as if they were old friends, sharing a mutual experience. My wife and I started talking to a young couple behind us who told us a funny story about how they had camped out during the summer to get wristbands for Springsteen's last show in Worcester, Massachusetts. We talked about the impossibility of buying tickets over the phone through Ticketmaster, about Springsteen's upcoming appearance on MTV, and about other concerts we'd been to.

The computers started up at about 9:15 or so, and the line finally began moving. People in line were entering the store one at a time after the security guard checked and then removed their wristbands with a pair of scissors. As people exited with tickets, those still in line would ask what seats they got, what night they had, and what the people behind the counter were doing. As we got closer to the door, the discussion turned to strategy: should we ask for tickets on Sunday night the thirteenth or Monday night the fourteenth? Tickets for Sunday night had moved from the floor to the upper balconies; most of us decided to try for Monday after someone said that Sunday was selling faster. One woman, who had drifted in and out of our conversation because her husband was elsewhere in line, had a map of Boston Garden; people were very interested in charting the progress of the ticket sales as people came out. On what side of the stadium was the stage going to be? Have you ever been to the Garden? What are the balconies like? Where's the loge?

Because my wife had the low wristband number, she went into the store while I waited outside. The slowness of the video man was a continual complaint. Some people were exasperated with him, others felt sorry for him. Soon after my wife went into the store, she poked her head out to announce that she was going to kill the people in front of her because they were wasting precious ticket-selling time by asking about the availability of Boston Bruins hockey tickets! People in line who heard her laughed nervously. But she soon came out with four tickets, two for us and two for friends of ours, Suzanne and Perry, who had expressed interest in going. We answered questions about our seats for people still in line, wished them luck, and left triumphantly, two hours or so after we first arrived. We were going to see Bruce again.

The Concert, December 14, 1992

For the next month and a half, my wife and I listened quite a bit to Springsteen's latest CDs to prepare for the concert. For her, it was more a matter of "getting psyched" for the event; she had fond memories of previous shows and was anticipating the fun she would have. For me, since I was thinking of doing my dissertation research on Springsteen fans, my listening was more about educating myself as much as I could about Springsteen and his work. I had gone to fewer concerts than my wife had and wanted to be sure that I would be prepared to observe intelligently what transpired.

Boston Garden is an old brick-and-concrete stadium on the north side of the city, home to the local basketball and hockey teams and used as a venue for various rock concerts, sporting events, and the occasional tractor pull.[1] Its front facade is somewhat obscured by the elevated tracks of a subway line, and the entrance itself abuts the divided lanes of Causeway Street, on which cars noisily speed by. As we arrived the night of the concert, several large trucks were parked in front—presumably for hauling stage equipment—as were a mobile radio station van and a couple of rented limousines. The restaurants across the street, which usually cater to those attending Garden events, were full; lines stretched out their doors onto the sidewalk. As we approached the doors to the Garden, several ticket scalpers walked toward us, mumbling surreptitiously, only as they came close, "Need tickets?" I shook my head and heard them move on to others arriving near me. "Need tickets?"

We found our seats in the first balcony, and we waited. It was a half-hour before the concert was supposed to start, and people were continually arriving. Setting up a rock concert in an arena like the Garden is an awkward situation; it is built like a coliseum, with the performance space in the middle and the audience surrounding it on all sides. While several bands have tried the theater in the round, using a circular stage, it poses many performance difficulties and remains rare. Most rock bands use an amphitheater arrangement, with a stage and audience facing one another. For this concert, the stage was set up at one end of the floor; people could sit behind it, but the view was partly obscured by large lighting scaffolds and black curtains. In front of the stage, filling the rest of the floor, were rows of folding chairs and, behind them, a large soundboard. The stage was a huge black platform with wings. Openings behind the wings revealed stairs leading downward; underneath the stage I could see televisions and electronic equipment and several people. Above the stage, members of the light crew were crawling up and down ladders from the suspended lighting boom, checking spotlights. On the stage itself were several amplifiers and various instruments. Numerous "roadies" were busy adjusting microphones and testing the equipment.

At a show I had attended in New Jersey during the past summer, many of the audience members arrived early in order to tailgate in the parking lot, cooking hot dogs and burgers, drinking beer, playing Springsteen tapes, and socializing. Since it was December and quite cold, however, most people coming to this show quickly entered the Garden and did their socializing inside. People up in the balcony were busy waving their arms at people they knew down on the floor or on the other side of the Garden; other people with binoculars were watching the roadies and each other. Every once in a while someone exclaimed someone else's name loudly or jumped up and down in excitement. There was a great mixture of people in the audience: young teenagers looking at tour books they had just bought; college students in sweatshirts or flannel grungewear talking and laughing; many middle-aged couples wearing old Springsteen T-shirts, casually watching the stage and talking to each other; and even a few older folks, looking confident but somewhat out of place.

Immediately surrounding us were two middle-aged women, engaged in serious conversation; two young men and a woman, drinking boisterously; a thirtyish couple in front of us, snuggling; and an older man in a three-piece suit reading the newspaper. As they had arrived around us, they all first assessed with each other the quality of the seats—that is, whether they could see the stage and, presumably, Bruce. "This isn't too bad," they said, or, "Well, it's better than the last time." I had already gauged that our seats were on the same level as the lighting boom. The center mike on the stage didn't look very far, though I knew that it was several hundred feet away.

Suzanne and Perry arrived shortly after we did, and we exchanged greetings, talking for a bit. Perry reminisced about the time he saw Bruce do his legendary "I'm just a prisoner of rock'n'roll" shtick, and I talked about how good Bruce was in the last concert I saw. Music was constantly playing from speakers on the stage: Van Morrison, Bob Marley, some grunge bands. When a song ended, people called out "Bruce!" and random cries of anticipation. Indeed, the crowd kept up a pretty consistent whistling and screaming to build enthusiasm. When the lights dimmed momentarily, the crowd applauded and cheered. While nothing happened, the excitement built even more: the music seemed to get louder, people's conversations intensified, and the activity around the stage got busier. Near 8:00, there were about thirty stagehands working throughout the floor, getting things ready, and the Garden really began to fill up. It was a sold-out show.

Springsteen concerts are legendary among both fans and nonfans as long, energetic, and always surprising events. However, this concert had added meaning because Springsteen hadn't played in the Boston Garden since *The River* tour in 1980; Springsteen's more recent New England appearances had been at the Worcester Centrum, a newer venue in Worcester, Massachusetts, approximately forty-five miles west of Boston. So, for the audience, it was Springsteen's return, a homecoming of sorts. At least for many of the fans there, it was their first glimpse of him in five years since the *Tunnel of Love* tour in 1987. So when the lights suddenly went out shortly after 8:00 the crowd roared wildly. In the faint, colored light of the equipment displays, figures moved on the stage. Then my wife poked me and said, "There he is! There he is!"

A spotlight clicked on and illuminated Bruce standing alone in the center of the stage with his black acoustic guitar. He yelled, "All right, Boston!" and, waiting for the crowd roar to die down, strummed a few chords. "There must be some red-headed Irish girls out there tonight," he teased and immediately started playing a solo version of a new song called "Red-Headed Woman." He strummed his guitar furiously, not paying much attention to the crowd, closing his eyes, and attacking the words to the song with country-style hiccups and enthusiastic yelps. Nevertheless, there was still a lot of background noise, as if Springsteen had interrupted everyone's socializing.

When he finished, the lights went out again, and the crowd roared "Bruuu-uce!" over and over, a response developed by fans in earlier years and often misinterpreted as booing by those unfamiliar with the ritual. The band walked on stage. Then, as if reciting some sort of incantation, the audience and Springsteen together counted "One! Two! Three! Four!" and the band exploded into the opening, heavy guitar chords of "Better Days," a song from *Luckytown* (1992) about Springsteen's newfound happiness.

> Now a life of leisure
> and a pirate's treasure
> Don't make much for tragedy;
> But it's a sad man my friend who's livin' in his own skin
> And can't stand the company.
> Every fool's got a reason
> for feelin' sorry for himself
> And turning his heart to stone;
> Tonight this fool's halfway to heaven and just a mile outta hell
> And I feel like I'm comin' home.

For almost his entire career, Springsteen played with the E Street Band, a collection of musicians predominantly associated with the New Jersey area, but during this tour Springsteen had assembled a new band in order to make a change in his musical sound. He retained his keyboardist, Roy Bittan, but added a rhythm guitarist–percussionist and three backup singers in addition to a new guitarist, drummer, and bassist. For the audience, many of whom viewed the E Street Band as family and were initially outraged at the change, this appearance was their first chance to judge the new band in action. Most of the people around me were excitedly silent, watching with wide eyes.

The first half of the concert lasted an hour and a half and, while filled with energy, had a relaxed pace, in which Springsteen paused frequently between songs to introduce them. The crowd was initially less enthusiastic than I thought it would be; some people sat in their seats, passively listening, while others (on the floor, mostly, as such a move was dangerous in the balcony) stood on their seats to watch Bruce or half-stood, leaning forward and gyrating to the music by bending their knees and moving their arms up and down. Nevertheless, both Springsteen and the audience—particularly older fans—had some fun interacting.

At one point, after playing a string of songs, Springsteen halted the music, wiped his face with a towel, and started to tell a story: "There I was, all alone, driving on the back roads of the great state of New Jersey," he said, and immediately the older fans in the audience roared enthusiastically, recognizing it as part of one of his famous "Growin' Up" stories. Springsteen always tells a story about becoming a rock'n'roller during performances of "Growin' Up," a song from his first album, *Greetings from Asbury Park, N. J.* (1973). Typically, the plot involves some sort of quest: he and his saxophonist, Clarence Clemons, feeling down and deciding that they need relationships with "members of the opposite sex," drive south through New Jersey in search of women. Unfortunately, they get a flat tire. Heading for a gas station on the other side of some nearby woods, they encounter all sorts of werewolves, lions, and killer cows (fans usually imitate the sounds of the animals as Springsteen names them, roaring or mooing appropriately). However, they also stumble on a magical grizzly bear who says he can make their dreams come true. The bear brings them to a clearing and then, out of the sky, in the middle of the forest, produces a guitar and a saxophone. When Springsteen and Clemons pick up the instruments and touch fingers, they become rock superstars.

That night, Springsteen didn't tell the whole story but rather cryptically referred to it, repeating various sentences and cues. He first said, "I was scared of the sounds coming out of woods," and then paused with a grin as fans in the crowd started making the low, spooky noises of ghosts and goblins. Then he said, "And I dreamed that I was a teenage werewolf!" and started playing the opening arpeggios to "Growin' Up" on his guitar. The crowd cheered wildly. When Springsteen started singing, many in the audience sang along with him, as if remembering an old family favorite. This song was usually played with a full band, but this time Springsteen was accompanied only by his keyboardist, Roy Bittan, and the voices of the entire audience could be heard clearly. Indeed, the crowd was performing as much as the band on stage; at one point, when Springsteen sang, "When they told me to sit down, I stood up," one fan in the balcony to my right suddenly stood up and gestured with open hands to the crowd to do the same. After the last verse, however, the crowd stopped singing, and Springsteen, playfully referring to the metaphors of flying throughout the song, simply said, as he always does, "And it was bye-bye New Jersey! We were airborne!"[2]

Later, Springsteen and the band also played "Trapped," a cover of an old Jimmy Cliff song, which had been released to the public on the *We Are the World* benefit album (1985).[3] The song began slowly, with warm synthesizer chords, as Bruce sang about dreaming of better times. It gave the crowd an opportunity to catch their breaths a bit and clap lazily along. However, the lull soon shifted with a dramatic, drawn-out crescendo of guitars and drums; a flash of bright, white lights on the audience from the stage; and a loud, resounding burst of a chorus, which everyone sang angrily, punching a fist in the air to punctuate the lines:

> But now I'm trapped!
> Ooh, yeeeeee-aaaaaah . . .
> I'm trapped!
> Ooh, yeeeee-aaaaaah!

As the bright lights turned off and the music returned to its earlier quiet, people cheered and whooped excitedly, acknowledging the power of the moment. This happened four times during the song; each time, the lights shined on the audience and seemed to acknowledge its role in the performance. The song gave me a sense of being part of something greater. I was mesmerized not as much by the energy of the band as by the sheer physical force of listening to a crowd of ten thousand or so people suddenly singing at the top of their lungs in unison and throwing their arms up into the air. Their collective voice repeatedly drowned out the band and shook the cement floor of the balcony.

Also in the first set, Springsteen shifted into the role of an evangelical preacher, an act he had used often in tours past. In an urgent, emotional voice, he called out to the crowd, "Does anybody believe in *love* out there tonight?" The audience responded with a resounding "Yeah!" "Does anybody have any *faith* out there tonight?" ("Yeah!") "Does anybody have any *hope* out there tonight?" ("Yeah!") "Does anybody believe in *sex* out there?" ("Yeah!") "Well then whatta' we waitin' for?" After the ritual counting off of "One! Two! Three! Four!" with the audience, he and the band played "Leap of Faith," a song from *Luckytown* about looking for romance. During the song, Bruce leaned forward into the front row to kiss several women and at one point pretended to swoon, lying still on the stage and simply allowing the lyrics to go unsung as the backup singers continued the song. Amid cheering and calls of "Bruuuce!" he also jumped from the stage into the crowd. People caught him and tried to hold him above their heads, passing his body from person to person in a wide arc. He looked a bit awkward, legs and arms flailing for balance, but he was grinning wildly. One woman jumped up and kissed him passionately on the mouth before he was guided back toward the stage and unceremoniously thrown onto his face to roars of laughter.

The first half of the concert had some serious moments as well. Springsteen's song "57 Channels and Nothin' On," recorded as a rockabilly story of modern boredom for *Human Touch* (1992), was transformed into a loud and furious attack on racism and social violence. And he introduced "The River," from the 1980 album of the same name, with a poignant talk about life in the United States. He said:

> I wrote this song when the country was in the middle of hard times in the early eighties. Now it's the beginning of the nineties and there are still so many people— I know guys that work construction who are out of work again. And I was thinking about our troops that are over there in Somalia now [some people in the audience cheered] protecting people from all those teenagers with guns, and I was thinking about people here, in this country, who need protection from teenagers with guns, too. Anyway, this is—I guess this is my song about hope in the face of hopelessness.

During these songs, I noticed a clear division between people in the audience. In particular, while many older fans sang along to "The River," many other people got out of their seats and moved into the aisles to get another beer or some food. In fact, from my seat I noticed for the first time that the audience was not entirely riveted to Springsteen and his presence; instead, from my seat high in the balcony, it looked like a huge, seething mass of insects swarming a hive: some people were watching quietly, some were walking up and down the stairs, and others were talking and eating. I wondered whether those people walking around and not paying attention were fans. It seemed to me that all the activity was evidence that the audience was composed of all different sorts of people: fans, those mildly interested in Springsteen, and those simply out for a good time.

After Springsteen played "Roll of the Dice" (1992), a new song which he performed in a gospel style with call-and-response breaks and several false endings, and which fans likewise "performed" by throwing twenty large, stuffed, fuzzy dice on stage, Springsteen ended the first half of the concert. He yelled rapidly, in the manic speech of a carnival barker, drawing out the last syllable of each phrase:

> We're gonna take some half-time, right here: go back*stage*, get on the tread*mill*, lift a few *weights*, get on the stationary bicycle for a few *miles*, box a few *rounds*, and then we'll be back out here with some more rock'n'*soul* entertainment for you!

With that, he and the band disappeared beneath the stage.

Intermission lasted a half hour. As soon as the house lights came on, the audience seemed to collectively exhale with relief. People generally emptied their seats and milled about. Many stood to stretch their knees. My ears were ringing from the volume of the sound and I felt a little dizzy, but I stood also, looking around. After chatting briefly with the couple behind us who were quite drunk and rowdy—I knew that they weren't fans because a true fan would never ruin the experience of a concert by risking being so trashed as to not remember it!—I turned to my wife and Perry and Suzanne, who were talking casually about work. As before the concert, people waved to each other and intermittent yelps of enthusiasm rose from the floor, but, on the whole, the audience was tired and sat quietly, waiting and watching the roadies retune the instruments on stage.

The second half of the concert began when Springsteen and the band suddenly walked back up on stage and launched into "Prove It All Night," a defiant rocker from 1978's *Darkness on the Edge of Town*. As with other songs, people clapped along to the beat, danced in their seats, and sang along. I even noticed one security guard down at the front of the stage moving his head perceptibly up and down to the music. His behavior looked inappropriate next to the other guards, who were stoic and unmoved, standing with their arms crossed in front of them, watching the audience wildly dance and wave and jump.

The second set was shorter than the first, featuring a rapid-fire presentation of many more songs from Springsteen's later albums. Instead of the pauses and lingering introductions of earlier in the evening, Springsteen played with a sudden urgency, as if wanting to get in as many songs as he could before the night was through. As a result, I felt less relaxed nostalgia and more strong feelings of empowerment and energy; the rapid transitions between songs filled me up with electricity and sound and a strange sensation that I could do or be anything I wanted.

One of the highlights was a performance of "Brilliant Disguise," a song about the doubts and struggles of married life, which Springsteen sang with his new wife, Patti Scialfa, a former member of the E Street Band. Springsteen had been married to actress Julianne Phillips when the song was written; when it first came out in 1987 on the dark and contemplative album *Tunnel of Love*, many fans interpreted the song as a sign of trouble in Bruce's personal life. Unfortunately, due to no fault of her own, there had been widespread sentiment against Phillips among fans; besides the fact that she, a stranger, had taken Springsteen "away" from them, many fans felt that she wasn't "right" for him, was too West Coast, too show-biz, for a "regular guy" from New Jersey. Sure enough, Springsteen's marriage troubles soon made tabloid newspaper headlines. His marriage to Phillips was eventually annulled, and he quietly married Scialfa and started a family.

That night, at the concert, Springsteen started "Brilliant Disguise," as usual, by counting the beat with the audience. While it looked as if he was going to sing it alone, Patti then walked up onto the stage, playing acoustic guitar, and stood next to him by the microphone. The crowd roared their approval. "Brilliant Disguise" is a heart-wrenching song about never really being able to know someone, yet the chemistry between Springsteen and Scialfa transformed it into an erotic song about the risk of romance. When Patti harmonized with Bruce during the refrain, leaning into his body, putting her leg between his, sparks flew:

> Well I've tried so hard baby
> But I just can't see
> What a woman like you
> Is doing with me
> So tell me who I see
> When I look in your eyes
> Is that you baby
> Or just a brilliant disguise

Appropriately, perhaps, for the first time during the concert, a couple on the floor left their seats and ran to an empty corner by the soundboard, where they danced with each other.

During the song "Light of Day" (1992), a hard-driving, blues-rock number Springsteen had written in the early eighties, Springsteen and the audience once again performed for each other. The song was a powerhouse, filled with briefly yelled lyrics and scorching guitar solos over a thundering, bass-heavy rhythm. After about five minutes of this sonic assault, however, without any warning, Springsteen halted the music. While the waves of sound echoed into silence over the audience, Springsteen remained completely still, frozen in a kneeling position with his guitar on his lap. After the audience realized what was going on, they broke into thunderous applause and cheers, whooping and yelling, calling out "Bruuuuce," pounding their seats in rhythm, and trying to get him to react.

Springsteen remained frozen for a full two minutes and then, finally, with an unintentional smile—clearly he was enjoying himself—he turned his head and looked into the audience at one side of the stage. The crowd there exploded with a roar, waving their arms and jumping up and down. Springsteen then turned his head to the other side of the stage with the same effect. Eventually, he alternated his gaze from one side to the other, eliciting a rhythmic applause in time to the song. Jumping to his feet, he started it up again.

"Light of Day" fired up the crowd to amazingly high levels. People were screaming at the tops of their lungs, dancing in a frenzy, and the whole auditorium seemed to move up and down in rhythm to the song. After several humorous pauses, in which Springsteen seemingly ended the song but then suddenly started it up again, he slipped once again into the role of an evangelical preacher. "I came thousands and thousands of miles just to get here tonight!" he called out and paused as the band punctuated the phrase, call-and-response style, with a brief, single note and enthusiastic calls of "Yeah!" The audience also chimed in as he continued:

> I came around the world and a half just to get here tonight! (Yeah!)
> Via Sweden via France via Italy via Rome via London, England, via Dallas, Texas! (Yeah!)
> Just to get here tonight! (Yeah!)
> I came through some real shitty weather just to get here tonight! (Yeah!)[4]
> And I'm here for just one reason! (Yeah!)
> I'm here for one reason *only*! (Yeah!)
> [rapidly] I came through the great State of New Jersey! (Yeah!) Dallas, Texas! (Yeah!) San Francisco! (Yeah!) Los Angeles and Radio City Music Hall! (Yeah!) San Diego! (Yeah!) Canada! (Yeah!)
> I'm here because I know you're downhearted! (Yeah!)
> I know you're disappointed! (Yeah!)
> I know you're depressed! (Yeah!)
> I know you're low in spirit! (Yeah!)
> And I'm here tonight because I—(Yeah!)—I got something I need to testify to! (Yeah!)
> I've got something I got to tell you! (Yeah!)
> I got something I need to witness to! (Yeah!)
> [call-and-response getting faster and faster] I said I! (Yeah!) I! (Yeah!) I! (Yeah!) I! (Yeah!) I! (Yeah!) I! (Yeah!) I!
> [pauses while crowd cheers enthusiastically, and then in drawn-out, hoarse cry] *I'm just a prisoner!*
> [the band holds a minor chord dramatically for several seconds and then stops] *Of rock'n'roll!*

With a cymbal crash, Springsteen and the band then finally finished the song to wild cheering and applause. My wife, Suzanne, Perry, and I all exchanged looks because we had been discussing Springsteen's "I'm a Prisoner" act before the concert started. I thought to myself that it is uncanny how Springsteen always seems to know what you're thinking.

The concert went on very late, past midnight. Like his songs, Springsteen concerts have many false endings and are drawn out with multiple finales and encores. The fun is that you never know when they will actually finish. That night, the concert first appeared to wind down when the band played a loose and fun performance of "Glory Days" from *Born in the USA* (1984). The performance followed tradition, the band all wearing hats which fans had thrown onto the stage and walking through the audience while playing the last chorus. Springsteen introduced the members of the band, including his manager, Jon Landau, who had come on stage earlier and strapped on a guitar.[5] The concert didn't end there, though. Springsteen, looking as if he didn't want the fun to end, immediately followed "Glory Days" with his first commercial hit in the 1980s, "Hungry Heart," which he let the audience sing alone, simply pointing his microphone away from him with an outstretched arm.

"I just want to take a second to thank everyone for coming to the shows," Springsteen said next, apparently finally ready to leave. "The support we've gotten from the fans in the Boston area has meant a lot to me. I appreciate it." He didn't move, however; and after tuning his guitar for a couple of minutes, he said, "This is for all the fans out there. I guess I've been coming up to Boston since about 1973; I played at a place called Joe's Place and a place called Charlie's Place. I've been at this for a long time, and when you get someplace, it's nice to see some folks there when you get there." Springsteen laughed and played a few arpeggios on his guitar before launching into an acoustic version of a widely acknowledged fan favorite, 1975's "Thunder Road." The crowd, oddly, didn't cheer but became quiet, softly singing the lyrics along with Bruce. A lone spotlight shined on Springsteen, but the darkened Garden sparkled magnificently with the tiny flames of thousands of cigarette lighters, held up in the air by fans.

At the end of "Thunder Road," the crowd cheered with abandon. Springsteen just smiled and said, "Well, we can't let you go home without *this!*" He then launched into the opening guitar riff of his popular 1975 anthem, "Born to Run." The house lights came on and everyone sang and clapped along, watching each other. It felt less like a concert than a private party. When Crystal Taliefero played E Street Band member Clarence Clemons's trademark saxophone solo, the audience cheered her on. Springsteen fans often refer to themselves as "tramps" so, during the refrain, which includes the line, "Tramps like us, baby, we were born to run," the fans in the crowd sang with all their might.

The concert definitely seemed to come to a finish with a subsequent haunting performance of "My Beautiful Reward," the song that ends *Lucky Town*. With a spare arrangement and subdued blue and red lights, Springsteen sang:

Well I sought gold and diamond rings
My own drug to ease the pain that living brings
Walked from the mountain to the valley floor
Searching for my beautiful reward
Searching for my beautiful reward.

Indeed, after a quiet harmonica solo, Springsteen and the band lined up on the stage and took a bow. A fan down in front gave him roses. And people clapped tiredly, stopping from time to time to gather their coats.

However, after several minutes of applause, Springsteen paced back and forth in the front of the band as if he couldn't leave. It was almost Christmas, and the fans knew that he hadn't yet played his version of "Santa Claus Is Comin' to Town"—something he always does in December concerts. Finally, Springsteen said slyly, "Do I have to *say* what time it is?" Donning a Santa hat left on stage by a fan during "Glory Days," he picked up his guitar. "We can't leave without playing this one for you!" He and the band then launched into "Santa Claus Is Comin' to Town," complete with a metallic tree lowered from the ceiling. The crowd responded gleefully, singing the lyrics and laughing when the lights on the tree didn't work. "Looks like a power outage!" Springsteen remarked happily.

At the end of the song, Springsteen thanked the audience with a wave, but as he was about to leave, he turned and noticed the large digital clock on the front of the lower balcony by the stage. "It's not even twelve o'clock yet!" he exclaimed. "I don't know. . . ." He paced back to the middle of the stage. "I think we need to pull out a stocking stuffer, now!" He smiled and gestured to the side of the stage. "I'm gonna have an old friend of mine, a great Boston musician, Mr. Peter Wolf, come up and sing something." With roars of applause and recognition, Peter Wolf, the former singer for the J. Geils Band, hesitantly came on the stage.[6] "Looks like we're gonna make it to the midnight hour!" Springsteen yelled happily, gesturing to the clock and introducing Wilson Pickett's "In the Midnight Hour" with a pun. As they played the old soul song, people were no longer in their seats but were dancing in the aisles; the Garden was a sea of moving bodies and limbs.

Wolf, Springsteen, and the band stretched out "Midnight Hour" for about five minutes, Springsteen repeatedly yelling out "One more time!" until the digital clock flashed "12:00." The performers then waved to the audience and, amid thunderous applause, walked off stage. The crowd applauded for about five minutes more, waiting just in case Springsteen came back out, but the house lights came on, and it was over. People were smiling, wiping the sweat from their foreheads, and gathering up their things to go home. Whereas most rock concerts last two hours at the most, this one lasted four.

*A*fterward

The only way to leave the Boston Garden is through several wide, winding tunnels that descend to exits. My ears were still ringing with music ten minutes after the concert had ended, and my wife and I just walked quietly. I did hear several people talking excitedly, evaluating what they had just seen—"Wasn't it funny when he was kissing those women?" "Remember when Bruce jumped into the crowd?" "That was a good show!" "The last tour was better." Most people, however, were fairly silent, a little dazed and tired from dancing and singing so much. We said goodbye to Suzanne and Perry and made our way to the train station and home.

The concert continued resonating for me over the next few days. We listened to Springsteen's latest CDs again, finding in them a renewed meaning. In particular, I found that some of the songs he had played during the show sounded different to me; I heard the lyrics and sound with a new sense of intimacy. I also read with relish the positive review in the *Boston Globe*, knowing that I had been a part of what the writer was discussing:

> In a time when the word "populist" seems to be bandied about with giddy aban-
> don, Bruce is the quintessential people person, just wanting to sing, needing peo-
> ple to hear, and then—hope against hope—needing them to believe. He's a
> preacher with a subtle approach, a gravely growl and the legs of a rocker, someone
> who sneaks up on you with the message, slaps you across the face with it, then he
> comes up clutching roses. (Smith 1992, pp. 67, 70)

The concert was also a hot topic of discussion among other fans. On the Springsteen fan computer discussion group, *Backstreets Digest*, fans posted the set list for the show and their reviews. Two fans remarked on the unique event of Jon Landau's playing guitar on stage; in a discussion that followed, others revealed that he had done this before at the end of a tour. These fans also talked about Crystal's satisfactorily playing Clarence Clemons's saxophone part on "Born to Run," the "Growin' Up" story references, and how the band "really rocked out" on "In the Midnight Hour" with Peter Wolf. Their evaluations were generally good; as one fan remarked, "Although I truly missed 'Real World,' I thought that this was one of his better shows that I have seen. The first set was incredibly energetic" (see Joergensen 1992; Lewis 1992; Purlia 1992; Slovin 1992).

Months later, the Springsteen fanzine, *Backstreets*, published fans' reviews of most of the shows on Springsteen's 1992–1993 tour. Among many other reviews of concerts in places like St. Louis, Indianapolis, Philadelphia, Pittsburgh, and Lexington, the reviewer who went to the Boston Garden show on December fourteenth, wrote:

> *Backstreets* has mentioned that when the audience is really into the show it fires
> Bruce up and he gets into it, too. Well, this was certainly the case last night. High-

lights included a blistering and gritty "Atlantic City," a bring-down-the-house, sing-along "Trapped," scorching guitar on "Badlands," and a beautiful poetic rendition of "The River" with an extended harp solo. Bruce dedicated this song to the soldiers and families trying to bring peace this time of year in Somalia. ("Can You Testify?" 1993, p. 22)

While the details were important to me, the mere appearance of such a review among others affirmed my vague feelings that the concert had been a significant and special moment of shared experience, something that positioned me among other fans and closer to Bruce.

In the following spring, I began my fieldwork, contacting fan friends and acquaintances for interviews, putting ads—asking people to contact me—on the computer network and in *Backstreets*. To my surprise, I met a few fans who had been to the concert at the Boston Garden. Invariably, in each encounter, after establishing where we had sat and whether we had liked the show, we excitedly exchanged reminiscences of our favorite moments: Bruce freezing during "Light of Day," the crowd trying to hold him up after he jumped off the stage, Peter Wolf coming out to sing.

Over the course of the next year, I talked with fans who were involved in many different activities, from collecting to listening, and who had different kinds of relationships toward Springsteen and his music. Some were interested only in his music, and others paid close attention to his personal life; some studied his lyrics as a kind of philosophy, whereas others admired his musical talent. But all talked about seeing Springsteen in concert. Even when fans had not had the chance to attend a show—because of age, the lack of tickets, or lack of money or because Springsteen did not appear near their hometown—they still eagerly talked about what it would be like to go to a concert and vowed that they would someday.

For fans, whether they've seen Springsteen live or not, a concert represents a powerful meeting of the various forces and people and ideas involved in their participation in musical life. The excitement of participation, the feeling of connection with Springsteen, the interaction of fans and other audience members, the rituals, the energy, the empowerment, the communal feeling, the evaluation and discussion: together, they enact the meaning of fandom. They shape and anchor fans' sense of who they are and where they belong.

2 Touched by the Music

Defining Fandom

"Fan" is a confusing word. Although it is regularly classified as slang, it has been used in English for almost three hundred years and has appeared in a variety of historical and social contexts.[1] Most scholars trace the origin of "fan" to late-seventeenth-century England, where it was used as a colloquial abbreviation for "fanatic." "Fanatic" connoted religious zealotry and was widely used at the time to refer to those who were mad, frenzied, or possessed (*Oxford English Dictionary* 1989, pp. 711, 712–713). "Fan," however, became obsolete and did not reappear until the late 1800s in the United States, when sports journalists used the term to refer to early baseball spectators. It then quickly spread to other kinds of commercial hobbies and amusements. In 1907, "fan" was used in print to refer to spectators at a boxing match (Partridge 1956, p. 265) and to those attending a racetrack (Thornton 1962, p. 301). In 1913, it was first used in print in England to describe the audience of a soccer match (*Oxford English Dictionary* 1989, p. 711) and also to describe film viewers in the United States (*Random House* 1994, p. 725). By 1930, "fan" had become a widely accepted American colloquialism, used in reference to sports, film, theater, and even politics.

There are two explanations of the appearance of "fan" in the United States. The traditional view, represented by the *Oxford English Dictionary* (*OED*), is that American journalists in the nineteenth century revived the term from its earlier use as an abbreviation for "fanatic" to metaphorically describe the devotion of early baseball spectators. "Fan" described the degree of one's participation in public performance; thus the *OED* defines "fan" as a "keen and regular spectator of a professional sport."

Other scholars, however, disagree with this etymology and argue that sports journalists in the 1880s and 1890s were more likely to have derived the term "fan" from "the fancy," which was, in the words of etymologist Robert Barnhart:

a collective noun meaning all who "fancy" a certain hobby or pastime [which] originally applied to pigeon fanciers and later (1807) to boxing fans. "The fancy" was a popular phrase in the 1800s, used by Southey, DeQuincey, Thackeray, and Herbert Spencer. (Barnhart 1988, p. 368)

In particular, historian Elliot Gorn explains that at the turn of the century, as boxing lost its brutal, working-class roots and became a respectable, middle-class sport, "the fancy—the old sporting fraternity that had lived beyond the pale of respectable society—became fans, paying spectators in search of entertainment" (1986, p.254). In this alternative view, the word "fan" was not used to benignly describe the *degree* of audiences' participation in commercial amusements but rather to negatively describe the change in the very *quality* of their participation.

Whatever the historical truth of the origin of "fan," people tend to view fandom from these two different poles. On the one hand, many people today use the word "fan" to refer rather neutrally to anyone with a significant degree of enthusiasm, saying, for instance, "I'm a big fan of Italian food" or "My friend is a fan of horror movies." On the other hand, many people use the word "fan" to negatively label someone who eagerly participates in the mass media, often prefacing it with adjectives such as "crazy" or "deranged." On the whole, it is used both descriptively and prescriptively to refer to diverse individuals and groups, including fanatics, spectators, groupies, enthusiasts, celebrity stalkers, collectors, consumers, members of subcultures, and entire audiences, and, depending on the context, to refer to complex relationships involving affinity, enthusiasm, identification, desire, obsession, possession, neurosis, hysteria, consumerism, political resistance, or a combination.

To label oneself a Springsteen fan in such a confusingly diverse terrain of meaning can be frustrating. Springsteen fans constantly have to deal with preconceptions about who they are and what they do. As one fan told me in a letter, "It's hard to generalize about people's reactions. It has ranged anywhere from approval to mystification." Judi Johnson, a middle-aged administrative assistant from Michigan, explained:

> Some of them think this is a fun thing . . . others are uncomfortable with it. It is actually a mixed response. My husband tolerates it, my children (all grown) find me an easy ice-breaking conversation piece at parties, and my co-workers are a bit in awe, most especially at my willingness—drive—to follow any shows and to travel any distance I can to see a show. (interview, November 4, 1993)

Andrew Laurence, a 21-year-old college student from southern California, likewise reported: "My brother seems to enjoy/tolerate the music; I think he recognizes it as 'quality,' but it's just not his cup of tea. My friends, on the other hand, mostly just want me to turn it off. Lord save me from the uninitiated" (interview, October 23, 1993).

Despite this variety of definitions and perceptions, however, all of the Springsteen fans to whom I spoke agreed with startling consistency that, in the end, being a fan is about having a special feeling of "connection" with Bruce Springsteen. J. D. Rummel, a 33-year-old helpdesk manager, explained:

> For me, that is the bottom line. I identify with Springsteen the man as I understand him through his work. I have never met him, and maybe I'd be disappointed, but the thoughts he expresses, the way he delivers his creative force is very involving to me. He seems to ask many of the same questions I find myself asking about the world. He is perplexed by the pain he sees, the things we inherit from parents, the need for love that is universal, yet the strange troubles we have finding it and keeping it. He seems to be a very human being who is sharing what he has found on his journey through this life. I have learned much about being alive and living day to day from listening to his input. I feel very much like it's a shared journey. (interview, May 14, 1993)

Louis Lucullo, a 22-year-old insurance underwriter from New Jersey, agreed:

> The fan knows the stories Bruce told in the seventies of the fights he used to have with his father while the country was telling him to give his life to something he didn't even have any particular opinion towards. The fan, who might have been in the same situation, knows somebody in the same situation, or simply understands what it would have been like, is attracted to the music because there is something in the music that the fan can relate to. (interview, April 20, 1993)

For some fans, this basic quality of "connection" is true not only for Springsteen fans but also for other music fans. Al Khorasani, a 30-year-old software engineer, explained:

> To me, there are various versions of fans that people think about. There's groupies. That I don't know what—I don't consider that a fan. I don't know, I don't want to talk for anyone. But I think they're just in it for a good time. I think a lot of them probably couldn't care which band, you know? [laughs] Then, there is a group that is all to itself, and that is the Deadheads. I think in a weird way they might have the same connection to that music that I would have had to Bruce. I think a lot of true Deadheads are older than I am, because they date back to the seventies or even earlier than that. And I think that, let's say, Grateful Dead music and Dylan music, had the same effects on those people, maybe. . . . I think people that were really heavily into Dylan—the music did something to them. Most of those people are still true to that. They still enjoy it. They don't grow out of it, you know? Because it meant something more than just "party on" and "good times" and then forget about it. Because when the music touches people in a certain way, then it stays with them. . . . Don McLean wrote "American Pie" I think twelve years after Buddy Holly had died. He's still—you can feel in his music the way that that music had affected him. He hadn't grown out of it. I don't know. Now, that's a fan. That's a real fan to me. (interview, March 23, 1993)

The idea of Springsteen fans having a connection with Bruce Springsteen and his music may seem to be an obvious explanation of fandom. But among Springsteen fans, the idea of connection means more than just having an affinity for Springsteen's music; it means making the music a deeply felt part of one's life, of having an ongoing, shared relationship with Springsteen the artist. Indeed, fans talk very specifically about the process of forming a connection with Springsteen and what it means to be "touched by the music." Examining these ways in which they talk about the moment of connection, of becoming a fan, is vital to understanding what fandom is all about.

ℬecoming a Fan

Very few studies address the origins of an individual's fandom; for many scholars, "fan" is a kind of consumer category into which someone simply falls or does not fall. Several studies, for instance, only deal with fans as the logical result of advertising or a "star system" (e.g., Adorno [1941] 1990; Buxton [1983] 1990; Vermorel and Vermorel 1989; DeCordova 1991; Staiger 1991). In such studies, there is no "becoming a fan"; rather "being a fan" simply appears as a mode of audience participation, part of a larger historical context of industrialization or the rise of mass entertainment. Even in works about the psychology of fandom, most scholars often only vaguely refer to the development of an individual's fandom as a behavior that "stems" or "comes from" unavoidable "contact" with media figures. As Jib Fowles cryptically explains:

> We admit stars into the *sancta sanctora* of our minds to work on our emotions. We permit them access to ourselves in ways we permit no others. Perhaps because we allow them such license with our innermost selves, Americans come to revere them. Such admiration easily leads to emulation. (1992, p. 165)

A few recent works, using ethnographic research, have addressed in more detail the ways in which people become fans of television shows. Henry Jenkins talks about how viewers of science fiction television "watch a series, off and on, for an extended period of time before deciding to make a regular commitment to it" (1992, pp. 58–60). Jenkins quotes a few accounts of how people became fans, but he is primarily interested in the general "intensity of emotional and intellectual involvement" of such accounts and how they disprove previous theories of television viewing. Camille Bacon-Smith (1992) discusses her own entrance into *Star Trek* fandom by outlining her movement through different stages of "initiation," including learning about fanzines, videotaping, and various types of fan fiction. For her and for the *Star Trek* fans she met, becoming a fan is primarily a social phenomenon that involves "an extensive mentor-apprentice system for training newcomers in the structures and customs of the community."

Springsteen fans understand the process of becoming a fan a little differently than either of these explanations. While the process often includes "intensity of involvement" and mentoring, such phenomena are only elements of a more specific and personal transformation, which fans quite consciously shape through frequent and regular sharing of "becoming-a-fan" stories or what Bacon-Smith calls "initiation narratives." As I explain later, "becoming-a-fan" stories represents a specific genre of fan discourse and is one of the many types of stories fans tell each other in fanzines, over computer networks, and when fans meet. In particular, such stories are popular forms of introduction between fans; often, when fans write letters to the editor of a fanzine or send a message to the fan mailing list for the first time, they include an account of how they "discovered" Springsteen. Indeed, I learned quickly in my fieldwork that, when meeting a fan for the first time, one of the best ways to put a person at ease and start a lively discussion was to share our becoming-a-fan stories.

Stories of becoming a fan are personal narratives that center on a "conversion" or significant change in one's attitude and behavior toward the music and image of Springsteen. I use the word "conversion" deliberately; fans often talk about introducing someone to Springsteen's music as "converting" them. For example, Laurie McLain, a college student in Oregon, explained:

> I spent a while as a lonely Bruce fan with no one to talk to about it. I managed to convert a friend of mine over a period of several years and now he's on our side, though he's never seen a show, poor soul, because he didn't quite come around until after the [1987] *Tunnel* tour and then he was in England for the duration of the '92 U.S. tour. I tell him it serves him right because he told me once before his conversion that he hated Bruce. (interview, March 11, 1993)

Often fans use the idea of conversion in a specifically religious sense, logically seeing the act of introducing someone to Springsteen's music as a kind of proselytizing. As Alan Levine, an advertising and marketing executive from New York City, told me about taking his sister to a concert:

> LEVINE: My sister, my younger sister, didn't understand it, and finally I got her tickets. She was then a believer. She has gone to numerous shows.
>
> CAVICCHI: A conversion!
>
> LEVINE: A conversion, yes. She had a religious experience. (interview, April 2, 1993)

Twenty-year-old college student John O'Brien likewise talked about taking his sister to a concert:

> That was a huge event. That was the first concert I think she'd seen of anybody. And after, she said it was a "religious experience." She came home and told my Mom that, and my Mom was like, [clapping] "We got another one!" (interview, March 15, 1993)

On the whole, fans use the idea of conversion only as a metaphor to signify the degree of dedication and commitment Springsteen usually inspires. However, a closer look at fans' accounts of their experiences shows that the concept of conversion serves as more than simply a metaphorical description of fans' degree of feeling; it actually describes in detail the process of becoming a fan. In particular, the descriptions of transformations found in narratives of becoming a fan are remarkably similar to those found in the conversion narratives of evangelical Christians in the modern United States.

There have been many descriptions of what happens when a person is "born again"; perhaps the most famous is William James's outline of Protestant Christian conversion in *The Varieties of Religious Experience* ([1902] 1925, pp. 189–258). He described two types: the self-surrender type, in which a person, after a great deal of frustration and unhappiness, gives up the will to change and then suddenly is converted, and the volitional type, in which the change is gradual and consists of building up, piece by piece, a new set of habits.[2] These types have been criticized by subsequent scholars of conversion for being limited in their applicability. In my research, however, I have come across people whose descriptions of their experiences might be clearly divided into these two poles. Some people I met spoke of becoming a fan as something that happened suddenly; they could often pinpoint the exact moment and talk about how they felt and what they did. Other people, however, spoke of becoming fans gradually, either through getting to know other Springsteen fans or simply by buying albums and going to concerts over a period of years. For such people, isolating how they became fans was difficult; there was no one "moment."

Stories of the self-surrender type begin with a "setting," which is loosely similar to the period of "crisis" or "conviction" in conversion narratives; as people describe being lost or unhappy before converting, fans negatively describe their activity or attitude in the period before the actual "discovery" of Springsteen. They mention hearing about Springsteen but having feelings either of dislike or indifference toward him; others talk more generally about how they were interested in music but not satisfied with the music available, how they were bored one night while watching television, or how they were feeling lonely while at work or in some foreign locale.

This indifference or negativity is then radically altered. An individual hears a song on the radio, reads a line in a book, or is dragged to a Springsteen concert and simply becomes "hooked." Such a transformation is an epiphany, often described as mystical and inexplicable; it is rarely detailed but rather described using dramatic recreation of speech ("Yes! I understand now!") or, if written, using textual devices such as "all caps" or multiple exclamation points to convey the excitement of the moment. William James's description of how a convert "undoubtedly seems to himself a passive spectator or undergoer of an astounding process performed on him from above" could easily apply to the feelings fans indicate in their stories.

Finally, after the moment of transformation, fans describe a subsequent period of exploration. Like religious converts who intensify their participation in the activities of the religion with which their conversion is associated, fans describe a period of exploration after converting in which they intensify some previous musical activity, such as listening to recordings or buying collectibles. And like many religious converts who feel "unified and consciously right, superior, and happy," as William James describes it, people who have just discovered Springsteen describe their new intensity of activity with feelings of widened perception, especially about the worth of Springsteen as an artist.

David Merrill, a 34-year-old computer repairman and former soldier living in Vermont, told me a becoming-a-fan story which quite closely followed this structure, moving from a setting of indifference in Long Island and then misery in Iceland, to a sudden transformation after reading a book on Springsteen by Dave Marsh, and finally to a period of intense exploration:

> My first exposure to Bruce was through a roommate when I was stationed in California in 1977–78. My roomie was from Long Island, and he played nothing but Beach Boys and Jethro Tull until I thought I would gag. Then he brought home two albums; one of them was the Jackson Browne album with "Running on Empty" on it. The other was Springsteen's *Darkness on the Edge of Town*. I can recall sitting down with headphones on, listening to this new music. I didn't get it. . . . I preferred the Jackson Browne record.
>
> Bruce didn't grab me, shake me, or move me. I was actually a big Doors fan, at the time, and was into testing my limits, both physically and intellectually. I abused alcohol and drugs, fell in and out of love several times and basically just enjoyed being young and free in the California sunshine. I don't recall Bruce being a big part of this scene at all. The music we listened to at the time was, along with the Doors, Zeppelin, Hendrix etc., was new bands such as Van Halen, The Cars, Dire Straits, and Foreigner, who all had their first albums out at that time.
>
> In 1979, I was transferred to Iceland. The NATO base at Keflavik is stuck out on a peninsula in the North Atlantic, with no protection from the high winds, and of course it is dark and cold during the winter. After I had been in Iceland for about a year, Bruce released *The River* album, and "Hungry Heart" was a big hit, getting a lot of airplay on Armed Forces Radio. I borrowed the album from a friend and pirated a copy. I also bought a cassette of *Greetings from Asbury Park*. A roommate had the *Born to Run* LP. So I started listening to more Bruce, but still he was just another rock'n'roll singer at that time and I didn't get much beyond the "everybody's got a hungry heart" and "tramps like us are born to run" stage.[3] Then the guy next door lent me a copy of Marsh's book, *Born to Run*, and everything changed.
>
> Once I started reading about Bruce I realized how deep his music really was and how much I had been missing. I went back and listened to the albums again and "rediscovered" them, so to speak. What I had thought was simply good rock music

took on new meaning. It's really difficult to put this into words, but I'll try. Some of the lines that I had never really "listened to" before began to jump out at me. The characters in his songs nearly came alive for me, or they were people that I *knew*, I had seen them, they were everyday people wrestling with the things that we all face in life, looking for their own drug to ease the pain that living brings, to paraphrase Bruce. My admiration for Bruce grew the more I listened (and learned). The fact that this rock & roll singer/songwriter could write these semi-autobiographical songs about his own life, and yet have it come so close to *my* life, and teach me things about myself, was mind-blowing. (interview, May 6, 1993)

Al Khorasani told a similar story about his discovery of Springsteen while growing up in New York City, describing a setting in which he doubted Springsteen's worth and then, after seeing him live, becoming a devoted fan who would buy Springsteen albums as soon as they were released:

Well, it was right at the beginning—like 1974–75—the start of the *Born to Run* hype. Where before that he was pretty much local to the East Coast, sort of like what Southside Johnny is now. And I had heard of him playing around. I was like thirteen or fourteen at the time. I had heard him but I had never seen him. I had never seen him in the local clubs or anything. 'Cause of my age and everything—[chuckles] that's why I didn't go to clubs that much at that time. But heard of him. And a friend of mine had bought his album called *Greetings from Asbury Park, New Jersey*. And he told me that when *Born to Run* had come out and everything, "Yeah, this guy has another album. I have it and I've been listening to it and it's really great! Just listen to it—it's *Greetings from Asbury Park*." Well, you got to put it in perspective: Asbury Park, New Jersey, now to Bruce fans is like a shrine and everything. But back then, I said, "Oh god, if this guy calls his album *Greetings from Asbury Park*, he has no future! Obviously the guy isn't going to make it!" So he said, "Just listen to it." So I listened to it. Then I went out and bought *The Wild, the Innocent and the E Street Shuffle* and I bought *Born to Run*. And I saw him first on that tour in Madison Square Garden, and that was it. That was just all she wrote! I was, like, hooked. I just couldn't get enough of the music. It was just amazing. I had never experienced anything like that; I had never heard anything like that. Ever since then . . . like albums would come out and I'll go the first day and get the album, come home, put the album on, get the sheet out with the lyrics, and play it until I memorized the whole thing. Just over and over again. So that was the routine. [laughs] (interview, March 23, 1993)

Laurie McLain's account of her becoming a fan was not so much a narrative as a commentary on her transformation, yet it refers to the three-part structure: her indifference, sudden "needing to know what was up with this guy," and a subsequent period of intense listening:

I became a fan in the spring of '85. I was only 13, so it's not like I could have gotten into it sooner than that. (I can be a little defensive about being a *Born in the USA* person). I had heard most of *Born in the USA*, of course, by that time, but it hadn't impressed me much. My family had just gotten cable and I used to make fun of the "I'm on Fire" video, thinking, in my young, deluded state, that it was boring. I was intrigued by his part in *We Are the World*, but that was about it. Then one morning I woke up and I was a fan. I can't even begin to explain what happened because I don't know. I remember absolutely needing to know what was up with this guy, and I pulled out my brother's almost unplayed *B-USA* and listened to it over and over again one day, then borrowed all the other albums and had them memorized almost immediately. It's been a defining feature of my life ever since. Very strange. I've always sort of half-heartedly believed that it was somehow predestined that I would be a Springsteen fan since there's no logical reason for it at all. One minute I didn't care who he was and the next he was the most important thing in my life. (interview, March 28, 1993)

While a majority of fans' stories follow this self-surrender pattern, a small number of fans also told me stories which reflected James's "volitional" type of conversion. Such stories had a looser, more free-ranging pattern: instead of describing a setting from which one was suddenly transformed, many fans talked about a longer process in which they slowly came to attach a positive meaning to Springsteen's music over time. In such stories, fans "discover" Springsteen repeatedly, and each time they feel that their fandom deepens. David Mocko, a graduate student in atmospheric science at Colorado State University and a New Jersey native, told me a narrative over electronic mail which was quite long but nevertheless a good representation of this type of story, covering a lengthy period and involving several different life experiences:

I became a fan during the BitUSA years [1984–1987]. I remember watching MTV with my friend Tom (remember, I was 15 at the time). I never was really all that interested in rock music before 1982, other than occasionally listening to Casey Kasem's Top 40. I am the oldest of 4 boys, so my brothers were never much of an influence on my musical tastes. My parents were country fans, so that wasn't much help either. Also, all my friends were my age, and none of them had older brothers/sisters to get me into music. Anyway, from 1982 to 1984, I began to get interested in rock, primarily through MTV. I don't remember seeing "Atlantic City" [a Springsteen song and video from 1982] at the time—just a bunch of Brit synth bands who I never much cared for, although I liked one or two of their songs. My brother, Steve, who is a year-and-a-half younger than me, was also watching MTV during this time period, and he was getting fanatical about certain bands that I just couldn't understand. Pretty much anything that had a "cool" enough video for him, he became obsessed with, turning up the volume when it came on the TV or radio. I remember him into acts as diverse as Madonna, early rap (Run DMC), and Mötley Crüe (when they were wearing all that ugly makeup). He tried to get me into some of these bands, but I was still uninterested. Then in spring 1983, I started really digging Def Leppard. A friend of my bother's gave me an extra tape of *Pyromania*, and I was hooked on rock'n'roll. Songs (and videos) like "Photograph," "Rock of Ages," and "Foolin'" helped me become an actual *fan* of a rock group in a way I hadn't understood before. Def Leppard is my favorite act after Bruce.

To return to how I became a Bruce fan, Tom [his friend] and I were watching MTV, specifically Peter Wolf's solo video, I think it was called "Lights Out," but I remember the chorus of the song being something like "Dancing in the dark, oh, oh, oh, lights out, uh huh, flash, flash, flash." Anyway, the song was popular at the time. Right after the video ended, the VJ came on and introduced a world premiere video, saying that this was the first video that Bruce was actually in.[4] Of course, it was Bruce's "Dancing in the Dark" video. I had never even heard of this guy before, never mind hearing any of his music. Pretty much from the first notes I was interested, and by the end of the song, I completely loved it. I started watching MTV more often just to see the song, as well as listening to the Top 40 stations hoping to hear the song. I actually remember being disappointed when the song peaked on the charts at #2. Next, "Cover Me" came out (no video!!) and by then I had abandoned the Top 40 station in favor of 102.7 WNEW (mostly because they were playing more Springsteen). The "Born in the USA" video and song came out right before Christmas, when I received the tape of the album. I played that tape over and over and over during 1985. I thought it was the greatest album ever—I loved every song. My brother liked a few of the songs, but not anywhere near to the degree that I did. Tom also had the album and we both liked it. By the time the stadium tour came around that summer, the hysteria of the whole BitUSA thing was at its peak (especially in the NJ area). I tried like H*ll to get tickets for Giants Stadium, but the phone lines were impossible to get through and my parents wouldn't let me stay out all night for tickets. They wouldn't let me go unchaperoned either! So, I missed out (but not for the first time).

I never really bought into all the flag-waving crap associated with that tour, however. Not that I was a kid genius or anything; I just read the lyrics to "Born in the USA." However, I didn't really notice all the pro-American stuff going on at the time, so I wasn't upset about it. I even thought it was kind of cool when the President mentioned Springsteen's name in his campaign, although I didn't think that Bruce was therefore endorsing the Prez. Of course, I wouldn't have thought it was okay if Bruce had released some statement rebuking the President.[5]

Anyway, I never got around to getting more of Bruce's albums until after the *Live/75–85* set came out. I remember begging my father to buy it for me as soon as the box set became available. The day it went on sale, he came home with a copy for me that he said he bought at a record store in the city. Actually, the record store was selling them to people as the sets were unloaded from the truck out on the street outside the store!

I played the box set over and over until the tapes just about wore out. During the summer of 1987 (right after I graduated high school), I bought some more albums: *Born to Run, Darkness, Greetings.* When *Tunnel of Love* came out that fall, I was a freshman at Trenton State College (TSC). Before Christmas, I had purchased all of the "legal" albums on cassette.

I tried to get my girlfriend at the time into Bruce that summer. She was more of a U2 and Bowie fan, but she was starting to like the box set. I even made a copy of those tapes for her dad because he liked them so much. I remember looking at her *vinyl* copy of *Born in the USA* and being amazed (don't forget I didn't own *any* music until 1983–84).

When the *Tunnel of Love* "Express Tour" came around in May 1988 to the Garden in New York City, again my parents and I tried to get tickets over the phone, and again no dice. I remember pricing scalpers' tickets, but they were way too expensive (I refuse to pay more than 25% more than the face value of *any* ticket). Besides, I thought, I'll just wait until the tour comes to the Meadowlands. Needless to say, *it never did*. Bruce joined the Amnesty Tour. That fall, one of those dates was in Philly, but I didn't have any cash to get into the show.

All the time before the *Tunnel of Love* album came out, I was definitely a fan, but to a lower degree than I think I am now. The lyrics to the album really hit me in a way lyrics never have before (remember I was dating my high school sweetheart at the time), especially songs like "Tougher Than the Rest" and "Tunnel of Love." These songs seemed so passionate and beautiful to me, and I loved sharing them with my girlfriend. I also *really* listened to albums like *Born to Run* and *Darkness* in a way I hadn't before. The next spring ('88), my girlfriend and I broke up, and I listened to the *Darkness* album continuously. I just couldn't stop playing it. Songs such as "Badlands" helped me be upset, enraged, consoled, and saddened all at the same time. Then, in the spring of '89, I was a sophomore at TSC. I completely fell for this freshman, who I had known the entire academic year, but, well, spring fever got me. She was a bit of a Bruce fan before I started dating her, but that wasn't what attracted me to her. I was playing *The River* album over and over at the time; it helped me fall in love. Even though we only dated that spring and summer, I love taking that album out and blasting it out my car speakers every spring.

When I broke up with the freshman girl, I was again totally depressed (especially over the way it happened, which I won't go into here). Don't get the wrong idea, I'm not this way with every girl I've dated!! Anyway, instead of playing the *Darkness* album as I sulked, I listened to the sadder songs on *The River* and on *Born to Run*. I remember one time she came over to our apartment at school and she wanted to talk after we broke up. I refused and sat in my room listening to "Stolen Car" and "The Price You Pay" for over an hour straight while she talked to my roommates. In particular, the song "Backstreets," I felt, applied to our relationship, and I took the lyrics to that song to heart, as well. Don't get the wrong idea, again, way less than half of my strong attraction to Bruce's lyrics/songs is as a result of relationships with women.

From the end of the Amnesty Tour [1988] to the release of the *Human Touch/Lucky Town* (*HT/LT*) pair in March '92, my fandom grew, not faded. Although none of my closest friends at TSC were more than passive Springsteen fans, I did meet a couple people who hooked me onto [concert tapes]. I got copies of a BitUSA show at the Meadowlands, and a *Tunnel* show in California. This music showed me a side of Bruce I hadn't seen before—a *live* performance. I thought his showmanship was great, and the band really rocked (as opposed to some acts that I had seen in concert by this time).

By Feb/Mar 92, I was in the first year of my Masters' program here at Colorado

State University. There was this one girl I was interested in dating around this time. We were spending a lot of time together. I even gave her a copy of *Darkness* and *Born to Run* for Christmas. Anyway, the night the *HT/LT* albums came out, the local record store was having a midnight opening to begin selling them. I convinced her to come out with me, so for two hours, the store blasted the new albums through the store and offered food and drink. At 12:01 A.M., I bought the *HT/LT* albums (and the new Def Leppard which went on sale at the same time). For being first in line, the store gave me a *Lucky Town* promo poster. The local paper sent a reporter out to cover the story; he interviewed me, and I was quoted three times! For reasons beyond my control, that was the last time I was friendly with this girl, although some part of me thinks that when the album came out, I had something personal and private that I no longer needed as badly from a relationship (especially her). My instant reaction to the new albums was positive, and has been ever since. (interview, May 17, 1993)

Throughout his becoming-a-fan story, David mentions the influence of other people: his friend, Tom; his brother; women he was dating. In fact, stories that involve a gradual transformation are often tied to relationships with others. Lofland and Skonovd (1981) have labeled religious conversions which involve bonding with another "affectional"; other scholars have cited such bonding as integral to any conversion process (Lofland and Stark 1965; Lofland 1977; Stark and Bainbridge 1980; Ullman 1989). At any rate, for many fans who described a gradual transformation, the presence of another was an important catalyst for the development of their fandom. John O'Brien's transformation happened over a period of years while he was growing up in Washington, D.C., beginning with exposure to Springsteen's music at home through his mother and then through media exposure during the success of Springsteen's *Born in the USA* (1984). As he explained:

Actually, my mother listened to Bruce. *Born to Run* I remember. She played it sometimes before I'd go to school in the morning. Like "Jungleland"—and she loved that. She would just play it over and over again. And so I just listened to that and started liking it. But I wasn't really kind of a from-the-beginning Bruce fan. Actually, I was one of the people who, after *Born in the USA*, really started listening. She continued to buy until *Born in the USA* and then I was like, wow this is pretty cool, and so I got the *Live* one. And the *Live* one had all the old stuff, so then I got the old albums—the original versions of the live ones. And so I kind of backtracked which—I know people make fun of people who just join in with the big albums, but that's what's I did, basically. [laughs] (interview, March 15, 1993)

Jackie Gillis, a 26-year-old graduate psychology student in Colorado, told a story in which she first discovered Springsteen after going to a concert in her freshman year of college. She liked him so much that she went out the next day and bought the *Born in the USA* album. "But," she explained, "that was the extent of my devotion for the time being." She continued:

In 1988 (senior year undergrad), I took a small Psych class and met a guy named Chris who seemed nice enough, but who had a beard (not a plus in my book), and a leather beret-type hat and jacket. I would find out later that this was his attempt at the Bruce '75 *Born to Run* look. I ended up dating his best friend for a while so we became acquaintances. In June '88, I finished my B.A. and immediately came to Boulder, CO, for a 5-year Ph.D. program in Behavioral Genetics (which, of course, I am just finishing now). My Springsteen look-a-like friend, Chris, decided to stay in touch so we began writing and calling each other long-distance. By April '89, we were beginning to realize that this was a "relationship" (my fling with his friend ended with my graduation, of course, and he had shaved the beard by this time). He came out to visit me in Boulder and this was when two things happened: (1) I fell in love (we are getting married this coming July 24th :-)), and (2) I was "Bruce-ified". Chris totally swept me off my feet but he has to give some of the credit to Mr. Springsteen. As typical of most males I know, he had memorized almost every line to every song he had ever heard, especially those by Bruce. For example, his favorite B. S. song is "Night" [from *Born to Run*], so after he left, I got this humongous card with [a line from the song] "She's so pretty that you're lost in the stars . . ." and my very own copy of *Born to Run* through Federal Express. As he explained, I shouldn't go another day without owning *Born to Run*. This continued . . . messages on my answering machine ([Jackie] let me in, I wanna be your friend, I wanna guard your dreams and visions, etc.), cards, etc. After he graduated, he decided to move to Boulder to go to grad school also. During the next two years, we spent many hours listening to Bruce and we even took a road-trip to Utah via Wyoming and listened to nothing but "Badlands." We accidentally stumbled upon a used record store at one point. This was a turning point in my life. I had *enjoyed* Bruce up to this point, but now I was really transformed. Since that time, I regularly go to that store to pick up any Bruce recordings available. Our collection isn't as large as some people's on the net but it's growing. I only recently stumbled upon the *Backstreets Digest* but I have loved every minute of it and feel like it has even strengthened my admiration for Bruce and his music. (interview, May 14, 1993)

My own story of becoming a fan is of this type. I first learned about Bruce in high school when I took some of his albums out of the library. I was into jazz at the time and liked all the horns and funky rhythms of his earlier albums: *Greetings from Asbury Park* (1973) and *The Wild, the Innocent, and the E-Street Shuffle* (1973). I eventually went out and bought *Born to Run* (1975), but I wouldn't say that I was a fan; I just listened to it occasionally. Then, in 1985, when I was a sophomore in college, a group of people in my dorm were going to a *Born in the USA* concert in Toronto and had an extra ticket, which they offered to me. Two were die-hard Bruce fans who had been to many concerts on that tour and, while I enjoyed listening to stories of their adventures during the seven-hour drive to Canada, in the end I didn't really like the concert. I thought it was too long and too big. However, I did become friends with the people who went. I used to tease one in particular about the Bruce posters hanging in her room, but as I came to know her better and to understand how important Bruce was to her, I found myself becoming interested in him myself. I remember playing my old *Born to Run* album, really listening to the lyrics for the first time. I read about Springsteen in magazines. I studied Springsteen's guitar solos. After we got married, I truly became transformed. I remember listening to all of her Springsteen albums and tapes for the first time and being astounded by the music's breadth and energy. In particular, I latched on to a b-side song off the 1987 "Brilliant Disguise" single, "Lucky Man." It was a basic twelve-bar blues, but I played it over and over until I knew every echoing beat of the bass drum, every sharp-edged guitar slide, every catch in Springsteen's gravely voice. I loved it. Now I share my fandom with my wife; we both eagerly await new Springsteen releases and announcements of a concert tour, regularly listen to his music, watch for any news stories about him, and generally make his work a part of our lives.

The Meaning of Conversion

The correspondences between narratives of religious conversion and becoming a fan can easily devolve into pat generalizations about "media idols replacing religious figures" and discussions of the secularization of modern society. That is not my intent, here, and I think we ought to be careful about such inferences. I do think, however, that while religion and fandom are arguably different realms of meaning, they are both centered around actions of devotion, which may create similarities of experience. In fact, fans themselves are aware of the parallels between religious devotion and their own devotion.

At the very least, the discourse of religious conversion may provide fans with a model for describing the experience of becoming a fan. The fans to whom I spoke could possibly know of the language of conversion from their own religious traditions. All except one were brought up with a religion, including evangelical Protestantism, mainstream Protestantism, Catholicism, and Judaism. In fact, 65 percent claimed to be currently practicing members of a religious faith. Even then, one does not have to be necessarily religious to pick up on elements of religious conversion; as John Lofland and Norman Skonovd (1981) have pointed out, the "self-surrender type" of conversion, or what they call "mystical" conversion, is among the oldest recorded and most studied forms of conversion in the West, stemming from the New Testament accounts of Saul's transformation on the road to Damascus.

Another explanation is that fans are copying other secular models of conversion. Springsteen's songs themselves contain many references to spiritual rebirth and renewal, from the temporary escape of "Thunder Road" (1975) to the enduring change described in "Better Days" (1992). And in various interviews and concert stories, Springsteen has alluded to his sudden discovery of rock'n'roll through Elvis Presley. As Dave Marsh (1987, p. 40) quoted Springsteen: "I remember when I was nine years old and I was sittin' in front of the TV set and my mother had Ed Sullivan on and on came Elvis . . . I remember right from that time, I looked at her and I said, 'I wanna be just . . . like . . . that.'"

Rock critic Jon Landau's highly publicized story of becoming a Springsteen fan, which borrows from religious discourse by portraying a renewal of "faith in rock'n'roll," follows the self-surrender type of conversion narrative even more closely. He first told it in a published concert review in the midseventies; while the story is currently unavailable in its original form, it was the central part of Columbia Records' advertising campaign for *The Wild, the Innocent, and the E-Street Shuffle*, Springsteen's second album in 1973, and is featured in a chapter of Dave Marsh's *Born to Run*, one of the most cited Springsteen biographies among fans (Marsh 1979, pp. 126–131). The story begins with a negative setting in which Landau is "feeling old . . . and remembering that things were different a decade ago." He is transformed, however, after seeing a Springsteen concert. The transformation is described as instantaneous—he says he "saw rock'n'roll flash before my eyes"—and as inexplicable; he describes the concert only in terms of the sores on his thighs where he had been pounding his hands. (In Marsh's book, the chapter describing Landau's experience is called "Thundercrack!" which is the name of one of Springsteen's early unpublished songs and one that captures the suddenness of Landau's transformation.) Finally, he closes the story with a period of exploration, in which he is listening to Springsteen records until 5:00 in the morning, feels younger, and rededicated to "telling strangers about rock'n'roll."

One of the most important themes in narratives of evangelical conversion is realizing a new and special relationship with God through Christ. People report a strong and direct feeling of connection with God, which they refer to as being "filled with the Spirit" or "feeling the Lord's presence." In most cases, converts regard their discovery of God as a deeply personal event, something which they experience internally, in their hearts, and which is unique to them. Springsteen fans, while obviously not claiming to experience a revelation from God, are nevertheless claiming to experience a new and special relationship to another with whom they have not had any conventional contact or interaction. Most fans have not physically met Bruce Springsteen and, in fact, often describe his distance from them, as a singer they only stumble across, on the radio, or learn about secondhand from a sibling. Yet, despite that distance, they report feeling an odd closeness to him, referring to him by the familiar "Bruce," as if he were some sort of close friend whom they have known for many years. Indeed, despite Springsteen's singing to a large audience composed of many different people, fans feel that he is singing to them personally.

Among those I interviewed, many mentioned that Springsteen's lyrics were about familiar experiences, things they had done or thought themselves. For example, John O'Brien said,

It always happens that the latest single or album that comes out from him in a way matches up with how I'm thinking. It's almost uncanny. It's weird! I don't know if I'm just such a nuts fan that I make it my philosophy after he comes up with it. But it does always seem like—and I guess this is what really good artists do—he expresses something to me that I've been thinking all along but haven't really known how to say it, you know? (interview, March 15, 1993)

Others found that Springsteen empowered them with some sort of energy or philosophical stance precisely at the time when they needed that support. David Mocko, for instance, continually found that Springsteen's music "applied" to various difficult moments in his life and helped him to endure. Still other fans described intense feelings of regional or class identification with Springsteen, mentioning the importance of Springsteen being from New Jersey or identify-ing with Springsteen's—as one fan put it—"blue-collar working man image." J. D. Rummel even mentioned reacting to Springsteen's role as a performer:

Bruce first impacted my life when I saw him live in '78. The night has taken on a wholly fanciful quality in my life. Never had I been so moved by a performance. I couldn't understand a thing he was saying, but the energy, the power of that man, his music, and his band were just gripping. Part of me wanted to be that guy up there, part of me wanted to be the star. There is a certain aspect of vicarious living involved here; he is doing something that I would like to do. Not so much playing music, but having a passion and reaching out to people, contacting others and communicating through that passion. (interview, May 14, 1993)

Like religious converts and God, fans consider their relationships with Spring-steen to be solitary. For example, the fans to whom I spoke consistently described *individual* transformations, something that happened while they were alone, even in those cases in which another fan was involved as a catalyst. Thus, John O'Brien described buying his own albums after being introduced to Springsteen by his mother, and Jackie Gillis, despite the strong influence of her fiancé, talked about going on her own to used record stores and solely participating on the fan com-puter mailing list. Even in the few instances in which fans were close friends and shared most of their fan experiences, they each nevertheless talked about be-coming a fan as a personal event, not something which was able to be shared. Throughout my fieldwork, I did not come across any stories about groups of people becoming fans en masse while, say, at a concert or listening together. In fact, I would surmise that many fans might frown upon such an occurrence as too connected with the uniformity of a mass audience (something I discuss in chapter 4).

Fans also see each of their developing relationships with Springsteen as dif-ferent, based on the specifics of each person's particular experiences and values. Unlike other narratives fans share with each other—about concerts or about meeting Springsteen, for instance—becoming-a-fan stories are always highly introspective and carefully framed with phrases like "Well, for *me*" or "My own story is," which limit the significance of what is being described. While fans do not see such stories as inappropriate for public discussion, when they are shared among fans on the Internet, they are frequently marked as a special kind of idiosyncratic discourse with apologies like "Allow me a little leeway, here" or "Thanks for bearing with me."

Indeed, all of the fans I interviewed told me stories which varied in detail, length, and intensity of feeling. Part of the variation in people's stories might have had to do with the fieldwork process: some people enjoyed telling a story, while others were uncomfortable doing so, particularly to someone they had met only recently. In addition, when I was starting my fieldwork and still searching for the best ways to get people to speak, I did not ask the open-ended question "How did you become a fan?" but rather the question "When did you become a fan?" which elicited answers limited to one's specific moment of transformation.[6] Nevertheless, the variation among the stories was too well crafted to be simply reactionary; it purposefully served to signify individual personality. I spent much time with other fans thinking about the differences between their stories and my own story, about our different values and experiences that led us both to Springsteen and his music.

Of course, having a personal relationship with Bruce Springsteen does not mean that fans actually know—or have deluded themselves into believing that they know—the actual person called Bruce Springsteen. Indeed, many fans are wary of any sort of "deification" of Springsteen or fawning over him as a person. As Monty Smith, a 31-year-old engineering manager, told me:

> I've found that many fans tend to deify their idol. I've never deified Springsteen (or
> other performers, for that matter) nor do I have that burning desire to meet and
> talk to him that others share. All we fans see are his image, and the image por-
> trayed doesn't always show us the real person. So I'd have to say I don't feel as if I
> know Springsteen the man at all. His music, his shows, his image I know quite well.
> But since I don't know a thing about who he really is or what he's like, I'm content
> to stay within the bounds of fandom and enjoy the music only. I view Bruce, the
> man, as some guy a million miles away that I'll never get to really meet, much less
> know. (interview, May 1, 1995)

This sentiment is not isolated. *Backstreets* even has an editorial policy which states that the magazine will not publish anything having to do with Springsteen's personal life and instead will focus entirely on his music and performances.

While I have met many fans who *are* interested in Springsteen as a person, on the whole such fans are well aware that they do not really know him, and most talk about such interest respectfully, hesitantly, and with some embarrassment. For example, in a conversation about meeting Bruce, Judi Johnson told me about several of the "tricks" fans use to find out what hotel he is staying at during a tour. But she warned that there are "real-strict rules in terms of seeing him off-stage":

JOHNSON: In no way would I wish to stalk him. I mean, to be in a public place and to know he's there is very exciting; I would never go up to him and ask him for an autograph or bother him in any way. Now, the times that I met him in Toronto, at the hotel—we stayed at the same hotel. And when he came down to leave for the show, we were in the lobby, which we had every right to be—we were staying there. There were all these fans that gather at the hotel. And he's very amicable about it. He usually talks to them and signs autographs and everything. So, in Toronto, there were only two of us, so he was even more open. I've seen him do this where he's very nice and friendly, but he kind of has a veil up that shuts himself off somehow. I don't know. Maybe, if there's too many people, he gets uncomfortable with it. But he seems—

CAVICCHI: Well, he always seemed shy anyway.

JOHNSON: I think he is. But it was very nice to have this sort of—he didn't seem to have the veil up when he talked to us. And he was very nice to us, very friendly. So, I've been fortunate, and I think there are definite rules. You know, like yes, I've driven past his house, but [whispers] I'd never stop. [laughter] I just wouldn't. (interview, January 13, 1994)

Unfortunately, such rules regarding fans' "relationships" with Springsteen are lost on many nonfans; to them, having any sort of relationship with someone known only through the media connotes abnormality and even danger. As I have mentioned, many media critics have used the idea of having "relationships with the stars" to shape arguments about the dangers of celebrity and fandom. Richard Schickel (1985) has called stars "intimate strangers," characterizing knowledge of them as a "self-deception" or a "falsity." Daniel Boorstin (1972) has railed against the ways people are entangled in a "thicket of unreality" populated by "pseudo events" and celebrities who are "known primarily for their well-knownness." James Caughey (1984), while not entirely critical of people's relationships with stars, has nevertheless characterized such relationships as "artificial social relations" because they are relationships with people known only through fantasy or the imagination.

To characterize Springsteen fans' relationships with Springsteen as "false," "unreal," or "artificial" is, I think, to mistake their very nature. Such adjectives, instead of descriptively characterizing the connection fans feel *in their own terms*, prescriptively assign the connection a negative value by comparing it with supposedly more real, more genuine, "face-to-face" interaction. It is like calling parents with adopted children a "pseudo family" or an "artificial family" because their relationships are not based on blood. Having a personal relationship with Springsteen means that one feels deeply about Springsteen the performer; in becoming-a-fan stories, fans are not so much touched by Springsteen himself as by his performance. As Al Khorasani explains about his becoming a fan:

I know this is cliché, that I could relate to the music and all of that, but the thing that made me feel a certain way was: most people that like a rock star, they think of the person—well, I can't talk for most people—it seems that they picture the person as some kind of a deity, as some kind of a God. The thing about that music was that it never made me feel that way towards Bruce. He just seemed so . . . normal. I felt like if I see him on the street, I wouldn't react like trying to run over and grab him or something. Like, I've seen Michael Jackson concerts where they have to have a row of security across the front of the stage, because if his fans managed to get their hands on him, they'll just rip him apart. Bruce leaps into the middle of the people, and they hold him up, pass him along, and no one does anything. I think that's how most people feel. . . . I used to go and hang out with my friends on the Jersey Shore, and it was just the lyrics, the music, the lyrics were just amazing. That's what really appealed to me—the fact that it made me feel like this wasn't some kind of a god, it was just an ordinary person, writing how he felt. (interview, March 23, 1993)

In addition, the idiosyncratic nature of becoming a fan does not mean that becoming a fan is not a social phenomenon. Psychologists have long been interested in religious conversion because of the insights it gives into the nature of identity development. It is a phenomenon which seems to expose both the self and the social. In particular, converts often talk about their experiences as deeply personal yet also as part of their entrance into a specific social group or context. As Chana Ullman (1989, pp. 191–195) has argued, changes in a convert's "objective self"—that is, in social roles and cultural beliefs—go hand-in-hand with changes in the convert's "subjective self," or the way one experiences reality.

While fans see the personal details of becoming-a-fan stories as indicative of different personalities, they expect that the structure of such stories will be familiar, signifying membership in the fan community. As I've mentioned, fans purposely tell becoming-a-fan stories to each other at their first meeting to announce their fandom. Many fans in computer discussion groups are aware that they are telling similar stories of epiphany; many, for instance, make reference to Jon Landau's transformation when talking about their own.

I met one fan before he had become a member of the Springsteen fan community. He was in high school, didn't know any other fans to speak of, didn't subscribe to any fanzines, and had been to only one concert. While he told me his story of becoming a fan, the narrative was primarily framed in terms of his responses to particular songs. In fact, he emphasized all sorts of details about when he listened to them and how he felt about each. Later, however, after he had subscribed to *Backstreets Digest*, and after he had interacted with other fans for a while, he posted his becoming-a-fan story to the *Digest* for everyone to read. In this version, however, he changed his narrative so it fit with the structure of a "self-surrender" type of transformation. In particular, he began with a much clearer "setting" in which he was first exposed to Springsteen through his brother, and then, instead of detailing what songs he liked and didn't like, he rendered his transformation as instantaneous and ineffable. He simply talked about how he decided to buy another Springsteen album and said, "The rest is history, as over the next year and a half I bought every Springsteen CD I could get my hands on." Here is clearly a case of a fan who, while maintaining the idiosyncratic nature of his discovery of Springsteen, learned to shape his description of becoming a fan in terms acceptable to the fan community in which he was participating.

*O*nce a Fan, Always a Fan

At the turn of the century, popular observers of religious conversion often focused on the "duration" of someone's newfound faith and linked variation or changes in intensity as a sign of conversion's unreality. But many psychologists of religion have argued that duration is not the point of conversion and that it can be quite deceptive. As Edwin Starbuck said, conversion brings:

> a changed attitude towards life, which is fairly constant and permanent, although the feelings fluctuate. . . . In other words, the persons who have passed through conversion, having once taken a stand for the religious life, tend to feel themselves identified with it, no matter how much their religious enthusiasm declines. (qouted in James [1902] 1925, p. 258)

So it is with becoming a fan. Several fans told me that their feelings for Springsteen changed over time while insisting that such variation did not alter their fandom. LeAnne Olderman, a college student from Texas, for example, explained that while she used to listen to one Springsteen album every day when she was a teenager, as she became older she found she had less time to devote to Springsteen and became involved in other activities. Yet, despite this change in her habits, she explained that Springsteen still meant a lot to her:

> It's like when you hear your name in a conversation. People are talking, and you hear your name. You're automatically on this other plane of consciousness where you're alert; you turn your head because somebody spoke your name, right? Well, that's what it is with this music. Only you hear Springsteen's name. I just automatically—it's like, "What? Did you say something about Bruce Springsteen?" I still do that. It's like an automatic response! (interview, May 13, 1993)

Other fans talked about losing interest in Springsteen or being disappointed by his work. For instance, Mark Van Atten, a 20-year-old Dutch university student, told me that he stopped listening to Springsteen for a period:

> I selected fewer tapes, and those that I did play, I often stopped after 5 or 10 minutes; then I realized what I was doing, and I took a short cut and stopped playing him at all. The problem was that I didn't make much progress in elaborating my

more philosophical views on some things, views that were in part based on what I get from Springsteen's music.

But after taking a long break from his listening to Springsteen, Mark discovered that his connection had never left him: "When I came back to Springsteen after a while, it became clear how much I really liked it. It felt like 'it's been a long time'" (interview, December 9, 1993).

Al Khorasani told me that he didn't really like Springsteen's newer songs, especially those about marriage on *Tunnel of Love* (1987). But while Al longed for the "old" songs, he also found that his connection with Springsteen remained:

> We had a day of mourning when we heard that he was getting married. We said, "Oh no, It's over!" But then when I listened to the album, again, I said to myself, I said, "Well, I've always liked his music and I've always respected him as an honest musician because he wrote what he felt like. I always thought he didn't write what he thought people wanted to hear. He wrote what he felt like. And that's how he was. I mean, he had grown up; he wasn't a teenager anymore. It was quite different. Especially on these last two albums, when I think about it more, I see that the change is true to him. It would have been fake at this point in his career to write about "well, they closed down the auto plant in Mauwau." He is a multi-millionaire! He talks about [how] "he bought a bourgeois house in Hollywood Hills." So, again, it came back to: even at first when the change was kind of disappointing to me because I still wanted to be the protest–*Born to Run*–personal declaration of independence, he had changed and remained true to what he has always been—to write about how he felt at the time. And that's what I respect: his honesty. I felt—I don't know him personally, I don't know how he feels—but I always felt that he was honest and true to his music. That his music to him came first, before what he might have thought his fans would have liked him to do. And that I respect. (interview, March 23, 1993)

Most Christian theologians agree that "conversion" comes from the Latin verb "convertere," which means "to turn around" or "to return" and that it generally refers to a turning toward God. As Wayne E. Oates has written:

> To be converted is an inward but objective change in man in that he confronts and comes to terms with God. Conversion is not a ritual, an outward deed, or a purely subjective experience inasmuch as God is working in the processes of man's life to will and to do his good work. It leads to an observable new way of life, but this is the result of a spiritual transformation and fresh identification with God in Christ. (1978, p. 150)

Studies in the psychology of religion frame this "turning" more secularly as a radical change in the direction of one's beliefs, behaviors, or affiliations. As William James wrote:

To be converted, to be regenerated, to receive grace, to experience religion, to gain an assurance, are many phrases which denote the process, gradual or sudden, by which a self hitherto divided, and consciously wrong, inferior and unhappy, becomes consciously right, superior and happy, in consequence of its firmer hold upon religious realities. This is at least what conversion signifies in general terms, whether or not we believe that a direct divine operation is needed to bring such a moral change about. ([1902] 1925, p. 189)

Becoming a Springsteen fan also entails a radical, enduring change in orientation. It is not simply a matter of acquiring a new taste but is the development of a complex relationship with Bruce Springsteen through his work, a dramatic opening of oneself to another's experience. While fans often have trouble articulating exactly *why* they became fans, in their stories they dramatically portray the process of becoming a fan as a journey from one point to another; they indicate that it is a lasting and profound transition from an "old" viewpoint, dominated by ignorance and disenchantment, to a "new" one, filled with energy and insight.

In the end, while fans' feelings may fluctuate, connecting with Springsteen means that he becomes a part of each fan, a continuing presence to which they may turn again and again. On the whole, fandom is not some particular thing one *has* or *does*. Fandom is a process of being; it is the way one *is*.

3 Ignoring the Music Business

While many fans represent their connection with Bruce Springsteen in terms of his music "touching them," a very personal and immediate interaction, they nevertheless admit that their listening is part of a lengthy and elaborate act of commodified exchange. Fans know that when Springsteen writes a song, he cannot simply perform it for his audience; the song must travel a complex circuit involving band members, record company executives, managers, producers, recording technicians, mixing engineers, promotion people, designers, printers, record store owners, clerks, the press, radio DJs, concert promoters, roadies, and merchandisers before it ever reaches anyone's ears (see Darnton 1989). As 20-year-old college student Russ Curley told me, "Ideally, you would have music, and the people who were going to listen to it naturally gravitate toward it. But things are complicated when you have a capitalist society and system where music is big business" (interview, November 2, 1993).

Many scholars of popular culture focus on this circuit and accept as commonplace the importance of large, centralized, business institutions in the organization of fandom. As I have explained in the Introduction, theories abound in which fans are described as the product of, or response to, various kinds of business practices, from the creation of a star system to the development of media "hype." The music business is almost always portrayed as powerful and manipulative, while fans come across as either completely duped, obediently shelling out their cash for useless trinkets and shallow experiences (the view of Frankfurt School theorists and most champions of "good music"), or struggling to fight the good fight, resisting corporate greed and trying to create a better world (the view of postmodernists and neo-Marxists). In both cases, scholars tend to see fandom as something primarily shaped by a relationship with the mass culture industry.

Although the fans to whom I spoke did see some truth in these theories, they were hesitant to endorse any one. As Anna Selden, a law student in Florida, responded after I told her about the ideas of manipulation and resistance: "I think, to me, it's a little of both. I think in each, you're going to find some truth—I don't think Bruce bootlegs are as big now, just because he hasn't played in a while—but it seems that there's a little bit of each" (interview, January 12, 1994). Indeed, Russ Curley explained to me that such theories tended to paint too bleak a picture of the business:

> You have the good, the bad, and the ugly, here. The good is this is a person—like you take Bruce—he's got unlimited studio resources, he can play with anybody he wants to, all of the expenses are covered, and he has the time to put out whatever he wants to. But when you have to package something and you have to sell them, they're gonna compromise the artist's integrity to an extent. Also, the fans are going to suffer. Ideally, Bruce will write a song and say, "Let's get it out to the fans. I don't have an album, but here's a song." That would be the best. But the way the system is set up, that can't happen. You've got to put it out as an album and sell it for $16.99 as a CD or whatever; that's where the money's coming from. So, yeah, fans are at the whim of the record companies to an extent. But I think you have to look at it broadly and say, "Well, you've got to take your good with your bad." Just like in life. (interview, November 2, 1993)

Al Khorasani added that the music business wasn't as bad as other businesses:

> I have to say that rock'n'roll is one business where they're not charging—as George Will said—they're not charging as much as they could and their customers are satisfied. How many businesses can make that claim? [laughs] I still think that probably the rock'n'roll fans—being, again, involved with a money-making machine—are getting a lot better deal than let's say, maybe some of the baseball fans dealing with baseball teams. (interview, October 28, 1993)

In fact, fans' general stance toward the music business could be better characterized as a kind of indifference or disregard. Many of the fans to whom I spoke acknowledged the presence of the music business in the production of popular music, but they saw the business as incidental to their connection with Springsteen. For one thing, many fans saw Springsteen as existing outside the business and its routine production of pop stars. As Russ Curley explained:

> If you look at his relationship with the music business—he's almost like a maverick. He does what he wants to do. And they indulge him in that liberty, because he sold so many with *Born in the USA*. *Born in the USA* saved him; it gave him a lot of freedom to do what he wanted. . . . And I think he took that freedom and said, "I'm going to do what I want to do with it. I'm gonna put out an album about love, I'm gonna put out these albums here about finding myself, because I think this is what's going to work." So, I don't think you're getting as much the bad effects of commercialism of the music industry and its effects on fandom with Bruce because he's afforded this luxury of doing it. (interview, November 2, 1993)

Al Khorasani echoed this sentiment, locating Springsteen's "freedom" not in his power from sales but in his steadfast resistance to musical trends:

> I've always felt that he wrote, you know, what was on his mind. Even with the *Nebraska* album—that was a time when the big thing was MTV and a lot of electronic gimmickry in the concerts and videos—and the guy records the album on an four-track tape recorder in his *kitchen*, uses black-and-white video shots of Atlantic City, and he puts it out. And that's it. So that's what he felt like doing. I never thought of him as a fake. (interview, March 23, 1993)

Furthermore, fans explained that the music business has little to do with, and is not geared toward, their needs and desires. In particular, fans agree that, rather than serving them specifically by releasing rare tracks or live recordings, the music business serves anyone willing to pay for its products and focuses only on "hits" that will sell. As Al Khorasani explained:

> It *is* a business. We can't delude ourselves. There *is* a purpose. It's like: someone at GM [General Motors] one time—I don't know who it was—said GM is not in the business of making cars, it's in the business of making money. So sometimes, you gotta remember that a lot of the promoters, etc., they're not in the business of making music, they're in the business of making money. (interview, October 28, 1993)

Linda Warner, a retired interior designer living in New Jersey, cited the business's haphazard success with marketing Springsteen's work—particularly the choice of singles to be promoted—as a clear indication of its ignorance of fans' needs. "I've been very disappointed at Sony's handling of *Luckytown/Human Touch*.[1] The singles were a joke," she wrote. "I guess I'm cynical when it comes to retailing. The bottom line is always money. Art is not well served" (personal correspondence, November 6, 1993).

It is easy to misinterpret fans' relationship with the business. For instance, one could argue that fans are ideal consumers. They automatically buy the latest works of a star, they avidly collect past works, they go to great lengths to purchase tickets for concerts, and they are the most likely to purchase record company merchandising, join official fans clubs, and participate in "special" promotional deals. In fact, since the beginnings of rock'n'roll, record companies have recognized that stars and fans are good for business. As Simon Frith has written:

> Record sales rise without the record companies having to lift a finger, and the companies' business is not just more profitable, but easier; "what the public wants" becomes a known, fixed quantity, and the buzz associated with big stars rubs off on little stars, and so on down the rock line. The most common music business cliché, when sales are slow, is that what is needed is a "new Beatles," someone who is "guaranteed platinum." (1981, p. 135)

Or, one could argue that fans are quite resistant toward the business. Every issue of the Springsteen fanzine, *Backstreets*, for example, proudly includes the disclaimer that it "is an independent publication and is not officially associated with any of the performers we write about or their record companies." Complaints about the production, marketing, and customer service of Springsteen's label, Columbia Records, are common on Springsteen fan computer discussion groups. And fans often spurn consumer culture for an underground culture of trading various bootlegged concert recordings and videos. Indeed, several of the fans to whom I spoke indicated that they were not good consumers at all. As Linda Warner explained:

> I've stopped reading *Rolling Stone* and can't afford to buy a lot of music. So I don't browse record stores or take a lot of chances. I have to know the artist or have something unconditionally recommended to me by someone I trust before I buy it. I'm a record company's nightmare. (personal correspondence, November 6, 1993)

However, in the end, such interpretations would be, as in the parable of the blind men and the elephant, mistaking parts for the whole and would have more to do with the interpreter's interests than with fans' interests.[2] Talking about fandom as dependence on, resistance to, or negotiation with the music business only gives the business an importance in the daily lives of Springsteen fans which it simply doesn't have. As college student Carrie Gabriel told me, "It wasn't the record companies or marketing that brought me into Brucedom. It was Bruce!" (interview, April 26, 1995). On the whole, Springsteen fans do not sit around and wait for what the record company is going to do next or scheme to come up with ways to subvert its intentions. They see Columbia Records rather as a bothersome nuisance, simply part of the way the music world works. What's important ultimately to fans is Bruce's music, not how one gets it.

Of course, it takes effort to keep that narrow focus, particularly in a world where the music business seemingly controls almost every aspect of popular music. Fans constantly work to devalue the role of the music business in their fandom: first, by creating a specific, shared understanding of Springsteen as a "common man," who has a life apart from the one promoted by industry marketing; second, by developing a number of complex tape-trading and ticket-searching methods which decrease the significance of record company products and services. Both activities help make the music business more of an absence than a presence in daily life.

*J*ust a Regular Guy

The early seventies is generally acknowledged as a time when rock music—the raw, passionate, and immediate expression of a youth culture—disappeared.

Rock had become something corporate and polished, something which, in the guises of singer-songwriters, bland top-forty, or glitter rock, was either safe and respectable or a parody of its past. So, when Bruce Springsteen appeared on the popular music scene in 1973, singing about swaggering hustlers, car racing, street gangs, and teen angst, all in an astonishingly vibrant street language filled with nicknames and alliterative rhymes, he was perceived as someone who was genuine and connected to *real* life, who—in a whirlwind of storytelling and powerful images—could conjure up what it meant to be young and struggling and alive in modern America. As rock journalist Bill Flanagan explained to me years ago:

> In 1974 . . . one way or the other, everything was either folky or everything was jazzy but everything was tasteful. Taste was the key word. And the top forty was incredibly bad: you know, "The Night the Lights Went Out in Georgia" and "The Night Chicago Died" and Helen Reddy and the Carpenters and just the worst, absolutely the worst stuff in the history of top forty. And there was nobody doing rock'n'roll with brains and balls. And Springsteen came out and it was like, "Who is this greaser?" I mean, here's this guy in the leather jacket with the short hair, and he had a band at the time with David Sancious and Boom Carter—it was a mostly black band. Actually it was three black guys and two white guys. And so they would do bits of the avant garde jazz stuff. They'd do a Lonnie Linston-Smith type-of-thing to open "Spirit in the Night." And they'd do these extended "New York City Serenade"s, as well as the fact that he'd sit down by himself at the piano, à la Neil Young. So, it was real like, "Oh well this kind of a jazzy fusion thing." Or, "No, no, it's a kind of a singer/songwriter thing." And then he'd just start rockin'. Then, as well, he was romanticizing New York at a time when the whole rock aesthetic was anti-urban, pro-"let's go down to the farm, Abby, and play Allman Brothers records." It was, to me in 1974, when I was nineteen, just startling what he was putting together. . . . Springsteen was the one who stood up, and he went, "What the hell is *this*?" (interview, March 21, 1989, quoted in Cavicchi 1989)

Ever since that time, Springsteen has always been someone who has been associated with a certain authenticity. From his early song-narratives about working-class life to his more recent self-doubt about being a "rich man in a poor man's shirt" ("Better Days," Springsteen 1992), from his acknowledged dreaming about being a rock star to his clear disdain of the machinery of stardom, Springsteen has maintained a reputation as a genuine, down-to-earth person, who, despite his rise to celebrity, has simply been trying to play the music he loves and share it with as many people as he can.

This authenticity has been a popular topic of discussion among both scholars and fans. For many scholars, such authenticity is almost always contrived, a marketing strategy meant to increase sales. Rather than talking about the actual person, "Bruce Springsteen," much academic discussion of Springsteen's authenticity primarily focuses on his "image" and how changes in that image—from, say, his early "greaser" look to his *Born in the USA*–era stance of a buffed-up worker—construct different, appealing images of realism (Lombardi 1988; Pfiel 1993; Bird 1994). As Simon Frith has said: "What matters in this post-modern era is not whether Bruce Springsteen *is* the real thing, but how he sustains the belief that there are somehow, somewhere, real things to be" (1988, p. 95).

For fans, however, authenticity *is* about Springsteen as a real person. Fans are not so naive as to deny that Springsteen has an image, and one which has changed several times over the years, but for them, that image is always part of Springsteen's performance, a way to establish a mood and theme for each of his recorded works. They insist that underneath that changing image is a human being with a continuing personality, someone with beliefs and talents and a life like everyone else. In particular, while critical discussions of Springsteen's authenticity make "Bruce Springsteen" synonymous with the production of a commodity, fans clearly see "Bruce Springsteen" as a human being who has had to deal with commodity-producing institutions like the music business and the media and has had to work through the consequences of having his work mass-produced. This difference—that is, seeing Springsteen not as a commodity but rather as a human being whose music is commodified—is crucial to understanding fans' view of the music business as incidental to their fandom.

Springsteen fans certainly understand scholars' assertion that Springsteen, as a rock star, is primarily a commodity, an image that is marketed and sold. In fact, many of the fans to whom I spoke talked about the typical rock star as someone who, by virtue of their stardom, was distant and unreal. As Russ Curley said, "A lot of rock stars—they get very obscure when they get to that level. Like Michael Jackson is not someone I could relate to; and I don't think most people could. He's just out there. People like his music, but as a person, people are like, 'Well, I don't want to touch that'" (interview, April 20, 1993). Paul Fischer, a 35-year-old graduate student in Ohio, told me about his old job working as a security guard at rock concerts in Chicago and meeting many stars who were not what they seemed:

> More often than not, I have been disappointed by the ones that I had some affection for or connection to via their work. It's like, "Here they are, and boy, they're assholes." . . . So, it's like, here I am, I'm assigned backstage, I know they're going to be there, and I know they have to deal with me and I get to be the fly on the wall. They came in and treated me like shit. (interview, May 25, 1993)

However fans may feel about many rock stars, they do not, on the whole, feel that way about Springsteen. In fact, they often characterize Springsteen as having qualities that are opposite to those of the typical rock star. For one thing, instead of being involved in the "star system" of the record industry, in which the promotion of a musical product is based on the creation of a particular, continuing image or "personality," fans see Springsteen as shunning such practices, and they often tell each other stories about Springsteen's indifference or anger toward the machinery of stardom.

For instance, most fans know the story of how Springsteen was initially promoted by Columbia as the "next Dylan," a characterization which Springsteen had to spend years living down. Or they know how Springsteen failed miserably as the opening act for the rock group Chicago in 1973 and, seriously jeopardizing his relationship with Columbia Records, refused to open for anyone ever again. In one of the most famous stories, Springsteen exploded against the hype and publicity accompanying the release of *Born to Run* in 1975 by storming through a theater in London and tearing down his own promotional posters and flyers (see Marsh 1987, pp. 12–13).

Springsteen's subsequent bitter contract dispute with his manager, Mike Appel, which prevented him from recording from 1976 to 1978; his daring and unconventional 1982 release of *Nebraska*, a collection of songs which he recorded on a four-track cassette machine in his living room and a commercial nightmare for Columbia; his move toward a wider audience with 1984's *Born in the USA* and then subsequent retreat with the quieter and deeply personal songs on 1987's *Tunnel of Love*—for fans, these events are evidence that Springsteen is not utterly controlled by the business and is more interested in making music than in making money.

In addition to these stories, fans point to Springsteen's discomfort with the record industry by citing his refusal to accommodate traditional record promotion with press interviews. Though he has granted more interviews in recent years and seems to be more comfortable talking about himself, the number of one-on-ones he's had with writers can still be counted on a person's fingers. And in the interviews he has done, he has always been less than a willing subject. As Fred Schruers wrote in *Rolling Stone* about his interview with Springsteen, "Accuse Springsteen of being a star and he'll flick his hand like he's just been splashed with pigeon shit" ([1981] 1987, p. 354). When interviewed by rock critic Kurt Loder in 1985 for an MTV special, Springsteen conspicuously avoided looking at the camera, hesitated to answer questions, struggled to find the right words, and generally looked like he was going to slide right out of his seat—and the camera frame—at any moment. Again and again in such interviews, whenever asked about being a star, he denied that such a status was of any importance. As he told Bill Flanagan, "Getting caught up in the iconography and all the hero worship and idolization of rock stars or movie stars or people who win game shows is a *distraction*" (B. Flanagan 1987, p. 151).

That fans do not see Springsteen as a typical rock star is also supported by their belief that he is someone whom they may contact directly, without having to go through representatives of the record business or the media. Indeed, fans believe that Springsteen himself values such a connection with his audience. Paul Fischer, for example, echoed many of the stories about Springsteen's dealings with fans when he talked about one encounter he witnessed at a concert he worked at in which Springsteen, like Shakespeare's Henry V going incognito among his troops before battle, snuck out into an arena and waited for fans to find him:

> He spent a couple of minutes chatting with . . . people. He even took a sip of a guy's beer. And just was as nice and wonderful and as natural with them as I'd seen him in all these other encounters. And it's real clear to me that that's what he went out there to do. I mean, he really did just want to talk to some regular Midwestern folks. And the opportunity presented itself without him having to wait very long. Then, you know, after they'd sort of gone around and gone through a couple of rounds of pleasantries—you know, "Oh, yeah, we're gonna do a good show tonight" and all that sort of stuff—he excused himself and drifted back through the curtain, and that was the end of it. As long as he's not being crowded or hounded, I think he welcomes that sort of contact. I think that's very important to him. Because he has said in interviews, probably from early on in his career and throughout, that the night you get up on stage and can't see yourself sitting in the audience is when you're done. And I think that connection for him is really important. (interview, May 25, 1993)

Unlike many fans, whose letters to popular stars are answered by personnel at a record company or by their management, several fans have corresponded with Springsteen himself. Judi Johnson, for example, told me about writing Springsteen a letter after she and her daughter had traveled to New Jersey from Michigan and caught one of his surprise musical appearances at a local bar:

> JOHNSON: I told him that we had been there on vacation. It was a short letter; it wasn't very long. I told him how fantastic it was to get to see him, and I told him how much I loved the new album, and "Could I please get two autographs?" [laughs] I said I'd never asked anyone for an autograph before. And I enclosed a self-address stamped envelope, two pieces of paper, and mailed the thing off. I thought, "Okay . . ."
>
> CAVICCHI: See what happens.
>
> JOHNSON: Yeah. If he's gonna do it, he'll do it right away. I simplified it as much as I can. And I kind of haunted my mailbox for about two weeks. Nothing happened. So then, I gave up. But two days before Christmas, I received a Christmas card addressed to just myself. Most of my Christmas cards are addressed to my husband and myself. So, this was just addressed to me. And I opened it up, and it had a little note saying, "Dear Judi and Chris, Bruce and I want to wish you a joyous and healthy holiday season." And it was signed Julianne and Bruce Springsteen. [laughter] Then, underneath, in another pen, a different pen was: "Merry Christmas, Bruce Springsteen." I looked at it and went, "That is the signature. I've seen pictures of it. Oh my God!" [laughs] And the envelope was postmarked Redbank, New Jersey, and it was real. I got a Christmas card! (interview, January 14, 1993)

Other fans have met and spoken with him in person. A college student in Pennsylvania wrote:

I finally met Bruce this summer. The funny thing was that about two weeks prior I had thought of writing him a letter trying to explain what he's given me and to thank him, because I knew I wouldn't be able to do so should we ever meet. Anyway, for some reason, I never got around to it. On a Wednesday night this summer I was in Long Branch at a bar and my brother said, "Bruce is standing right behind you." I was just like, "Yeah, right, Erik." For about five minutes this went on before he (Erik, not Bruce) physically turned me around. Before I knew it, Bruce was standing next to me at the bar! I'm still amazed that the words *did* come out. I said it was great to meet him. He said thanks and asked how I was doing. I just said, "Honestly, I'm shaking" and showed him my hand. He grabbed my hand to steady it and laughed. Later, as he was leaving, in the parking lot my brother chatted with him for a while and he signed my *Tunnel* CD—which I just happened to have in the car. It was incredible!!

Of course, fans have not been able to contact Springsteen anywhere, anytime. As he has become a bigger celebrity, he has had to limit his contact with fans, and visits to his house, for instance, have often met with resistance from the local police. But most fans, despite such difficulties, resolutely hold on to their belief in their ability to contact Springsteen directly. Al Khorasani explained this belief in a story about sending Springsteen a birthday gift:

We'd celebrate his birthday every year. And we're coming—this is around *The River*—we're coming back on the campus of Syracuse University, walking back. And we were feeling no pain. It was late at night. And we said, "We gotta send Bruce a gift for his birthday." And there's the U.S. flag on the pole! One of us was actually drunk enough to climb up and reach where the rope was, finally, and we cut the flag down. We stole the flag from the quad! We ran like hell, packaged it up the next day, and sent it to Columbia Records. We had no idea where to send it; we didn't know where he lived. So we sent it—just "Bruce Springsteen"—that's what's on the back of the album, you know, I mean, he *must* get it. So we sent it, and then we forgot about it and everything.

Then, years later, the *Born in the USA* album comes out. And there's the flag on the cover. I was like, "Oh, God, I wonder, I wonder!" One of my friends called me that I hadn't talked to in years. He said, "Did you see the cover? You think that's the flag?" I was like, "Oh, God, maybe we *inspired* him." [laughter] But then, the documentary came out that said he was inspired by Ron Kovic. [pause] And I said, "Aw, damn! It wasn't us." But it still could have been our flag. It still could have been our flag. (interview, March 23, 1993)

Likewise, Mary Krause, a 28-year-old human resource director from Syracuse, New York, told me a story about making a car trip from New York to Florida with her college roommate during a spring break. They decided to stop for a visit at Springsteen's house in Rumson, New Jersey, on the way back and, despite having a run-in with the police, believe that they "got through":

KRAUSE: We went to Disney World, and while we were there, we got—we said we'll get Bruce something. Can you believe this? [laughs] Shopping for our family in Disney World—we'll get Bruce some mouse ears with his name on it, and we'll stop in New Jersey on the way home. So, we did that. It's like two in the morning, and we get to Rumson, New Jersey. And it was raining a little bit, or spitting out. Bruce was in Japan. We stopped on a side—why did we stop? Oh, we wanted to write a note . . . to the Boss. So, we stopped on a side road, had the little inside light on, and wouldn't you know it, the Rumson Police were on duty, and they saw us. My roommate was driving at the time, and I was in the passenger seat. And I said, "Quick. Give me a map!" So, we get the map off the floor. We're going to pretend we're lost! [laughs] Like we've never been there, Dan! [laughter] And the little police guy comes with the big floodlight on the car. [in a deep voice] "Can I help you, ladies?" "Well, could you tell us how to get to route—" whatever it was, the main road which I knew was right down the street. [in a deep voice] "Yes, you just go right down here, take a right, and go"—you know, however many miles.

CAVICCHI: It's just a coincidence that you happen to be parked outside—

KRAUSE: Yeah, we're right around the corner from Bruce Springsteen's house, lost. [laughs] He followed us out of town. But we fooled him, because he went left and we went right, and we knew there was a little circle that you go around and you could go right back. [laughing] So, we drive right directly back to Bruce Springsteen's house, drove in the driveway. And it was windy and rainy, so we were like, "What are we gonna do with these Bruce ears?" So, I took the shoelace out of my sneaker, and we threaded the ears and tied them to his fence post and put a plastic bag over it so it wouldn't get wet and would last until he got back from Japan [laughs]. . . . I think Evan and Jessica [Springsteen's children at the time] share the ears to this day. (interview, April 30, 1993)

Finally, in addition to viewing Springsteen as disconnected from the music industry and as someone whom you can contact directly, fans believe that Springsteen is down-to-earth. For some fans, this down-to-earth quality is a kind of class allegiance in which Springsteen becomes a rich rock star but never forgets from where he came. As Louis Lucullo explained, "When you see Bruce, there isn't any flash or glamour surrounding his act. Just the man and his music. Someone who moved to Beverly Hills but still plays in the bars of Jersey" (interview, March 28, 1993). Russ Curley echoed:

Bruce is someone I could hang out with, I could sit in a bar with, or just hang out and be his friend. He's someone who's—I'm not going to say made it out. It's not a hard area; nothing like moving out of the 'hood [laughs] in Los Angeles, but it's a place where—he's a guy who wasn't special, not a great-looking guy as far as a movie star or something—Tom Cruise is from my area (everyone famous is from New Jersey!) but I think he was just someone who, you know, was the guy down the street. His father was a prison guard, bus driver, every job you could think of; his mother worked. He wasn't especially gifted in any one area, besides being a mu-

sician. And he practiced that. He just made it and became big. I think that's why
there's such a powerful, possessive feeling towards him. I know people who were
like him who never amounted to much. He always said, "I could have been a truck
driver or I could have been pumping gas." I know people like that from my high
school who are! [laughs] (interview, April 20, 1993)

For other fans, Springsteen's down-to-earth quality lies primarily in his
music, which makes much use of actual sites and streets from the areas in New
Jersey where he grew up. In fact, one of the major activities among fans is making a "pilgrimage" to the New Jersey Shore and locating all the different streets
and sites mentioned in his songs. *Backstreets* even has published tour guides to Asbury Park and Springsteen's home town, Freehold (Cross et al. 1989, pp. 45–51).
As Mary Krause explained after showing me photographs she had taken of sites
in Asbury Park, New Jersey, including the boardwalk and a card-reading shop
called Madame Marie's mentioned in "Fourth of July, Asbury Park (Sandy)"
(1973), "I just thought it was really neat. Like: 'There it is! Madame Marie's! It's a
real place! This is so exciting!' It was just neat. Everything he sings about—there
it was!" (interview, April 30, 1993).

Other fans admire that Springsteen himself has not severed his ties to small-
town New Jersey, even after becoming a star, and that one can, from time to
time, see him around town, going to the gym, getting a bite to eat, or showing
up at the local bar for a drink. Amy Thom, a 33-year-old retail manager from
Seattle, told me about visiting her friend Linda Warner in the New Jersey area and
seeing Springsteen "all over":

THOM: We met his mailman, and we went to his health club, and we saw him coming out of the health club. And he drove in his car right behind us!

CAVICCHI: I'm sure you tried to look inconspicuous.

THOM: Oh, God. Linda was driving. She said her clutch foot was shaking so badly, she
couldn't drive. I always get mute. I just get petrified. But it was funny. (interview, April
1, 1993).

Likewise, another fan, living in New Jersey, said on *Backstreets Digest*:

My friend (Danny) was picking his wife up from the Red Bank train station late
last week and as she got off the train he saw Bruce and Evan (his son) get off behind her. He walked up to Bruce and said: "I don't want to bother you but aren't
you Bruce Springsteen?" Bruce said, "Yeah." They shook hands and Danny asked
Bruce to sign his wife's shirt (say *what?*). Bruce did and then told Danny that he had
to re-board the next train back to Little Silver (where his mother was waiting to
pick them up). He told Danny that Evan had never been on a train so they took a
train ride from Little Silver back to Red Bank. I imagined Bruce with Evan sitting
on his lap looking out the window and singing "My Hometown" [from *Born in the
USA*]. Hey, it's a cool story. *I love living here!!!* (Shareshian 1993)

Still other fans locate Springsteen's down-to-earth qualities in the way he interacts with others. Paul Fischer, for example, emphasized this to me when describing what he saw of Springsteen's behavior backstage while working as his security guard:

> The way he handled the long string of public relations encounters—you know, where they were bringing in groups of people to talk to him. These were people he'd never met and knew nothing about, and he just had to take it on faith from the record company that these were important people he had to meet and be nice to. He was really wonderful with them! I've seen other performers go through that sort of a gauntlet. And I got the impression that he wasn't putting anything on; he was the same with them as he was with me at two o'clock in the morning, when we were just about the only ones left in the building. So, there's a real consistency there. (interview, May 25, 1993)

Indeed, in the stories fans tell about meeting Springsteen, they are struck again and again by how friendly and unassuming he is, ready to chat as if he'd known them for many years and making no pretenses about being more important or special. As Anna Selden said:

> There was one story that kind of stuck in my mind. It was after a concert—I don't even know when it was—but it was still at the time when they were going around in tour buses. And the tour bus was waiting outside, and he was signing autographs for fans. This one girl went ballistic when she saw him. Tears, crying, you know, falling all over the place. And she had a little stuffed animal for him. She was like, [whispering] "I want to give this to you." And she tried—you know, you imagine trying to talk like a sniveling idiot, it's not an easy thing to do. And so, you know, he was really concerned. [in a caring voice] "Just put it up on the dashboard, here," you know. I guess what also intrigued me about him was that he seems to care about his fans. All interactions that I've heard—well, for the most part—have been positive interactions with fans, not "Get the hell out of here" but very appreciative. (interview, January 12, 1994)

No one but perhaps Springsteen or his management really knows whether Springsteen's shunning of the music business, his willingness to meet fans, and his unassuming, down-to-earth qualities are genuine or contrived. Simon Frith is certainly correct in pointing out that such qualities ironically seem to sell records. But it would be a mistake to assume, as many people do, that Springsteen's business success automatically means that he is somehow dishonest or that the qualities fans see in Springsteen are a huge marketing hoax, a utopic "fantasy bribe"—to use Frederic Jameson's term (1979)—created by those in power to maintain their cultural control. Indeed, the cynicism of such an assumption is something I find far more troubling than the fact that Bruce Springsteen is making lots of money.

In the end, what is important is that fans believe that Springsteen, despite being a successful rock star, can and does exist independently from the music business as an authentic, living, breathing human being. Popular music scholar Andrew Goodwin has said that "pop fans generally appear to want their stars clad in denim, leather, and spandex, not ironic quotation marks" ([1988] 1990, pp. 272). My discussions with Springsteen fans support this statement. Springsteen fans are interested in Bruce Springsteen and his music; in their becoming-a-fan stories, when they see him on MTV, hear his songs on an album or on the radio, or even see him in concert, they are not interested in the *media or product* through which they come to know him and his work but rather they are interested in *him and his work* as they perceive them through the media and music industry products. Springsteen's negative feelings about the music business, his willingness to contact fans, and his friendliness and lack of pretension are all factors which enable fans to see the mediating presence of publicists, managers, or advertisers as incidental to what Springsteen is all about. While many scholars are busy talking about Springsteen's marketed images, fans are busy attending Springsteen's club shows, making pilgrimages to sites in New Jersey, and meeting Bruce on the street or at the stage door. In those moments, the images fade away and Springsteen becomes a real presence: a person who has moved them with his music.

Looking for the Whole Springsteen

If one accepts Bruce Springsteen's musical work as a commodity, then one has to look no farther than the Springsteen CDs and the concert tours promoted by Columbia Records. There are no "Springsteen performances" outside record company marketing; they are synonymous. However, if one accepts Bruce Springsteen as an artist who happens to have signed a recording contract with Columbia Records, then one has to take into account the possibility that Springsteen's creativity exists beyond what Columbia Records promotes. Officially endorsed CDs and concerts in this view become merely periodic, packaged summations of Springsteen's daily life as a musician. In addition to his CD releases and official concert tours, Springsteen's work may include all sorts of songs which did not fit into the theme of an album or songs he performed live but did not record, as well as unofficial performances at bars, at private occasions, during soundchecks at concerts, and on television shows.

Springsteen fans clearly embrace the latter view. Most fans, for instance, see Springsteen as an incredibly prolific songwriter; while they may complain that he often takes years to complete an official work, they know that the problem is not Springsteen's inability to fill up an album with songs but rather his perfectionism, his choosing from among many songs, figuring which ones best fit together, which arrangements are most appropriate, which lyrics have the most impact. For every album that Springsteen has recorded, he has usually had enough extra material for three more and has routinely given many songs away to other artists like Patti Smith, the Pointer Sisters, Gary U.S. Bonds, and Southside Johnny. Stories of "extra" Springsteen songs have circulated for years among fans, and several listings have been published in fan publications.[3]

In addition, most fans see Springsteen's live concerts on tour as varying considerably from night to night, shaped by different song lists, arrangements, solos, introductory stories, and, depending on the chemistry of the venue, the audience mood, the weather, and so on, different degrees of joy, rage, and introspection. Even when Springsteen presented highly choreographed and unchanging shows during the *Tunnel of Love* tour in 1987 and again during the 1992–1993 tour, fans—despite some complaints—continued to find and value differences from show to show. When not on tour, Springsteen often makes frequent surprise visits to bars and smaller venues, as well as appearances at various benefit concerts, where he tests out new material. In fanzines and in computer discussion groups, fans are constantly sharing reviews of every one of his appearances and posting varying set lists. To see one show is to see only a piece of what Springsteen is all about.

Many of the Springsteen fans I contacted found the music business especially inadequate in capturing what might be termed "the whole Springsteen." As Charles Cross wrote in 1989: "Springsteen is one of the most prolific songwriters of the modern era. He's written over 1,000 songs; the recorded work on his nine Columbia albums is just the tip of the iceberg" (Cross et al. 1989, p. 149). Every December, when record companies tend to release retrospective boxed sets of outtakes and rarities by specific artists for the holiday season, many Springsteen fans hope that a Springsteen set will be among them. It has never happened. While singles released to promote albums have usually contained an outtake or two (they are commonly referred to as "b-sides" by fans), fans complain that such outtakes do not even begin to approach the actual number recorded and have not always been the songs that they have wanted to hear. The singles for the *Human Touch/Lucky Town* albums in 1992 and 1993, for example, included outtakes and live tracks that had already appeared on previous releases.

In addition, despite the general acknowledgment among critics and fans that Springsteen's real strength is as a live performer, Columbia Records has released only two live Springsteen albums: *Live 1975–85* (1986), a boxed collection of live tracks from various concerts over a ten-year period, released internationally, and *In Concert: MTV Plugged* (1992), a recording of a small and somewhat contrived studio concert for MTV. The former has been particularly criticized by several fans and collectors for its blatant editing and remixing of songs. As writer Clinton Heylin wrote about the *Live* set:

> Springsteen's disappointing *Live* set . . . contained a healthy dose of cuts from his scintillating 1978 Roxy show. But they just don't sound right—drummer Wein-

berg is using that annoying mid-eighties "gunshot" drum-sound, suggesting that
some serious rejigging of the original performance had taken place. (1995, p. 407)

Despite the continual clamor from fans for full concert recordings, without editing and rearrangement of songs, which capture the skits, stories, improvisations,
and sheer magic of Springsteen's live shows, no official concert recordings exist.

Fans even see the structure of the music business as inimical to promoting
Springsteen's strength live. That musicians must create a work, a product, and
then go "on tour" to "support" it is belied by the fact that most fans see Springsteen's creative process the other way around: for them, the tour is primary and
the work—which the tour is supposedly supporting—is secondary. The CD releases, while treasured and highly anticipated, are usually not much more than
precursors to the tour to come. As Gene Chyzowych explained to me:

> I think, if I could, I'd love to be around him in concert. Because . . . there's noth-
> ing boring about that. Going to see him in concert is always a new experience
> whereas listening to whatever—*Born to Run*—over and over again. . . . I tend to
> want to go out and see him live. You know, I don't want to hear him on my stereo
> anymore; I want to hear some of the stories he has to say and see him jump around
> stage and play with energy. (interview, April 21, 1993)

To further exacerbate matters, tour promoters rely on a system in which a performer plays one or two shows in a city before moving on to another; the process
is based on the (correct) assumption that most people will go to see one show
and will do so if it is nearby. Fans, however—more interested in getting their fill
of Springsteen and experiencing the changes in Springsteen's shows over time—
often attempt to see multiple shows in a wide geographical region. The fact that
the system is not made for such attendance can cause problems in terms of acquiring tickets.

To address the inadequacies of the music business in maintaining and supporting fans' interest in Springsteen's work as a whole, fans have adopted practices which supplement record company products and services.

Bootlegging and Tape Trading

Not all fans collect and listen to bootleg recordings of Springsteen's work. Several people, for instance, told me that they owned a few bootlegs but found the
poor sound quality too distracting. On the whole, however, a good 80 percent of
those responding to the questionnaire I circulated indicated that, while they
owned all of the official releases by Springsteen, they nevertheless felt the need
to supplement such releases with tapes of unreleased songs and concerts.

The term "bootleg" is actually quite ambiguous; different groups of people
use the term to mean different things. Most major record companies consider

any unauthorized recording of one of their artists a bootleg, including "pirated" or "counterfeited" copies of existing albums,[4] unauthorized copies of outtakes from existing albums, illegally taped concert performances, and homemade tapes of various songs from official releases. Most bootleggers, however, distinguish their carefully packaged products from the deceptive and often shoddily produced pirate or counterfeit recordings of existing releases; they use the term "bootleg" to refer to only to recordings which have *not* been officially released by record companies. Most fans use the bootlegger's definition, but some music fans and collectors offer yet another distinction based not in the object itself but rather in how it is used: for them, a "bootleg" is any unauthorized copy of a concert or studio recording which is *sold* by one person to another. They contrast it with a "concert tape," an unauthorized recording of a concert performance which is copied and *traded* from one person to another.

The ambiguities of the definition of "bootleg" have to do with the general history of unauthorized recordings and with the moral arguments for and against such a practice (E. Flanagan 1994; Heylin 1995). Record companies, who obviously are against any sort of competition with their own recordings, are likely to label anything not official as a bootleg. Bootleggers and fans, who are making and collecting such tapes, are more apt to see the finer distinctions of the term, locating their activities in legal "gray areas" based on differing national copyright laws and public domain statutes or on the lack of money exchanged. On the whole, Springsteen fans avoid pirate or counterfeit bootlegs (see Cross 1994). Instead, different Springsteen fans are involved in (1) buying unauthorized studio or concert recordings, often made abroad and packaged with professional equipment; (2) trading such unauthorized recordings with other fans; or (3) making or trading unauthorized concert tapes, usually on blank cassettes without any professional packaging.

How do Springsteen fans enter this "underground" world of bootleg recordings and tape trading? While bootleg recordings of classical artists date back to the turn of the century, bootleg recordings of rock artists have been around since the late sixties; the first rock bootleg is generally considered to be a 1969 recording called *The Great White Wonder*, featuring an impromptu Bob Dylan performance at his girlfriend's apartment as well as several studio outtakes. Bootlegs of Springsteen's studio and concert performances didn't surface until his career took off in 1975; since then, he has remained one of the most bootlegged artists in existence, with more than eighty CD titles alone.

In any big city, usually several record stores carry bootlegs, as do various conventions and collectors' shows. Bootlegs can also be ordered from abroad through various music fan and collectors' publications. Most Springsteen fans who buy bootlegs told me about getting them at local stores or at shows. Their accounts, interestingly, often emphasize the illicitness of such an activity. As one fan told me about his first encounter with a bootleg dealer:

I remember being a kid and going to this flea market in Edison, New Jersey, where this guy had a booth. And he would sell bootlegs, but he was totally nervous about it. He was afraid of being arrested or something. When you wanted to see them, he would stand guard—he had an enclosed booth at the flea market—he would stand guard at the door! I never bought anything from him because I just kinda felt like, "This is so bad . . . [laughs] I'm doing something evil, here."[5]

Another fan talked about how she and her friend dealt with various shady characters:

We'd meet people who had bootlegs. Slimy people. There was one guy named Gary. [laughs] We bought these bootlegs from him; they were *bad*. You couldn't really hear it too well. Anyway, people at school had bootlegs. . . . We just started collecting stuff like that—anything we could find.

Many fans find it far easier to obtain bootleg recordings through the extensive system of tape trading. Rather than having to go to a store and purchase what is considered by most authorities to be an illegal recording, fans instead trade tapes of such bootlegs (bought by one fan collector at some point, of course), as well as their own homemade recordings of concerts from radio broadcasts. As one fan explained to me:

I taped stuff off the radio when I was a kid: the Cleveland-Agora show and a couple others, like the Bruce hours, one of which had the studio version of "The Fever" played on WPLJ in New York. So, I had a few of these tapes sitting around. Then, when I got on the [electronic mail] list, someone made the offer to do b-sides tapes. So, I wrote to him and said that I'd really like to get some of these and this is what I have, it's not much, but. . . . Anyway, we became pen pals. He sent me a trade list, and I was just blown away by all the tapes and things that I hadn't heard.

Tape trading is done far less surreptitiously. Fans frequently post messages on the Internet or in the classified ads of fanzines in which they offer or ask for tapes. In the course of my research for this project, several fans sent me their "lists" of tapes for which I might trade; a couple of them included more than three hundred items. Tape trading is also a little more flexible than buying bootlegs: even if a fan doesn't own anything to trade, most traders are willing to "get a person started" by accepting whatever they have or by taking two blank tapes in exchange for one concert tape. As one person explained:

In '88, was when I discovered [tape trading]. I kept seeing, "Your list gets mine, your list gets mine, your list gets mine." And I had found one guy in a record store here who made tapes and sold them, you know, under the counter. . . . And then I went to a record show. And somebody had some tape there, and I bought that. So, I think I had a few things on tape. Finally, in '88, I put an ad in *Backstreets* and said that I wanted copies—I only wanted the shows I'd seen. I wanted Cleveland and I

wanted Detroit. And I was absolutely bombarded by letters! People with everything from one page with a few shows on it to people with, you know, page after
page after page after page of tapes. I wrote them and said, "Well, here's what I have."
Which was nothing. And I said, "Can I get a copy. . . ." and I picked one thing on
each person's list. One thing only. "Would it be possible to get this?" I mailed these
things off, and [whispers] all these tapes piled in! It was incredible! Everyone—even
though I had nothing—everyone sent me what I asked for. I am certain some of
these people just didn't—when I made and sent them their tapes, all they did—I
know now—was just take those tapes and put them in and use them for blanks.
[laughter] Because they didn't need them and the quality I had wasn't that good.
But they were kind enough to do it.

Record companies have traditionally recognized bootleg recordings only in
terms of lost profits. To them, bootlegging is all about usurpation of their power,
which is based on an exclusive recording contract signed by an artist. This is, in
fact, the stance of many of the people who actually make bootlegs. As one anonymous bootlegger told Clinton Heylin:

> The way it works at the moment is totally wrong; the way a record company can
> say to an artist, "You can only release two or three singles this year as we don't
> want to flood the market." As far as I'm concerned, if someone wants to put out a
> single every week, then why not? If people have got great music in them, then they
> should be allowed to get it out. Monopoly capitalists don't like to have the secu-
> rity of their monopoly threatened in any way. And that—basically—is what boot-
> legging is all about. (1995, p. 385)

However, for Springsteen fans, bootleg recordings represent something
entirely different. For one thing, buying, collecting, and trading unauthorized
recordings enable fans to easily and repeatedly experience Springsteen's live performances, where they locate his greatest talent. As I've mentioned before, for
fans, the "feel" of Springsteen is different live; there is a passion and order to his
music that is missing on the studio recordings. One fan explained:

> Why live? Easy. Energy. There is more energy in one Springsteen show than in
> most groups' entire tours. Oddly enough, this even carries through to recordings
> of the shows. For me, Springsteen shows are a sure pick-me-up. Pop in a good
> show on the way home from a bad day at work and I'm ready for the evening! His
> energy and enthusiasm are contagious. There are many other bands with similar
> energy and enthusiasm, but a Springsteen show has additional elements (for me at
> least): a constantly changing set list and/or stories; a sincere feeling that he's play-
> ing for the audience, for the pleasure of it; music that I enjoy enough to hear again
> and again; insightful lyrics. . . .

Another said:

> I enjoy the power of the live arrangement as well as the fact that you know the
> songs are going to be played differently than on the studio release. Usually, the live

songs are much more powerful, making even the weaker songs (are there any?) more powerful.

Live tapes also allowed many fans to experience shows they could not attend. As one fan summed it up:

> Now, because, there are live tapes, I've been able to experience all of those shows that I never did see. You know, in '78. I know when I first got the tapes of the shows at the Masonic Theater here in Detroit, I sat here—[laughs] I said, [laughing] "Was I here in town? What was I doing then? Having a barbecue? I mean, where was I? Lost in the flood with the piano?"[6] [laughs] I've had a few moments where I was banging my head against the wall.

In addition to experiencing Springsteen's live performances, fans use bootlegs to piece together a better idea of Springsteen's total artistic output. Several fans explained to me that they were interested in collecting tapes of every one of Springsteen's live shows or a "well-rounded representation," which would serve to balance the studio releases. As a fellow fan explained to me after I mentioned a tape of a 1974 concert:

> That's my favorite. I kind of wish that Bruce would release something from the in-between years, because there were so many musical styles that never made it on the albums. That's one of them. Then there's the period between *Born to Run* and *Darkness* that's just not represented. There's so much of a shift between these albums.

Concert tapes also include elements of Springsteen's performances that have never been included on an official album. One person said about one tape he had:

> Especially after I started seeing the concerts, that tape became almost more important than the albums themselves. Because it was a recording of a concert, and I could relate more to some of these songs that aren't on the album that he played. Plus some of the shticks he does. I mean, the stories are just—we haven't even touched on that—but that just endears you more to him at the concerts, that he shares these fantastic stories.

As I've mentioned, some Springsteen fans totally reject the idea that bootleggers are usurping record companies' power, seeing both record companies *and* bootleggers as running businesses whose motivations have little to do with fandom. One person explained about bootlegging:

> It's an industry that—I mean, I think they take advantage of people. Like the Deadheads have circulating tapes. Obviously, it's much easier for them with the way they set up the tapers. But, it's—I don't know, the whole idea of charging money for this music! I'd probably buy it, but I just decided that I wasn't going to.[7]

In fact, many are quite adamantly opposed to the selling of bootlegs because it goes against the spirit of fandom. Another fan told me:

FAN: I have since decided that it is my obligation, if anybody ever needs tapes, that I will help people who don't have any. Because they bring so much pleasure! And I will do anything to put someone who sells them out of business. [laughs] I mean anything. Because I find that—I dislike that very much—people who are selling bootleg tapes. Never mind the legalities of it; I just find it—

CAVICCHI: It's just not nice.

FAN: Right. The sharing of the music is what it's about.

For such fans, trading unauthorized recordings is more of a social activity than a political one. Several fans told me about friends that they had met through tape trading. I myself contacted several fans for this project through tape trading networks. And, as a fan explained when describing a long-distance friendship, tape trading can serve to unite people: "It's really funny! . . . I'll say, 'Which one are you listening to?' And she'll go, 'Well, I'm listening to tape number two from night such and such—' [laughs]."

Ticket Strategies

Buying and trading bootleg recordings enables fans to supplement record company products. But fans have also developed other activities to address the inadequacies of the music business in organizing live performances. While fans are, generally, dedicated concert goers who will certainly go to any show involving Bruce Springsteen, they are frequently unable to go to such shows because of current ticket sales practices. In the seventies and early eighties, when Springsteen was not yet a "megastar," a fan got tickets for a Springsteen show by getting a good position in the ticket line, often by going to the local box office before tickets officially went on sale. This method rewarded the most dedicated of fans; the earlier the fan got in line, the better the chance of getting good seats. Many fans in the early years even camped out or arrived the night before tickets were to go on sale and formed a line on the sidewalk.

However, with the advent of Springsteen's stadium shows in the mideighties—which drew audiences from a widely expanded regional area—and the accompanying development of new ticket sales strategies to handle the volume, tickets have become more difficult to obtain. Because more people at many different outlets purchase tickets for the same show, blocks of the best seats may disappear within the first few minutes. The release of tickets has become networked into a central computing system; if one computer fails to function at a sales outlet, sales continue, and the people in line at that outlet lose out. To prevent camping out, which disturbed local vendors in the late eighties, a method of wristband sales was developed in which people have to go to an outlet a day before tickets go on sale, receive a nonremovable wristband with a random number, and come back the next day and line up according to that number. Further exacerbating matters has been the introduction of phone ticket sales, which, despite their so-called convenience, are often slow, limited, and accompanied by exorbitant "service fees."

On the whole, instead of rewarding the most dedicated, such new strategies treat every potential audience member the same way. This approach is a source of great bitterness among fans; indeed, whenever I brought up the subject of the music business during the course of a conversation, most fans initially responded by talking about the frustrations of obtaining tickets to Bruce Springsteen performances. Mary Beth Wilson, a 27-year-old insurance manager from New Jersey, explained:

> The first time I ever remember hearing about somebody who was going to a show
> . . . was during *The River* tour [1980–1981]. My cousin had gotten tickets, and that
> was something that interested me at the time, but I was much too young to pursue that on my own. By the time *Born in the USA* rolled around [1984–1985], I slept
> out one night in a town called Montclair, New Jersey, with some friends. We slept
> out on the sidewalk all night long, and it was cold and raining, and we never got
> tickets. (interview, January 17, 1993)

Indeed, Russ Curley explained to me that in New Jersey, tickets to Springsteen shows are often regarded with awe. "I was at work and I told people I was going to see Bruce and they were like, 'Oh, wow! You're lucky' and 'How much do you want for 'em?' [laughs] That sort of thing" (interview, April 20, 1993).

Several fans told me about being so desperate for tickets that they obtained them illegally through a ticket scalper, often for hundreds of dollars more than they would have had to pay ordinarily. Anna Selden told me about trying for years to get legal tickets for Springsteen shows where she grew up in Virginia. Finally, she couldn't take it any more:

> When it came around to [the 1992–1993 tour], I was down in Harrisonburg, Virginia, which is where I was in school at the time—this was during the summer.
> And it's a very, very small town. I had no *clue* that tickets went on sale. So, I came
> back home, and they had gone on sale like two weeks ago and had obviously sold
> out. So, I was like, "Be damned if I'm not going this time." And I perused the papers and, as much as I hate scalpers, I was like, "There's no way I can miss this one."
> I mean, it was worth every bit of it, but I hate the fact that I had to do that. Because
> it's just a business. Scalpers are people who go and buy two hundred tickets. And
> I *can't get two*. (interview, January 12, 1994)

Indeed, several fans raised the issue of ticket scalping as indicative of the music business's general attitude toward fans. As Al Khorasani said:

> These ticket scalping outfits—1-800-USATIX—I really wish, I really wish that fans
> could unite—"Fans of the World Unite!"—we could write a rock'n'roll manifesto,
> here, with a guitar and a drum instead of a hammer and a sickle [laughter]—and
> no matter how bad they wanted to see a show, not buy it from these people. Scalping! These outfits really get to me. Sometimes promoters take those tickets for the

front seats and sell them to these outfits. I mean, artists and the labels and the promoters are getting kickbacks on these things! And that's what gets to me. I don't
really respect much artists or promoters or people who knowingly do that. That
is really abusing your power. I mean, how much is enough? Aren't you making
enough? (interview, October 28, 1993)

Faced with such problems in simply seeing Springsteen in concert, fans eventually came up with various "ticket strategies" meant to find the loopholes in
new ticket sales practices. While initially spread through word of mouth, *Backstreets* has actually published a booklet, *50 Guaranteed Tips to Great Springsteen Tickets*
(Cross et al. 1990). These strategies include anything from befriending the local
ticket salesperson to traveling to distant outlets which might sell tickets to a local
show. (For instance, ticket outlets in Portland, Maine, sell tickets for shows in
Boston.) Because ticket sales in many cities are often limited per person, many
fans organize ticket-buying groups with many people fanning out to several regional outlets and then collectively sharing whatever tickets they are able to buy.
One strategy several fans told me about was to look for "extra seats." Not all rock
arenas are the same, and, depending on the setup of the stage, extra unantici-
pated seats often go on sale the night of the show. As Judi Johnson explained
about the 1992–1993 tour:

JOHNSON: Okay. Well, you know how the stage was sort of oval. Up on the side, there
were like four rows—sometimes three—three or four rows of seats near—they were
like the front rows. And then, up on the side of the stage, there were some on the floor
right up by the stage? We referred to those as the "magic seats." They released those
the day of the show, in all these cities.

CAVICCHI: So, it depended on how they set the stage up and all that? Yeah.

JOHNSON: And they would release the magic seats.[8] And I sat in those seats, like in
the second or third row. Never the first row, because the first row they gave out to people in bad seats. They went up and walked around up above and pulled people down
and sat them in the first row. But I got those seats in Tacoma, I got them in Cleveland,
Lexington, Pittsburgh—well, not Pittsburgh; I got an equally good seat, though. (interview, January 13, 1994)

David Mocko finally got to see his first concert through the same method:

That August [1992], I took my first break from working on my thesis all year and
took a trip back home to NJ. I arranged the timing of my trip to coincide with
Bruce's August 28/29 dates at the Spectrum. All week I was home, I tried to get
tickets (legitimately!), but to no success. The day of the Friday 28th show I was in
a local record store when I overheard the salesgirl talking about Bruce just releasing a few more seats for the show that night. I rushed to the nearest pay phone,
and ordered first row tickets behind the stage!! I went with one of my oldest friends,
John, and had a great time. (interview, May 17, 1993)

On a larger scale, ticket strategies have also included petitioning Springsteen's management for a reorganization of ticket sales. As the editors of *Backstreets* explain in the preface to *50 Guaranteed Tips*:

> What we've pushed for all along is for the Springsteen/Landau organization to set up mail order hotlines for the serious fans, along the lines of the ones organized by the Grateful Dead for their fans, which will help Bruce guarantee large crowds and which will assure that the true fans get the first shot at tickets. We've lobbied for this, and we hope you continue to do so too, but until change comes to the organization, you're on your own. (Cross et al. 1990, p. 1)

Calls for formally involving fans in the distribution of tickets crop up regularly on fan computer discussion groups. For example, in the spring of 1995, responding to a call from one fan about starting a fan club so that there might be more "official interaction between Bruce/management and us hard-core crazies," several fans on *Luckytown Digest* suggested that such a club might receive first chance at tickets, similar to systems recently set up by groups like U2 and Pearl Jam with their fan clubs. Such discussion led to several elaborate proposals. As one person said:

> I think it would be cool if Bruce did maybe three shows. Tickets would be distributed through fan organization—the one time the unofficial would interact with the official harmoniously. Bruce could do a show East (probably Meadowlands), West (LA Coliseum?), and the Midwest (say, Chicago). Maybe add an extra show in Meadowlands. Granted this isn't efficient because some parts of the country are getting left out, especially the down South. If the demand were great enough, perhaps a show might get added down there. But the key is to keep this to a minimum so as not to exert a lot of pressure on anybody and to keep costs minimum. Profits might go to a different charity at each venue, perhaps something local. So, you've got these shows and fans from areas would all commute to the venues to watch the show. (Stagl 1995)

In the end, little has come from such initiatives, and Springsteen fans have learned to rely instead on each other both for information on upcoming concerts and for obtaining seats to shows. *Backstreets* sends a special hotline number to all of its subscribers where they may find out about the latest Bruce information, including rumored and confirmed concert appearances. The old fan computer mailing list, *Backstreets Digest*, had a special address to which people might post crucial and late-breaking concert information. And in classified ads in fanzines, on computer discussion groups, and through word of mouth, fans often either ask if anyone has extra tickets to upcoming shows or advertise that they do have extra tickets and are willing to sell them at cost to other fans.

Both the buying and trading of unauthorized recordings and the use of various ticket strategies enable fans to correct the music business's ignorance of fan needs. Such practices are not the only ones fans have developed. One could talk about fans' circulation of their own CD and concert reviews and close monitoring of the music press as a way to supplement the sometimes brief promotional information provided by the Columbia Records, or one could interpret fans' collecting of various Springsteen memorabilia, including everything from ticket stubs to old promotional posters, as a way to supplement scant record company merchandise. What's important in these practices is that fans perceive the music business as unable to support fans' attachment to the whole of Springsteen's musical work and uninterested in trying. Instead, fans have had to develop extra products and services which supplement those of the record company.

The *Greatest Hits* Debate

In the spring of 1995, after twenty-five years of playing and recording rock music, Bruce Springsteen released a greatest hits CD; it contained most of his singles as well as several new songs with a re-formed E-Street Band (which he had broken up in 1988) and a new recording of a song from the *Born in the USA* (1984) sessions. While the music industry press greeted the idea with much excitement, and while Springsteen himself promoted the album with several interviews, many fans were not entirely happy. In fact, from the moment the album was announced in January, fervid debate filled the postings of *Luckytown Digest*.

For some fans, a "greatest hits" album was artistically empty and an indication that Springsteen had possibly "sold out" to the business and its profit-making mentality. As one fan said, appealing to Springsteen:

> Remember—one of your biggest appeals to both fans and critics is your integrity and your refusal to do anything to make a quick buck. We love you for that, and trust that you won't exploit our desire to hear new music by releasing something that most of us already have! (McCrae 1995)

Responses to such a judgment of Springsteen ranged from complete agreement to warnings that not liking *Greatest Hits* was an insult to Bruce, but most fans fell somewhere in the middle, posting messages which argued that the appearance of *Greatest Hits* was simply part of Springsteen's contractual obligation to Columbia Records and that it was intended to introduce his music to more people rather than to satisfy fans. As one fan wrote:

> You know, I was under the impression that the main reason I loved this artist so much was because of the music he writes. As wonderful as "integrity" and the "refusal to do anything to make a quick buck" are, I don't buy his albums or search out his bootlegs for those reasons. Whether or not an artist likes to make money is not a factor I use in selecting my music. And since when does making a greatest

hits package go against those ideals? We all complain that no one else appreciates his music. If he comes out with a new album and it gains mass appeal, we eschew the new fans from our group because they are just "jumping on the bandwagon." "Listen to 'Rosalita' or 'Thunder Road,'" we say. Well, now people will have the chance to do so without having to spend $150 on all of his CDs. They can see for themselves why we adore this man's music so much and perhaps gain some more mass appeal for Bruce. Then when we talk of how much we love his work, maybe people won't give us those strange looks anymore. . . . (Sanders 1995)

For other fans, *Greatest Hits* was not about Springsteen's integrity but rather about the continuing inadequacy of Columbia Records in its handling of Springsteen's work and recording career. Several fans found the idea of the CD and its rumored song selection to be lacking any merit:

I'm afraid that with *GH* [*Greatest Hits*], there will be no order but just one song after one song. Those who are saying that they finally have all the good songs on one CD sure have missed the boat. Bruce's albums are albums, meant to be listened as a whole, not one song here and one song there. Plus, *GH* doesn't even have the best songs. (McDonald 1995)

In addition, several fans mentioned the rumors of a new Springsteen album in the works and cited the release of *Greatest Hits* as an unnecessary detour. As one fan said,

For two months, the word has been circulating that there will be a new studio album this spring, and now we hear this. Forgive me for being cynical about the prospect of seeing a new studio album later in the year. Forgive me also for sharing Andy K.'s sentiment that perhaps Bruce's management could come off the mountaintop every two years or so and tell us what's going on. . . . (Svoboda 1995)

Few fans contested such claims except to say that it would be "difficult to choose" Springsteen's greatest hits. In fact, on *Luckytown Digest* as well as in *Backstreets*, fans spent much time compiling lists of songs they would select for the *Greatest Hits* album if given a choice. Not surprisingly, fans' lists mixed already-released and unreleased tracks equally; while the actual *Greatest Hits* CD contained a "bonus" of four, new, unreleased songs, fans had already heard two of them and often rejected those for ones of their own ("Best of Bruce" 1995).

These debates over *Greatest Hits* on *Luckytown Digest* clearly demonstrate fans' problems with the music business: on the one hand, many fans were concerned about Springsteen's authenticity, his distance from the music business; on the other hand, fans were concerned that this release was another flawed product, particularly since it purported to represent Springsteen's career and that many other songs—either new ones or those sitting in the Sony vaults—had been ignored. Of course, not all fans agreed about what Springsteen's "authenticity" entailed or how one might represent Springsteen's musical career. Nevertheless, at the foundation of such debates lay an ideal view of the music business as separate from Springsteen, as not a motivator for his work but rather a supporter of it.

However, the release of *Greatest Hits* did not lead fans to stand for or against the music business. Despite the volume of the messages posted on *Luckytown Digest* about *Greatest Hits*, and despite the ferocity of some of the debates, in the end, most fans bought *Greatest Hits* and put it on their CD shelf alongside their collections of Springsteen's other official (and, for some fans, unofficial) works. As Judi Johnson explained to me when I asked her about *Greatest Hits*:

> I started out angry . . . then I lost my anger and resolved the whole thing. There are certainly fans to whom this is targeted. I am not one. But to appease me he added the four new songs and at least gave some thought to what his hardcore audience has clamored for. The new-to-me songs were a pleasure. "Secret Garden" took me longer but it clicked after about 15 listenings. "Blood Brothers" was immediate. I really loved it. I loved the lyrics, the vocal, the whole thing. (personal correspondence, April 13, 1995)

Russ Curley wrote to me:

> As I described to you once in an interview, one of the things I truly admire about Bruce is his way of coming out with an album that has at least one song that describes *exactly* how I'm feeling at the moment. "Blood Brothers" is that song for me. I have been separated from most of my friends from Brown, and they're working and don't have a lot of time to keep in touch just like me—bogged down "with work to do and bills to pay." But there is something heroic I think in trying to keep those friendships and memories alive, and that song is a window into my feelings these days. I know we will always be friends and I'll always keep them in my heart. I'm sort of ambivalent about the *Greatest Hits* album—on the one hand, it does not say anything artistically, but on the other hand, I look at Bruce as an old friend whom I trust and grant a lot of latitude. So I say if he wants to do this it is fine with me. I'm just glad he has the band together again. (personal correspondence, April 5, 1995)

In the end, fans are aware that they are deeply involved in an economic process in which music is commodified and sold to them, and several fans have negative opinions about the music business and its practices. But to obsess about such things is not what fandom is about; most fans grudgingly accept the presence of the business in their lives. Some scholars might label such acceptance of the music business as a kind of "false consciousness," a deluded state of ignorance about what is really important. But when fans talk about Springsteen as just a "regular guy" who happens to have a record contract or about themselves as just a group of listeners who want to hear more good music, they do so because such characterizations place an importance on the one relationship that means the most to them: their connection with Springsteen. Ultimately, to be a fan, to connect with Springsteen, a fan has to ignore the commerce, let go of the intricacies and abuses of the business, and listen to the music.

4 *Fans in the Audience*

Performance and the Politics of Participation

In their becoming-a-fan stories, fans often begin by describing themselves as "ordinary" popular music listeners, casually using rock as a form of entertainment which accompanies, but does not necessarily shape, their everyday behavior. Springsteen is an indistinguishable part of the media background of their lives; even those who know of him do not give his identity or music much attention beyond seeing one of his albums in a friend's collection or enjoying one of his songs briefly on the radio. But then, something happens. Either suddenly or gradually, fans talk about moving away from that casual stance and becoming people to whom Springsteen's music deeply matters. As Jackie Gillis explained about her becoming a fan: "I had *enjoyed* Bruce up to this point, but now I was really transformed" (interview, May 14, 1993).

The distance created by this movement from ordinary listener to fan is an important element of fans' understanding of their fandom. Whenever fans go to a concert, a record store, or anywhere else where they may interact with the larger Springsteen audience, one of the first things that strikes them is how different and alien nonfan audience members appear. John O'Brien, for example, told me about attending a concert on Springsteen's 1987 *Tunnel of Love* tour:

> I remember going to *Tunnel of Love* and looking around and thinking, "Wow, these people must just know 'Tunnel of Love,' must just have heard that single." And I wondered if they really understood the words and stuff. I'm not trying to be condescending, because I don't know. But you wonder about that sometimes. (interview, March 15, 1993)

Mary Beth Wilson echoed:

> To me—and I've said this to my friends Joe and Dave a million times during the shows—I feel you should have to pass some kind of test to get into a Springsteen

show. Because these people don't care the way I do, so [laughs] I don't want them there! (interview, January 17, 1994)

Indeed, when describing concerts, fans often tell humorous stories about their encounters with members of the "general audience." As one person on *Backstreets Digest* opened his story about a concert in Dallas in 1992:

The night began auspiciously enough, as the guy directly behind us in line apparently held a Ph.D. in Bossology. "You know," he spewed, "the only reason Bruce got rid of the E Street is because they wanted too much money." I nodded in mock agreement and laughed internally. Anyway we got inside, bought our required Bruce paraphernalia, and settled in to enjoy the show. Our seats were only second row lower balcony, not great but we were on the side nearest to Gia [Ciambotti, one of Springsteen's backup singers]. About 8:10 the crowd finally started pouring in, and Bruce took stage soon after. The set was essentially the same as Atlanta, with his Santa garb. My only disappointment was that he didn't play "Atlantic City," but I was prepared since I had already read the set lists from earlier shows that didn't include it. The gentleman behind me however lacked the same advantage, since after every song he would scream "Spurrit in the Niiiightt!! Spurrit in the Niight!" in typical Texas drawl. (Stinnett 1992)[1]

This distinction, from the point of view of fans, is clear enough: fans have a connection to Bruce Springsteen that nonfans do not. However, in reality, the distinction is far more ambiguous and difficult to pin down. Having a special, sustained connection with Springsteen is a deeply personal and internal affair that is difficult to define or measure. How is one to tell between someone who likes Springsteen's music and a fan who feels a strong connection to it? Both types of people know the songs and something about their context, both eagerly go to see Springsteen perform, and both buy many of Springsteen's works. As I have shown, fans often tell stories to one another about becoming a fan, but not all fans are equally gifted storytellers or even have any coherent stories to tell. Indeed, many nonfans can probably pinpoint, and tell a story about, when they first came to like Springsteen.

Contributing to this ambiguity is the fact that, in terms of participation in the popular music events, a fan is really no different from any other audience member. Everyone who goes to a Springsteen concert has to go through the same process. Everyone has to wait for an official concert announcement from Springsteen's management, stand in the same ticket lines or call the same ticket agencies, and pay the same amount of money per ticket. At the concert itself, everyone who drives parks in the same lot, and everyone sits in the same arena, buys the same T-shirts and programs, and sees the same show. Likewise, everyone who wants to purchase any of Springsteen's works has to do the same thing. Everyone must wait for the same release date of an album, go to the same record store chains, stand in the same checkout lines, pay the same amount of money, receive the same mass-produced product, and play it on similar audio equipment.

Further complicating matters is fans' tendency to talk enthusiastically about Springsteen's audience on the whole. Fans are often concerned about the sales of Springsteen's records and the general response to them; the size and mood of Springsteen's larger listening audience are obviously important to Springsteen as a performer. Fans even talk about the importance of the larger audience in terms of their own fandom, and the power of being part of the audience is a common theme in accounts of concerts. As Gene Chyzowych said about one concert he attended:

> It was incredible. You have to think about Giants Stadium—you know, that was basically his home venue at that point. That was the largest stadium in New Jersey, so when he was going to be playing New Jersey, that's where he was going to be. And the energy, with 75,000 people on a summer night going to see Bruce Spring-steen, was pretty incredible. (interview, April 21, 1993)

Al Khorasani described being astounded by the audience at his first Springsteen concert:

> I hadn't been to too many concerts at that time of life—I had seen Pink Floyd. And the crowd was so different! I was expecting something quite different. I was ex-pecting more, I guess, subdued, I don't know, more mellow. I had this vision of like James Taylor or Jackson Browne in mind. And then when he came on rocking like that—it just—at first, I didn't know how to react. I think what was amazing to me was his control over the crowd. He could say—you know, he would just raise his hand like he wants to talk, and [whispering] Madison Square Garden is quiet. [re-suming normal tone] It was amazing. Madison Square Garden is never quiet! I mean, the way people—I think that people felt that he had something to say and they wanted to hear. (interview, March 23, 1993)

Fans see themselves as separate from the general audience yet also a part of it. While being a fan in the ideal depends on a distinction between the categories of "fan" and "nonfan," being a fan from day to day nevertheless depends on a complex and continuing relationship with nonfan audience members. In fact, changes in the composition of Springsteen's general audience over the past decade have sparked serious debates among fans about the definition of fandom itself.

a Part of and Apart from

Several contemporary scholars, in their work on popular culture and the media, have addressed the distinction between fans and more "ordinary" audience members. John Fiske, for instance, has characterized fans as "excessive readers," involved in a "heightened" form of all popular culture audiences' behavior. He claims that "fans may differ from less excessive popular readers in degree, but not in kind" (1989, p. 147). Conversely, Lawrence Grossberg (1992a) has characterized fandom as quite different in kind from other types of audience behavior. For him, fandom is based on giving a certain "significance," or weight, to popular culture, while ordinary audience behavior is based on the pleasure and enjoyment of it.

Despite their different views, both Fiske and Grossberg locate the distinction between fans and audience in the broad economic context of mass society. In particular, they emphasize how people act variously as consumers of mass-produced, widely marketed "texts" of popular culture like television shows, romance novels, and albums. This singular focus on the consumption of mass-produced products does not address Springsteen fans' own views of popular music. As I have already argued, Springsteen fans generally dismiss their role as consumers and see the music business as a mere conduit between them and Springsteen. Instead, it is the moments of direct connection with Springsteen—at concerts, for example—which are central to their understanding of what it means to be a fan. Indeed, for Springsteen fans, music is not a product to be consumed but rather a performance to be experienced, not a static "text" that is mass-marketed but rather a dynamic event of communication unfolding through various media in space and over time.[2]

In the context of performance, the difference between fandom and ordinary audience behavior is not about how one consumes a product but rather about how one participates in an event. One of the most important aspects of any kind of performance—whether play, television show, CD, or concert—is that it is a special social event which is bracketed off from ordinary life, operating in a certain "frame" that contains unique and specific rules for behavior (Bateson 1972; Goffman 1974, Turner 1988). At a rock concert, for instance, no matter what participants may be like in their "normal" daily lives, during the performance they assume new, specific roles: some people become performers, some people become crew members, and others become audience members. In each of these roles, people behave in ways that they would not outside the performance: performers jump up and down crazily and scream in the middle of a crowd of people; crew members wear black and silently move in the shadows; audience members clap and yell or hold up cigarette lighters to show appreciation and sing when a mike is pointed in air—all things which would be inappropriate in the context of everyday life. As Judi Johnson told me about attending a Springsteen concert:

> I can remember the next day, saying—you know, there I am, forty-two, forty-three years of age—and I said, "I stood on a folding chair, yelling 'Goobah, goobah,

goobah!' [laughter] I can't believe someone has that kind of power over me! [laughs] He made me stand on a chair and yell 'Goobah, goobah, goobah!' [laughter] But, I did!" (interview, January 13, 1994)

In addition, a performance generates certain feelings of connection or exhilaration which are specific to the performance. Many performers have mentioned the high that they get from performing; Bruce Springsteen used to say that the only place he felt right was on stage. Music listeners, including Springsteen fans, likewise report a similar kind of high, which includes feelings of exhilaration, connection with the performer, and a sense of unity with other participants.[3] As Gene Chyzowych explained about attending a concert:

> It's hard for me to verbalize what a Bruce Springsteen show is like, because it's an incredible experience. I mean, you could talk about—"Well, it could be just his music and his presence"—but I think it has a lot more. There's a lot of intangibles there. I think it's just this energy, maybe his smile, maybe his—[pause] It's very hard. There's something about his presence. . . . I think it's the whole area. It's him, his music, and his presence on stage, which does so much. It's a feeling of—I mean, for instance, there were 75,000 people at Giants Stadium! People of all ages. I mean, I was probably on the younger side, but there were families there, and I'm sure I saw people that looked like grandparents—older people. (interview, April 21, 1993)

This idea of a performance as a special, framed event is central to fans' understanding of their difference from ordinary audience members. In particular, fans see themselves as differently connecting their special experiences during performances with their daily lives. For most people, the role of audience is not very powerful. There are no special requirements for becoming an audience member; all one has to do is buy a concert ticket or a CD. Subsequently, ordinary audience members have no qualms about engaging in much "out-of-frame" or normal behavior during a performance, like talking with one another or getting up to get food. Indeed, while most people who listen to a Springsteen CD or attend a Springsteen concert abide by the conventions and roles of the performance frame and most have some kind of feeling of exhilaration or connection, these conventions and feelings are understood as only part of the performance frame and disappear once the performance ends. Being an audience member is a temporary role easily filled as the performance begins and then left behind as it ends.

Unlike ordinary audience members, however, fans see the role of audience member as very special and serious; they see the process of becoming a member of the audience as an elaborate ritual with many "requirements." Buying concert tickets or CDs involves lengthy road trips, camping on sidewalks, standing in long lines, and much strategy. In fact, fans feel that they *must* be involved in any Springsteen performance; those who are unable to attend a concert, for instance, see their inability as a failing. Appropriately, during concerts, fans are eager to engage in performance-specific, "in-frame" behavior, like swaying to the music, singing, and dancing. As we shall see, they regard those who get up to get food or talk as a nuisance and not deserving of the audience role. And while ordinary audience members easily drop the role of audience once the performance ends, fans tend to remain "in frame," making their role of audience a part of their daily identity. They relive specific moments of concerts by collecting and listening to concert tapes; they collect Springsteen memorabilia—including buttons, posters, and newspaper clippings—to amplify and sustain the excitement of a CD release or concert tour; they look for Springsteen on the street or make pilgrimages to the sites in his songs in order to support feelings of connection with him; and they read *Backstreets* and participate in fan computer discussion groups in order to interact with other fans and, as at a concert, maintain feelings of unity with people who would otherwise be strangers.[4]

This contrast between temporary role of audience member and the more permanant role of fan is an important feature of fans' discussions about fandom. Fans characterize ordinary audience members as people who only listen to records or periodically attend Springsteen concerts and who, in both instances, let the music "go in one ear and out the other." Conversely, they see themselves as existing both inside and outside the performance frame, as people who have "stuck with it" or for whom Springsteen is "life." As Amy Thom explained:

> I think an ordinary listener, for example, would go out and buy the new release because maybe they heard a cut or two on the radio that they liked, or maybe they were into the *Born in the USA* thing, and they'd give the new album a try or something. And they'd listen to it, and they'd put it down for a while and listen to it again here and there. Whereas a fan would be the first one in line to get the tape the morning it was available and would listen to nothing else for the next month and would be on the various hotlines that are available to find out when the shows were going to come and just really live it. (interview, April 1, 1993)

Russ Curley echoed:

> A lot of people I meet will say, "Yeah, he's okay. I like him. I listen to his records; he's okay." But unless you can delve into his major body of works, not the [singles] that are released off the albums—you gotta listen to the real stuff on the records, think about him, analyze him, and see him live. It is almost a requirement. (interview, April 20, 1993)

In addition to differently connecting Springsteen's performances to their daily lives, fans and ordinary audience members differently perceive the meaning of those performances. Fans see ordinary audience members as passively responding to the more obvious and superficial elements of rock performance, interested only in having fun, partying, and being entertained. But by strongly weaving their performance experiences into their daily lives, fans see their own participation in rock performance as far more active, serious, and interpretive, as shaped by something larger than the performance itself. As Louis Lucullo explained about listening to a song:

> "Born in the USA" is a good example to show the boundary between casual listener and certified "fan." The casual listener doesn't really bother to consider the lyrics of the song, but instead takes it at face value to be a pro-USA anthem. The fan, in contrast, puts the singer before the song and wants to know why the lyrics are not pro-USA, but in actuality an expression of resentment against a country and its treatment of those drafted to fight in Vietnam. So, the fan goes and buys books about Bruce, collects bootlegs of Bruce, and listens to all the Bruce music there is, including unreleased material. (interview, April 20, 1993)

Richard Schechner (1977, p. 87) has made the argument that any performance is either "efficacious," an event that makes things happen (like a ritual or religious ceremony, for example), or "entertaining," an event that serves to create pleasure (like a play). Fans see both these distinctions in the same performance event; while a Springsteen concert acts as entertainment for the general public, for fans it represents efficacy.

For fans, a Springsteen concert is not a single theatrical event but rather a ritual in which they regularly participate over time. Fans see any concert as connected to all other concerts and understand their concert going as a repetitive action, something they've done before and about which they have extensive knowledge. Not all Springsteen concerts are the same, of course, but the tension between what changes and what remains the same is very important to fans' experience of any show. Many fans even keep track of what songs Springsteen plays from concert to concert and study any variations in their structure or arrangement (e.g., Cross et al. 1989, pp. 167–218). As David Mocko explained, "A concert . . . seems more of a celebration, not to mention the fact that by the time I see him in concert, I have heard his latest albums and all his other albums. Thus, the songs are not truly 'new' to me (although they may be in a different musical arrangement)" (interview, June 8, 1993).

In fact, fans told me about their annoyance at nonfans who simply see a concert as a one-time, finite event. As Russ Curley told me:

> It's almost annoying, to certain extent, being with someone who doesn't know that much or doesn't appreciate it. I mean, the guys I went with the first time— the guy wanted to leave to beat the traffic before he [Bruce] was done with "My Beautiful Reward." I was like, "What?" [laughs] "We're not going anywhere!" (interview, April 20, 1993)

LeAnne Olderman told me of a similar encounter with a nonfan:

> Oh! Let me tell you about this. It was so funny! My friend had brought his roommate, and she thought it was too loud; she wanted to go. She'd never been to a

rock concert before. So I was upset—he should have known. That was kind of a bummer for me. So, I was aware that they wanted to go, and after the first encore, he gets up to leave! And I'm like, "No! He's not done, okay?" [laughs] I said, "I know he's not done, because he didn't say goodbye. I know he's not done." And I was right. He came back out. (interview, May 13, 1993)

For fans, a Springsteen concert is not something to watch passively from comfortable seats separated from the stage but something to actively join, and fans are constantly creating their own performing traditions. Such traditions are usually based on themes in songs and aim to break the invisible wall that divides performer from audience. For example, on the 1992–1993 tour, fans brought large "fuzzy dice" and threw them onstage during the song "Roll of the Dice" (1992) or brought baseball caps to throw onstage for Springsteen to wear during the song "Glory Days" (1984). In many ways, fans see themselves as performers along with Springsteen. They sing along with him, yell out his name and other messages between songs, and even act out some of the lyrics. One fan told me a story over electronic mail about his own performance at a concert:

> In 1985, I got a (very bad quality, but then I was very excited about it) tape of a show which I didn't attend, but a teacher at my school did. When "My Hometown" starts, he yells "Heeeeeeeey!" and I can very easily recognize his voice even now. So I decided to try the same thing. I didn't sing along too much, to save my voice for the Magic Moment. That moment came, of course, when he started "Darkness." So I yelled as loud and as long as I could, hoping to find myself on tape one day. The people around me looked at me laughing and thinking I went crazy; well, they were right. But the experiment failed. On the tape you hear so much screaming and yelling, I cannot discover myself. : (

Indeed, Springsteen fans consistently told me about feeling as exhausted and tired as Springsteen himself at the end of a concert. As Gene Chyzowych explained:

> I'm tired after seeing a Bruce show. I'm tired! Because I've been on my feet, I've been applauding and I've been yelling and screaming. I feel as I'm as exhausted as he is! That's why I'm saying it's not a passive experience for a fan. There's always a sense of relief when he's actually done with his second or third encore. I'm like, "Wow. He's totally exhausted me and I'm ready to go home. I'm satisfied. I'd love for him to come out and play some more, but I have to sit down at this point!" (interview, April 21, 1993)

Al Khorasani concurred:

> You come out of the show . . . tired! I mean, it's tiring to watch it. I was drenched. I came out and said, "I can't take it any more. I'm through. I'm *done*." If this show didn't end within five minutes, I probably would have gone to sleep. I couldn't take it any more! (interview, March 23, 1993)

For fans, a Springsteen concert is not a display of talent to be appreciated but rather an opportunity to reaffirm their belief in the power of rock'n'roll. Springsteen fans repeatedly told me that they did not perceive concerts as necessarily about putting on an entertaining show, at least not in the conventional rock concert sense of "entertaining." As David Merrill explained:

> Seeing Bruce in concert is like a religious experience. He doesn't really *do* anything on-stage. I mean, he doesn't bounce and dance around like a Mick Jagger, he doesn't have laser light shows like Aerosmith or Rush, he just sings and plays guitar and totally captivates 30,000 or so souls with his energy and emotion. (interview, May 6, 1993)

Fan criticism of a concert—while not unheard of—is always tempered by the fact that such judgment about quality is not ultimately the point. As Mary Krause told me about one concert she went to in Syracuse, "Bruce was sick. He had a cold, and he looked really scruffy. He needed a haircut badly. It was just not the same, in some ways. And the sound just wasn't the same. But it was still Bruce. It was still great" (interview, April 30, 1993).

Indeed, Springsteen fans often told me about falling into trancelike states rather than consciously attending to the events of the concert and evaluating them. Linda Warner explained, for example:

> I saw the *Tunnel of Love* concerts three times—no, four. Twice in Philly and twice in New York. And one of the nights in Philly we had front-row seats. It was really bizarre, because I didn't really *get* that I was there. I got like—it was too much for me, and I just stood there. I didn't say anything; I just stood there! Like I was in complete shock. And Clarence was right in front of me? Clarence kept looking at me, like, "Are you okay?" He was really concerned. [laughter] It was really funny. But I just couldn't get through my head that this was really happening to me. (interview, March 25, 1993)

Mary Beth Wilson told me about a similar experience:

> WILSON: I saw him when he opened the Meadowlands, and I can't even think of a song that I heard that night, but then right away, I know that when I get home that night, I think to myself, "Oh, I have to hear that again," because I was so caught up in the moment that I don't really know how it sounded. You know what I mean?
>
> CAVICCHI: Sure, sure. It's like you're not really there listening. Kind of. [laughs]
>
> WILSON: Exactly. [laughs] You kind of go somewhere else during that six minutes or so, and then it's like, "Oh, I hope I have the chance to hear that again so I'll know what it really sounded like!" [laughs] (interview, January 4, 1994)

Finally, for fans, a Springsteen concert is not about fun but rather about results. One of the most common themes in fans' accounts of concerts was the amount of "energy" they felt throughout the experience. In fact, when I asked the fifty or so fans who completed my questionnaire what three adjectives they would use to describe Springsteen in concert, the words they came up with mostly referred to an overwhelming sense of reinvigoration: "energetic" (11), "inspirational" (9), "intense" (8), "powerful" (7), "exhausting" (6), and "amazing" (6). Mary Krause explained:

> See, that's the thing about concerts: it gets you into it physically, because you're dancing, you're moving around, you're waving your arms, you're clapping your hands. You get into it mentally because you know the lyrics or you're listening to them again; maybe you're getting another meaning out of them, a new meaning or an old meaning, whatever. It's just such an energizing experience, and it's a spiritual experience. So, it gets you mind, body, and soul. (interview, April 30, 1993)

In fact, in interviews, fans often referred to a Springsteen performance as a "religious experience" or "spiritual experience." As David Merrill said:

> Bruce fans, I think, tend to concentrate more on the lyrics, the message of the song, as well as the way that Bruce plays it live, for them, that night. Also the stories which Bruce tells between songs contributes to the message. What's Bruce trying to tell us tonight? He's telling me that I'm not alone, I'm not the only one who feels lonely & downhearted. He's telling me that life throws bad turns at everyone now and again, but there's always hope around the corner. There's better days ahead. He's telling me to give money to a food bank in my hometown. He's showing me that he supports shelters for the homeless, and that Vietnam Vets have valid issues which the government should address. One leaves a Bruce Springsteen concert with the feeling that one has just been to a religious revival, and there is a reaffirmation of Faith and Hope and Joy! (interview, June 8, 1993)

On the whole, then, fans define their difference from ordinary audience members in terms of different kinds of musical participation. Everyone may attend the same concert, but fans and nonfan audience members come to that concert with different expectations, have different experiences, and leave with different feelings. Ordinary audience members are people who assume a temporary role before a stage to take a break from the hustle and bustle of their everyday lives and be entertained. Fans, however, are people whose role before a stage never ends; a concert is not a break from, but a continuing reaffirmation of, their everyday lives. In fact, being a fan is a lot like being a musician in that both live a lifestyle based on musical activity. Just as musicians are practicing, composing, and traveling between concerts or recording sessions, fans are collecting, writing fanzines, and making pilgrimages between concerts or listening to CDs. And as a professional musician might interpret a performance a bit differently than an infrequent performer—seeing it as only one part of a job rather than a uniquely exhilarating event, for instance—fans interpret a performance differently than ordinary audience members, seeing it as a ritual rather than as entertainment.

*D*egrees of Fandom

That fans and ordinary audience members represent clear and separate roles and occupy different frames of musical experience is an ideal in which most fans believe deeply. However, such an ideal is not always easily applied to the real world. For instance, when I first posted a message on *Backstreets Digest*, calling for Springsteen fans to participate in my fieldwork, I had not thought very deeply about what the term "Springsteen fan" meant. While I knew that not all fans were identical in their fandom—some fans liked to go to concerts while others liked to collect, for instance—I figured that the category of "Springsteen fan" was relatively clear, understood by all fans to refer to someone with a strong connection to Springsteen.

However, as I met and talked with fans, I realized that it was not so simple. While I expected fans to talk about going to many Springsteen concerts and collecting his work, several fans said they simply "liked" his music and listened to his records every month or so. As Kirk Anderson, a college professor from Massachuetts, explained to me, "He's not on the top of my list at all. . . . But some of the old stuff is some of my favorite music to listen to, some of his stuff that he did in the seventies. And I always like him. There's something about him that I like; he appeals to me" (interview, April 27, 1993).

Many of the fans I interviewed talked about similar encounters with people who believed themselves to be fans yet clearly had different relationships to Springsteen and his music. Amy Thom said about a friend:

> She's funny, because when we talk I pick up that she is as much a fan as I am, but she's not ever tuned into what's going on. Like she didn't know that he had a new album out, or she didn't know that the tickets went on sale for the concert. And I think if you are a serious fan, [laughs] you know, you'd know those things! (interview, April 1, 1993)

Another fan likewise talked about friends who turned out to be not quite what he expected:

> We went over to some friends' house for a barbecue. And I had loaned them *The Saint, the Innocent, and the Main Point Shuffle* [a Springsteen concert bootleg]. But they hadn't listened to it yet! And they had it for a couple of weeks. You know, if somebody were to loan me—I guess they're just not that into music, I guess. Overall, it's not a big part of their lives. . . . But they were real excited when I gave it to them.

Several fans had even developed typologies of fandom in which, rather than opposing one category (fans) to another (ordinary audience members), they posited a wide range of fan positions which derived their meaning in terms of their "distance" from the category of ordinary audience member. As Russ Curley explained:

I guess there's degrees of fandom. I would classify myself to the extreme. I'm an extremist. [laughs] You can't get anything more. He has a tendency to do that, to string them out. You can look: [gesturing] way over here you've got the extreme, and over here, you've got people who like him. Like the people I saw this summer at the Meadowlands tailgating in the afternoon before the show. They're all Bruce fans, and they like Bruce. They know what's on his records, and that's about it. They don't have old bootlegs and they don't have that, but they're still hardcore Bruce fans, and Bruce appreciates them. They probably, just in sheer numbers, make up most of the people going to the shows. I definitely think there are then the casual, the people who say, "Yeah, he's okay," but wouldn't go out of their way to see anything. (interview, April 20, 1993)

Louis Lucullo likewise divided fandom in different degrees. First, there are "obsessed fans" who, for instance, "literally would not think twice about flying to Europe the next day just to see his concert." As he explained:

I think you tend to find with the more "obsessed" fans, they see Springsteen as much more than a musician or rock'n'roll star. I think they find something in the songs that they can relate to, that is so directly a part of their lives, that they view the music as a means of expression more than anything else.

Second, there are "minimal fans" who simply appreciate his music. Louis Lucullo used the example of a friend from college, who "acknowledges Bruce's abilities but often thinks it is taken way too far by those . . . on the *Backstreets Digest*." Third, there are those who occupy the "middle ground," knowing a lot about the songs but, on the whole, feeling more connected to "the music than the myth" (interview, March 31, 1993).

Recognizing that not all fans have the same degree of connection to Springsteen makes it more difficult to isolate how all fans differ from ordinary audience members. In how much, and what kinds of, out-of-frame activity must a person participate to be called a "fan"? More important, how is one to measure or evaluate such activity? In particular, the type of fan considered closest to ordinary audience members, what Russ calls a "casual fan" and Louis calls a "minimal fan," is the subject of much debate in the Springsteen fan community. In *Backstreets*, computer discussion groups, and conversation, fans frequently argue about the legitimacy of the casual fan and to whom such a designation applies.

The term "casual fan" was first widely used during the *Born in the USA* tour in the mideighties, when Springsteen had become a megastar, selling out stadiums for three nights in a row and regularly appearing in the news. Many long-time Springsteen fans complained publicly that there were too many young "bandwagoners" buying up tickets and calling themselves "fans" simply because it was a popular thing to do. As one syndicated newspaper columnist railed in an editorial, "A Plague on Nouveau 'Boss' Fans":

> Since the Springsteen tour began last year, we . . . have suffered at the hands of
> a phenomenon that hasn't been reported: that thousands of you people jamming
> those concerts discovered Springsteen sometime last week and have proclaimed
> yourselves rock-ribbed fans. You are not. (Baker 1985)

Indeed, many older fans admitted that Springsteen's new and larger audience
represented a threat to the sense of ownership they felt toward Springsteen. As
another fan lamented in an article titled "A Steenian Tells Why": "In July 1975 his
records had yet to see the light of K-Mart. Cover stories of *Time* and *Newsweek* were
just pipe dreams of some public relations flunky. He was our secret. And our secret seemed safe" (Seely 1985, p. D-1).

This phenomenon was further exacerbated by the general hysteria surrounding Springsteen's rise to stardom, which encouraged a broader definition of the
term "fan" than Springsteen fans usually allowed. Instead of referring to a minority with a special, sustained connection with Springsteen, "Springsteen fan"
in the mideighties became a blanket term in common discourse, used hyperboli-
cally to describe the large numbers of people with any kind of enthusiastic interest in his work. As Laurie McLain told me, "As soon as *Born in the USA* came out,
everybody became a fan" (interview, March 28, 1993). In fact, during Bruce
Springsteen's appearances in large concert halls and stadiums for the *Born in the
USA* tour, newspaper headlines, captions, and reviews regularly emphasized the
sheer numbers of people who attended *Born in the USA* concerts with phrases like
"Bruce Springsteen performed Saturday night before 80,000 fans" or "Thousands
of fans waited for hours in long ticket lines."

While most prominent in the middle to late eighties, fans' concerns about casual fans have never disappeared; every time Springsteen releases a new work or
puts on a new concert, debates and discussions about casual fans invariably bubble
up in the letters to the editor in *Backstreets* or on the fan computer mailing list. In
some cases, the debates have to do with real disagreement between fans over the
criteria which distinguish fans from nonfans; in other cases, the debates have more
to do with the elitism of certain fans, who attempt to assert their fan identity by rel-
egating anyone who does not share their ideas about fandom to "casual fan" status.
Often, both motivations are inextricably intertwined as elitist statements by one fan
lead to a deeper, more widespread consideration of what "fan" actually means.

Debates about Age

Because of the length of Springsteen's career, the age of his fans can range anywhere from teens to fifties; the fans with whom I spoke were generally between
twenty and forty. Such age differences play an important role in determining
casual fandom; in particular, many older fans claim that a fan who is young
probably doesn't have that much experience out of frame and, in particular, has

not "paid dues" by following Springsteen on tour, collecting, learning about Springsteen, making pilgrimages to Springsteen's house, and the like. In fact, many older fans—particularly those who have been around since before the release of *The River* in 1980—are suspicious that younger fans may be only superficially interested in Springsteen because of the popularity and hype of *Born in the USA*. As I discussed with thirty-year-old Alan Levine about the 1992–1993 tour:

> LEVINE: With this tour, I found a lot of those people who sort of latched onto him in the *Born in the USA* tour were still coming to these shows. However, this music—I happen to love the *Lucky Town* album. I'm one of the few people who really like the new albums. I found these people were almost disappointed that it wasn't as commercial, but it was an "in thing" to still go to a Bruce Springsteen concert. I found the crowds—during the more mellower tunes, not the older tunes—would be talking, would go back—
>
> CAVICCHI: Go to get a hot dog, right.
>
> LEVINE: Yeah. In eighty, man, nobody would move for three hours! I remember—I don't remember which tour—but he did—the tour he was doing "This Land Is Your Land," the Guthrie song?—and I remember sitting in the Meadowlands, I think it was the last row at this concert, and it was a mellow song, but he asked for quiet, and you could hear a pin drop! He sang, and I'll never forget listening to that song at that point. With this tour, it was just different. People were moving about. You know, he did "Light of Day"—which is great—he's doing a lot of guitar work, which I appreciate—but a lot of the newer fans don't appreciate it. (interview, April 2, 1993)

Most younger fans greatly resent such characterizations of their fandom, however, calling such attitudes elitist. As one fan wrote into *Backstreets*:

> I am really sick of all the long-time Bruce fans telling me that I am not as good as they are since I am so young, and have only recently started becoming a Bruce fanatic. It's not my fault that I wasn't born until 1972. Since I was eight I have been interested in Bruce but when you're a little kid your parents aren't too thrilled with you listening to "all that trash." (Billings 1987)

In particular, to combat the stigma of being regarded as "casual," younger fans often point to the fact that they *do* have some sort of experience out of frame. For instance, many talk about having acquired extensive knowledge of Springsteen's work. College senior Laurie McLain explained:

> I know that it's dangerous to go and advertise the fact that I'm a *Born in the USA* fan. I haven't had any problems, but I always think they're going to be around. When I was waiting in line for tickets this last year, I was the [counts 1, 2, 3, 4, 5] sixth person in line. Incidentally, the woman in front of me was the same age as I was, but everybody else—there were like all these baby-boomers who—I mean, it looked like a Jeep Cherokee ad. There were guys sitting around talking about their wife and kids, and it was just so typical "Springsteen fan." They wouldn't even talk to us for a while. Then, they'd be talking, and they'd say something that was

wrong—I mean, little piddly things—and I'd correct them. We'd be listening to them or something and I'd say, "Oh, no, that was something else." And they would sort of look at me. After a while—by the time tickets went on sale, we had spent the night together and we ended up talking; everybody told their Bruce stories and everything. By the time we were about to go in to buy our tickets, one of the guys turned around and said, "How old are you?" And I said, "Twenty." And he said, "Well, it's really good that there's a new generation keeping up the tradition." So, I felt good about myself. (interview, March 28, 1993)

Other fans talk about having "paid dues" in a hostile environment, where, contrary to older fan belief, *Born in the USA* was not popular. One fan wrote in a letter to *Backstreets* in the early nineties:

> I take offense at how you think people who "jumped on the bandwagon in the 80s" are leaving Springsteen at this point in his career. I really didn't realize who Bruce was until 1984. I was watching MTV and saw this scruffy-faced leather-jacketed screaming man on my screen; I was a fan from then on. Don't be so high and mighty as to think that if you didn't discover Springsteen before '75 that that makes you less of a fan. It doesn't. Being a Springsteen fan in '84 at my high school was not easy. Only girls and a few guys were fans, and I took a lot of flak from the metal heads for my taste. Not seeing Springsteen in concert in your state is also hard. The last time he played in my hometown was in 1977 and I was eight years old. (Cosgrove 1992)

Finally, since the eighties, younger fans have vowed that they would remain fans and that the older fans could "check up on us ten years from now." Indeed, many younger fans proudly announced in 1994, ten years after the release of *Born in the USA*, that they were still fans. However, the debate has not disappeared; now, even newer fans (particularly those who discovered Springsteen in the early nineties when he branched out into film music and won several Grammy awards) are the object of suspicion. Indeed, whether current younger fans can understand Springsteen's "adult-oriented" music has been the subject of much discussion on *Luckytown Digest*.

Debates about Region

In addition to age, debates about whether a fan is "casual" revolve around the region to which a fan feels connected. Springsteen fans can be found in all of the United States and many foreign countries, but because Springsteen grew up in Freehold, New Jersey, and was an important figure in the Asbury Park, New Jersey, music scene for a number of years when he was starting out as a musician, many fans hail from New Jersey. In fact, a good third of those I interviewed either grew up in New Jersey or were currently living there. While not all fans play up their connection to New Jersey, several claim that such a connection made them less likely to be casual fans. For example, when I asked Gene Chyzowych whether he ever got any flak for being a *Born in the USA*–era fan, he replied:

> No, not at all. Because, I don't know, maybe I have a little more credibility being from New Jersey. You know, people make fun of me at times. Like, "You must love Bon Jovi and Bruce." And I'm like, "Well, Bon Jovi's not bad, but I do love Bruce." [laughter] It's weird. I was in the area this weekend, and I heard—I put on the radio when I was in the car, and I'd say one out of every few times I was in the car there'd be Bruce playing on one of the stations. So, it definitely has a lot to do with it. (interview, April 21, 1993)

Other fans echo this claim to credibility. Alan Stein, a 28-year-old computer engineer and New Jersey native, explained:

> I remember Bruce playing in New Brunswick at Rutgers and stuff, because I lived right by Rutgers. We used to go pick up my dad at the train station in New Brunswick every day—he took the train to work and we would pick him up—and The Ledge is a kind of a college club that was on the road on the way home. And we'd pass by it and see the signs. I remember seeing Bruce playing at The Ledge! You hear about him. It was different in New Jersey. (interview, May 24, 1993)

Amy Thom, despite never having lived in New Jersey, agreed:

> The fans in New Jersey are unlike fans anywhere else. That is not a myth. . . . I think that all the concerts attract a percentage of what I would call hardcore Bruce fans in any given town. But when you're in New Jersey, it's just a much higher percentage. So, the energy level is . . . serious. People are serious about it. There's a sense of ownership about him in that place. And pride. It's really kind of neat. I think you get more repetitive concert goers—people who went to seven shows, nine shows, whatever. What did he do, play eleven shows or something? And I think I saw three of them. I'm sure there were people who went to all eleven of them. (interview, April 1, 1993)

Of course, not every fan sees validity in such claims about New Jersey's special qualities. Some, like Washington, D.C., native John O'Brien, want Bruce to transcend regional prejudices: "For me, I think he is really more universal. He's not just about certain—obviously I can't say that I've experienced what his characters have experienced, you know, I can't say. . . . I didn't grow up in like Freehold, New Jersey" (interview, March 15, 1993). Other people cite connections between Springsteen and other parts of the country. For example, Mary Beth Wilson explained:

> The first time I saw him was in Philly, but I didn't even know enough about it then to know that it was probably different. But there was definitely a difference in the show between New Jersey and Philly. I felt that he gave a lot more in Philly, for whatever reason. You know, I'm not convinced that New Jersey *is* the place to see

him. I always wanted to believe that it was, and the reason that I got so excited when I heard him come on stage in Giants Stadium was because I wanted to, without fail, see him in New Jersey. That was like a goal. But after experiencing it several times, and seeing him outside of New Jersey. . . . It's different. He's got a big tie with the people of Philadelphia, for some reason. (interview, January 17, 1994)

Springsteen's move to a mansion in the "Hollywood Hills" in the early nineties took some of the power out of New Jersey residents' claims about region. In fact, Springsteen was perceived by many as "betraying" his roots and abandoning the idea that New Jersey really had any hold on him. Yet, the debates continued, as New Jersey fans pointed to Springsteen's unprecedented string of eleven shows at New Jersey's Meadowlands Arena in 1992, as well as his subsequent appearances in Jersey Shore clubs, as evidence of his loyalty and connection to them.

Debates about Attitude

For many fans, "casual fan" refers to the person's attitude toward Springsteen. During the *Born in the USA* tour, "casual fans" were, in the words of J. D. Rummel, "not in love with the music so much as the event, being part of the *Born in the USA* phenomenon" (interview, May 14, 1993). Since then, the criticism has been applied more generally to anyone without a serious approach toward Springsteen. Casual fans are, in the words of LeAnne Olderman, those who "only have one or two albums and don't listen much" (interview, May 13, 1993). Several fans even told me about the necessity of having an "obsession" with Springsteen; anyone without that obsession is somehow not quite a "real" fan yet.

Several fans, however, caution that endorsing a "reverence" for or "obsession" with Springsteen is far from what being a fan should be all about. As Alan Stein said, "I'm still amazed that people call up the hotline phone everyday. I can't imagine. Would you be interested? Every day? Getting [e-] mail every day is kind of strange; I kind of want to filter it out!" (interview, May 24, 1993). John O'Brien agreed:

> I know some people who follow bands around and get every bootleg, and I never really thought—maybe I never wanted to admit it [laughs]—there was something kind of frightening about making something that big a deal. And I think Bruce would agree. . . . 'Cause it's almost like a drug! You can just sit in your room and listen to this music and you're not really dealing with the real world anymore. Then again, maybe it helps you deal with real life. Now, I'm starting to find some kind of balance with it, which is good. (interview, March 15, 1993)

Such debates over what it means to be "serious" about Springsteen are quite ~plicated, since "seriousness" itself is difficult to define. In particular, does ~val of Springsteen's work indicate earnest engagement and caring or merely waning interest? When Springsteen released two new CDs in 1992, after a five-year silence, many older fans, in *Backstreets*, criticized the works for not living up to the standards of earlier releases. This criticism provoked a huge outcry from younger fans, who implied that outspoken criticism of Springsteen was a clear indication of casual fan status. As one person wrote:

> I've seen several reviews by those who call themselves "dedicated" fans of Spring- steen that trash him and his new albums. Everyone is entitled to their opinion, but this isn't right. It's almost as if they think Bruce owes them something. . . . The fact that some of us can identify with and find something special in his music is fantastic. But just because Bruce's life or ideas take a different turn than those of some of his "fans," I don't think that warrants negative comments and criticism. If Bruce Springsteen doesn't speak your language anymore, move along. (Lausch 1992)

Another group of fans even accused older fans of going overboard in their ob- session, being unable to let go of their past and follow Springsteen in new direc- tions:

> We European fans are sick and tired of superfans who, every time Bruce Spring- steen makes a move, come up with their reactionary "I still prefer *Born to Run*" at- titude (it's a superb album but so are all the others). What's the point of setting the albums against one another? . . . If Bruce doesn't get full support from his core fans, then you can hardly blame him for turning his back on us. (Weber and An- dersen 1992)

Such debates show little sign of abating. Despite the ambiguities involved in try- ing to determine the quality of someone's attitude, similar accusations accom- panied criticism about Springsteen's *Greatest Hits* release in 1995.

Debates about Behavior

For most fans, someone's behavior offers a more tangible indication of status as a fan than attitude does. In particular, "casual fan" is a label which is often given to someone who clearly acts like an ordinary audience member—for example, not paying attention or partying too much at a Springsteen show. As one fan ar- gued on *Backstreets Digest*:

> I don't have a problem with fans who only see one show and own no bootlegs or tapes. There are lots of people who aren't fanatics like some of us, and that doesn't bother me. What bothers me are the "casual fans" who scarf up the good seats, simply because it's "the thing" to do (to go see Bruce), and then when they get to the show, don't even stay in their seats to see it, but spend all night walking around buying hot dogs and beer. The ones who scream "Born in the USA!" dur- ing "If I Should Fall Behind" or who make a mass exit for beer during "Book of

Dreams." The ones who sit behind you and chatter incessantly about everything and nothing. The ones who keep asking, "Which one's Clarence?" The ones who are yelling and making noise as Bruce tells a poignant story about his old man. The ones who throw things at Bruce and yell "Fuck you!" when he notes the hell the last two administrations put this country through and expresses a hope for a better tomorrow. Those are the kinds of "casual fans" that I can do without. As for the other kind of "casual fan" who perhaps has never seen Bruce before (and won't again until the next tour), I don't mind. Not everyone will become a fanatic. Some may not see him again. But at least they will witness a great show with great songs played by a great band sung by the master of all stage performers. (Papleonardos 1993)

However, other fans claim that such an argument reads far too much into a person's actions and worry about the rigid behavioral restrictions implied by this sort of approach. As someone said in response to the previous argument:

What I don't understand is the hostility directed toward those in the audience who went to the trouble to get tickets but who the devoted think are not showing the appropriate amount of reverence for Bruce. While I think that the man has a lot to say and that he says it better than most, at the risk of blaspheming, he is not god-emperor. Being rude to a performer is one thing and I'm not trying to excuse that if that is the problem at these shows, but condemning people for not standing up? Is that such a serious transgression? I may be wrong, but the impression I get from his music is that Bruce is the kind of person who would prefer honest feedback, even if it is negative, to pure devotion. (Goldspiel 1993)

This debate was most clearly spelled out in discussions about the 1993 charity concert Springsteen performed at Madison Square Garden for a large audience of fans. Members of the E Street Band were rumored to be appearing that night; apparently, when Springsteen introduced a surprise guest performer, Terence Trent D'Arby, the fans, expecting Clarence Clemons, booed. Springsteen became obviously angry and cut the show short. In *Backstreets*, many fans sent letters that interpreted the event in very different ways. For some people, the fans who booed were not really fans at all. As one person wrote to *Backstreets*:

I will bet that this is not the first letter about the concert at Madison Square Garden in New York on June 26. I also hope that Bruce fans will continue to voice their anger at the rudeness of the concert-goers (not fans) who so rudely booed during Terence Trent D'Arby's appearance. I am sure that a lot of people were expecting members of the E Street Band to show up. I am sure that it would have been great if they did, but to boo another performer because they thought Bruce said "Clarence," not "Terence," is just rude. (Skeen 1993)

Or, as another wrote:

The spirit of the night was ruined when fans (if you can call them that) began to boo Bruce's guest singer, Terence Trent D'Arby. My heart sank as I listened to the rude, selfish audience surrounding me. I couldn't believe these were Springsteen fans. They had absolutely no class. (Feinberg 1993)

For others, the booing was not indicative of "casual" status but rather pointed to problems with the show itself. As someone wrote:

I don't condone the behavior of those few fans who booed D'Arby, but what ever happened to Bruce's beliefs about freedom of speech? Why do the real fans have to settle for less because of the actions of these morons? Why didn't Bruce foresee that allowing D'Arby to sing a song of such slow tempo as "I Have Faith in These Desolate Times" seemed totally out of place in between rockers like "Who'll Stop the Rain" and "Jolé Blon"? I think the general public deserves a little bit more, and for those who saw each show we really go to see two different sides of the "new" Bruce. (Holzhauer 1993)

A fan who had booed expressed an even stronger opinion:

I bought a ticket to a Bruce Springsteen concert, not a Bruce Springsteen/Terence Trent D'Arby concert. Don't misunderstand, I am and always will be an avid Springsteen fan. I have seen many of his shows and have an extensive collection. However, I was disappointed when he introduced D'Arby to perform and felt the best way to show my displeasure was to boo. Yes, I booed and I would boo again. If I wanted to hear D'Arby sing a song I'd go to see one of his concerts. The last time I checked this was America where I have a right to express my opinion publicly. (Marciano 1994)

As with debates about attitude, determining what is "proper" fan behavior can be quite controversial, particularly when it involves criticism of Springsteen's music.

In the early seventies, when Springsteen was a relatively unknown musician with cult status, playing to small, local audiences along the Jersey Shore, most of his audience was fans. The quality of someone's fandom was not much of an issue; being a fan meant, basically, knowing his songs and going to his shows. However, with the success of *Born in the USA*, Springsteen's audience became far more diverse, including many different people who were calling themselves "fans": those who own all of his works and camped out six weeks before to get tickets, curious friends or parents of fans, "teenyboppers" infatuated with Springsteen, people eager to drink and have a good time, reporters and reviewers for local and national newspapers, record company executives, activists interested in Springsteen's political message, and radio listeners who like Springsteen's latest single. Such myriad interests continue to be present, and the quality of someone's fandom remains a highly charged issue. Age, region, attitude, and behavior are all criteria for debate; future changes in Springsteen's performances and role as a musician undoubtedly will bring about new criteria and new debates.

*A*m I a Fan?

As I have mentioned, the whole idea of "degrees of fandom" reveals a certain elitism among some Springsteen fans, who assume that if not all fans have the same degree of connection to Springsteen, then some people must be more important, more knowlegeable, more of a fan, than others. Indeed, as the debates about the term "casual fan" show, "extremist" or "obsessed" fans, who have an intense interest in Springsteen—and, say, have collected tapes of every concert Springsteen has ever done or memorized the lyrics to every official song he has released—often feel some disappointment when they encounter fans who do not have concert tapes or who struggle to remember the lines to songs. Intense fans find it difficult to communicate with such fans and relegate them to "casual" or nonfan status as a way to maintain the integrity of their values.

An important consequence of this elitism is that many fans worry about whether their activities and thoughts place them closer to the ideal of the fan or to an ordinary audience member, about whether they are true fans or merely casual fans. For instance, when I first started meeting fans, I encountered not only people who I thought were more casual than I was but also many who had greater commitment and intensity. While I had all of Springsteen's works and was familiar with most of his songs, I met fans who were attempting to collect tapes of Springsteen's every performance during the latest tour so they could compare his various arrangements or fans who could trace characters as they appeared in different songs and had devised elaborate theories about the evolution of Springsteen's lyrical style. Such encounters usually left me with a sinking feeling that I was not really a fan at all.

Likewise, in the spring of 1995, a fan named Antonia posted a message on *Luckytown Digest* explaining that the computer mailing list had made her feel a bit inferior:

> As I sift through the digest I can not help but wonder. . . . *What is wrong with me?????* I have loved the music and lyrics of Bruce from the moment I became wise enough to listen to it. Yet, I must be doing something wrong. I must be half a fan. I have no "*bootlegs*," I haven't a clue what songs were played in what order during any particular show, I have no idea what would make a good "b" side and yes I shall even admit . . . I did *not* set my VCR for "record" during the Grammy's [sic] or the Melissa Etheridge "Unplugged" show.[5] Before I started reading *Luckytown Digest*, I considered myself a very good fan. I purchased every (commercially available) LP, CD, video tape, book, and magazine that possessed information on my favorite fellow. Somehow I feel like I should have done more. Forgive me Bruce. I will work harder at my fanhood! (Antonia 1995)

This message triggered several others in which people also worried about whether they were "good enough to be a true Bruce fan" or reported feeling "intimidated by all these postings of incredible Bruceology."

On the whole, worry about one's status as a fan rarely leads to a serious crisis of status; in fact, worry instead tends to encourage a reassertion of the general feeling of connection with Springsteen which all fans share. As Mary Beth Wilson explained, "We all have varied levels but, at some point, we all kind of come back to the same place" (interview, January 17, 1994). After Antonia worried publicly about whether she was a fan, several people offered her not only sympathy but also an answer. "Yes you are a fan!" one person wrote. "It is not the things and the trivia that makes one a Springsteen fan, it is the love of the music" (Mills 1995). Another fan echoed:

> What you feel about Bruce is in your heart, your soul, your inner core. Material possessions and number of shows seen have nothing to do with it. Does his music speak to you? Has it touched you? Do you know what it's like to drive through the darkness at the edge of town? If you answered yes to any of those questions, well, tramps like us. . . . (Dropdog 1995)

However, worry does indicate that fandom is, in practice, less of a ready-made category that clearly separates one person from all others and more of a process of distinction in which a fan must constantly question and monitor his or her experience, background, attitudes, and behaviors, relative to all the other people involved in any rock audience. Fans' acknowledgment of different degrees of fandom and their debates about casual fans do not erase the basic distinction between fans and ordinary audience members. Rather, such activities are part of a process of working out the ideals of fan and audience member in the real circumstances of the social world they inhabit, about creating a category of fan while acknowledging the different adjectives which might be applied to that distinction: "true," "real," "obsessed," "casual," "minimal," "semi," and so on.

In the end, all fans share a special feeling of connection with Springsteen's performances, which, in the ideal, shapes a specific kind of participation in those performances. However, that ideal, the feeling of connection between fans and Springsteen, is always influenced by other kinds of connections: between fans and the music business, between fans and ordinary audience members, between different groups of fans. Ultimately, the definition of music fandom lies not in any terse phrase or single image but rather in the *tension between* all of these relationships at any given moment. That is why fandom is so difficult to grasp. It is also why fandom is so central to understanding popular music.

5 *Listening and Learning*

In the song "No Surrender" (1984), Bruce Springsteen sings that "we learned more from a three-minute record than we ever learned in school." While clearly an indictment of the irrelevance of American education to the lives of many teens growing up in the sixties, the lyric also affirms the power of rock'n'roll music to shape dreams and ideas, to serve as a place where people can find inspiration, knowledge, and guidance. Indeed, Springsteen himself has attested to this power; as he told rock critic Robert Hilburn:

> When you listen to those early rock records or any great rock'n'roll, or see a great movie, there are human values that are presented. They're important things. I got inspired mainly, I guess, by the records, a certain purity in them. I just know that when I started to play, it was like a gift. I started to feel alive. It was like some guy stumbling down a street and finding a key. (Hilburn 1989, p. 79)

Most Springsteen fans are quite aware of Springsteen's belief in power of rock-'n'roll to awaken and transform; the lyric from "No Surrender" is frequently quoted, shared by fans at the end of e-mail communications and letters as a kind of reminder of what being a Springsteen fan is all about. In fact, just as Springsteen found meaning and direction in early rock'n'roll records, his fans find the same kind of meaning and direction in his music.

Whenever fans meet, whether in person, through fanzines, or on computer networks, they inevitably become involved in discussions about the meanings of particular songs. The editors of *Backstreets* and other guest writers regularly write short interpretive essays on Springsteen's music in a column that begins every issue. Fans regularly post inquiries on *Luckytown Digest* about Springsteen's songs and engage in heated and lengthy debates about how to interpret symbols and images, including everything from the idea of reincarnation in "Atlantic City" (1982) to what Springsteen meant by the term "Bar-M choppers" in "This Hard Land" (1995).

Many of the fans to whom I spoke explained that they spend much time studying Springsteen's songs. For instance, Laurie McLain, who labeled herself a "Bruce scholar," told me about making different connections between songs' characters and situations:

> I have read just about every word about Bruce printed in English and I have so much information about him and his career in my usable memory that it's mind-boggling. In my spare time I consider themes, trends, etc. This is my passion and I study it more thoroughly than I do anything else. (interview, March 11, 1993)

Other fans, often students, shared with me their own thinking and writing about Springsteen's work. Zach Everson, a high school student in Massachusetts, wrote an analysis on the American dream in *The Great Gatsby* and "Born to Run" (1975) for an English class; college student Russ Curley was working on a lengthy and wide-ranging analysis of love in the development of Springsteen's work; and Paul Fischer, as a graduate student, had written a paper on the role of narrative in Springsteen's performances.[1]

This discovery of meaning is not simply academic. Fans are consciously engaged with the ways in which Springsteen's music works to shape their experiences and perceptions. As Laurie McLain and I discussed:

> MCLAIN: I think it definitely affects my thinking. I think in Springsteen. [laughs] It's pretty embarrassing, sometimes.
>
> CAVICCHI: Well, no one can hear that, Laurie.
>
> MCLAIN: Well, people that aren't Springsteen fans don't notice it. Except sometimes the words I say rhyme too much. [laughs] There's too much meter to them, they're not regular speech. [laughter] (interview, March 28, 1993)

Others, like David Mocko, explained to me that the music represented a sort of "philosophy" or a value system:

> Some of the philosophy which I share, and the feeling conveyed in Bruce's music, are strong commitment to an idea, (emotional) directness and honesty no matter how "cold," the "beautiful loser syndrome" (to a degree, especially that we are both Jersey boys), and the idea that romantic love can help one to deal with life's problems and give one greater sense of fulfillment and purpose. (interview, June 3, 1993)

In fact, when I asked fans what they might say to Springsteen if they met him, most said the same thing. "I'd somehow try to communicate to him how much meaning his music has had for me in my life," one fan wrote. "I'd tell him how much his music has made an impact on my life and to keep it up," another said. "I would tell him how much his music means to me and how much he has helped me at certain times in my life," yet another echoed. One fan simply put it, "Thanks for getting me through!"

When most people listen to music, they find it meaningful, associating it with certain emotions, memories, and sensations. However, few people study the music's details, lingering over passages and memorizing lyrics, or shape their thinking and values around its themes. For fans, music has a unique depth and power; it hits them with such force that it becomes an important part of their daily lives. Part of this impact is due to the perceived qualities of the music itself—most fans told me again and again about the importance of Springsteen's writing, playing, and performance—but another part of this impact seems due to the ways in which fans use the music, constantly tying the songs to their experiences, both individual and shared. Indeed, fans' study of Springsteen's music and the ways in which they use the music to make sense of the world around them both fit together to form a complex kind of listening: while fans interpret Springsteen's music in terms of their experiences, the music works to influence and shape their experiences.

*L*istening to Music

In the early stages of my fieldwork, I attributed the meaning or "message" of Springsteen's music to the lyrics of his songs. The fans I was meeting seemed almost obsessed with what Bruce was *saying* in his music. They were memorizing lyric sheets, reciting lines to each other, and discussing his descriptions of characters and situations. Having grown up listening to instrumental jazz, I never paid attention to lyrics and instead found meaning in the mood or groove of the music, but so many people were telling me how important the lyrics were that I simply assumed that I was an anomaly among Springsteen fans, a lost jazz listener who had somehow found a connection with Springsteen's sound. In fact, after repeatedly encountering fans who talked about Springsteen's lyrics, it became clear to me that most fans shared a view of Springsteen's music as being about the themes of his lyrics: desperation, decay, loss, and the need for a balancing hope, faith, and redemption. As Laurie McLain explained:

> I think overall in Bruce's music there's a sense of people trying to do their best and not always succeeding, that there are forces out there that really can have an effect on who you are. It's not like you can do anything you want. In "Highway Patrolman," the tragic thing about the song is that there is no right decision that he can make. He has a job to do, he has to uphold the law. His brother has screwed up, and he knows it. And he knows his brother is bad and is going to keep screwing up forever and has no reason to expect otherwise. So, he should do something about it. On the other hand, that's his brother. Ethically and morally, there's no way he can win. That, in a lesser degree, runs through all of his songs. Or not every single one—not necessarily "Pink Cadillac."[2] [laughter] But it's a difficult world to live in. And you have to do your best and go out and actually do it. You can't just

go and, as Bruce has always said, "You can go and sit in front of your TV with a six-pack of beer," you have to engage in the world. And do what is the best thing you can. And you're not always going to do what's right, but you have to try. (interview, March 28, 1993)

Gene Chyzowych likewise talked about Springsteen's music in terms of finding hope despite the sadness of the world:

Yeah, he went through some tough times. And I think his songs show that. But he's also trying to show a better side of things. He's trying to put some positive things in his songs. And I think a lot of his songs at the end are saying "Keep your head up," you know? "There are better things coming your way." There are a few songs on his newer albums, too, that are definitely—"Roll of the Dice" and stuff like that. He's saying that "it's a gamble out there, sometimes you're going to win, sometimes you're going to lose, but just keep on moving. Don't give up." Stuff like that. So, there's definitely a message to his songs. (interview, April 21, 1993)

However, this consensus and clarity I thought I had found regarding Springsteen's lyrics and themes started to fade away about six months into my field-work. First, I began to meet people who, like me, didn't listen to Springsteen's lyrics yet still found his work deeply moving and meaningful. For instance, after I mentioned how my wife, to my great consternation, focused on lyrics, memorizing them, and singing along, Jackie Gillis explained:

It sounds like Chris and I are very much like you and your wife with regard to what we "listen" to, only I am the one, like you, that concentrates on the music and Chris hears the lyrics. I think I mentioned this before, but I tend to focus on the keyboards especially since I played myself . . . especially David Sancious on "New York City Serenade" and Roy Bittan on "Point Blank." . . . I must confess that, like you, I love these songs but I can't sit down and write (or even sing along, for that matter) *all* of the lyrics. Chris, on the other hand, and like your wife, knows the lyrics to every song he's ever heard. It's incredible. I kid him and tell him that it's a waste of brain memory storage space and that's why I'm the one getting the Ph.D. (just a joke; really!). (interview, June 10, 1993)

Of course, this attachment to the music over the lyrics was not always intentional; several fans humorously said that they found themselves drawn to the sound because they couldn't understand Springsteen's garbled delivery of the words. But, nevertheless, for such fans, the meaning of the music was clearly not to be found in any sort of coherent "message," but rather in qualities like his "energy" live or in more personal terms such as how it "fit" various moods or represented certain memories. As J. D. Rummel explained, "I couldn't understand a thing he was saying, but the energy, the power of that man, his music, and his band were just gripping" (interview, May 14, 1993).

In addition, most fans who professed to pay attention to lyrics *resisted* the idea that the lyrics were primary in shaping the meaning of the music. For instance,

I had a conversation with Gene Chyzowych in which he explained to me, with some exacerbation, that the appeal of the songs "Johnny 99" and "Reason to Believe" on *Live 1975–85* (1986) was not about lyrics alone but also about the sound, his anticipation, and the whole unfolding of the performance:

> CHYZOWYCH: I just love when those [songs] come around on the stereo because it gets my heart beating real fast. He's telling a great story, and there's some fantastic harmonica playing on that, and I can just picture him singing that live. I don't think I've seen him do it live. He could have done it back when I first saw him and I don't remember. I don't even know if he plays them anymore. But when I saw him recently, I thought, "Wouldn't it be incredible if he just went into 'Johnny 99'?"
>
> CAVICCHI: Well, is it the lyrics? I mean, you said it was the story, right?
>
> CHYZOWYCH: The lyrics, yeah. The story grabs me. . . .
>
> CAVICCHI: The sound?
>
> CHYZOWYCH: I mean, it's the whole picture, Dan. The lyrics are telling the story that is just—a fantastic story. And it's his music. I mean, the E Street Band on that is just fantastic. You know, and then, it kinds of fades you out and gets you into—it tells you a really sad story, a kind of frustrating story—but then it gets you into "Reason to Believe." (interview, April 21, 1993)

Furthermore, as I talked with fans, I found profound disagreements over the meanings of songs, which really precluded any sort of isolated, single "message" in Springsteen's work. David Merrill explained:

> Not everyone likes the same songs. Not all of Bruce's songs speak to me on a personal level, and some songs which other folks rave about I simply tolerate. Songs such as "My Hometown" and "Bobby Jean" not to mention "Born in the USA" got so much radio play when [*Born in the USA*] was released that it just ruined those songs for me. In fact, I have not listened to the *BitUSA* album for several years. I am just now back to the point where the songs would be tolerable again for me and am considering purchasing the CD and "rediscovering" the album. I know there are other great songs buried on the album which did not get as much air play, such as "Downbound Train" which I always liked. Anyhow, my point is that not all of Bruce's music speaks to everyone the same way. Some folks rave about [songs on *The River* like] "Point Blank" and "Jackson Cage." Me, I prefer the "banal ditties" such as "Sherry Darling" and "Cadillac Ranch," or the haunting "Wreck on the Highway," which signaled a change in the way Bruce, and perhaps his fans, were looking at life. (interview, May 6, 1993)

Springsteen fans clearly see Springsteen's music as communicating meaning, but what is that meaning? And where does the meaning come from if it does not come from lyrics alone? How do we explain meaning in terms of the consensus and difference I found among fans? Unfortunately, much of the scholarship on musical meaning is of little help in answering such questions because it focuses solely on the "syntax" or symbolic qualities of musical form (see, e.g., Langer

1942; Meyer 1956; Nattiez 1990). While people might talk about Springsteen's use of various kinds of chord progressions, delayed endings, or lyrical structures as the source of his music's meaning—and many fans do focus on such things— this approach does not account for fans' differing interpretations of the music. If they all hear the same music, the same "syntax," then why don't they under- stand it in the same way?

Several scholars have criticized such theories' narrow focus on musical form and, instead, have emphasized the role of historical and social context in shaping musical meaning (see especially Keil [1966] 1994; Shepherd 1977, 1991; Walser 1994). One theorist in particular, anthropologist and ethnomusicologist Steven Feld, has developed a model of listening which helpfully accounts for how lis- teners can find multiple meanings in multiple places for any piece of music ([1984] 1994). Basically, Feld argues that music is not an autonomous "thing" from which listeners simply "take" meanings, but rather music is always con- structed by listeners as they encounter it. In other words, while any organized sound may have noticeable structural qualities (loudness, texture, progression, etc.), that sound only becomes meaningful, only becomes music, when a listener brings to it certain ideas and perceptions about what it is and how to understand it. These "interpretive moves," as Feld calls them, are both social, drawing on shared conventions and ideas about music, and individual, based on personal ex- perience and knowledge.

Feld's model sheds much light on the complexities of Springsteen fans' lis- tening and interpretation. Fans do clearly employ a general set of interpretive moves which create a shared understanding of what the music is and how it has meaning. At the same time, fans combine those interpretive moves in different ways and at different times, and such combinations can lead to very different conclusions about the music. The general set of interpretive moves shared by fans has six elements.

Situating the Listening Experience

Fans share several conventions about where and how they should listen to Springsteen's music. During a typical day, one is apt to hear Bruce Springsteen's music in variety of places, each of which shapes a different experience of the music: on the stereo at home, in the background at the supermarket, live on tele- vision during a talk show, during the opening of a movie, on the car radio, at a crowded party. In each of these instances, Springsteen fans automatically evalu- ate the situation: Have I heard this song quite this way before? Is this the best way to listen to Bruce? Am I ready to listen to this song again right now?

The amount of time fans spend listening to Springsteen is not, as many peo- ple might expect, necessarily high. Most fans indicated in interviews and on ques- tionnaires that Springsteen occupied only 30 to 50 percent of their total listening, and every fan to whom I spoke listened to at least one other performer. The other performers, who were difficult to pinpoint either stylistically or thematically as having any relationship to Springsteen, included Billy Joel, Kate Bush, Iron Maiden, Pink Floyd, Debussy, Ice-T, Metallica, the Monkees, 10,000 Maniacs, Kiss, Prince, Sting, B. B. King, the Pogues, Nirvana, and Neil Diamond, to name only some. In fact, to answer a question about how many hours they listened to music *in general* per day, most of the fans I contacted said they listened only two to four.

The reasons for this limited listening to Springsteen varied. Several listened less because of restrictions at work, and others listened more because they had radios or tape players in their offices. On the whole, though, many fans indicated in interviews that they were self-regulating their listening, not wanting to "go overboard." As John O'Brien explained, "You shouldn't listen to music in that way . . . because it can really make you screwed up. 'Cause it's almost like a drug! You can just sit in your room and listen to this music and you're not really dealing with the real world anymore" (interview, March 15, 1993). Instead, many fans talked about getting their fill of Springsteen in small daily doses or in listening "blocks," where they would focus on Springsteen for a while and then move on to other artists. As Gene Chyzowych explained:

> Well, I have a six disc magazine. So, for instance, I'll fill it up with six Bruce discs and hit "random." I'll leave it in there for a couple of weeks and get my fill of Bruce. Then I might not listen to him again for another couple weeks. What happens is I go through stages of my music listening. So, when I'm interested in hearing a group—for instance, when I want to hear Bruce—I'll leave them in for a while, get my fill of them, fill myself up to the brim with it, then take a little rest from it. Hopefully, I'll hear him a couple times on the radio before I put them in again. (interview, April 21, 1993)

Even though fans may not spend an inordinate amount of time listening to Springsteen, when they do listen, they tend to concentrate intensely on the music rather than use it as background. Russ Curley explained:

> I wouldn't want to be reading or talking to someone on the phone or listening to someone else while [Springsteen] was on. I'd want to focus on it. Other artists, other people, I can put on and it's background. I can do other stuff and there's music. But, if I'm going to listen to him, it's purposeful. And I end up constantly rewinding. I want to hear it again, I want to go back again and listen to it. (interview, April 20, 1993)

This doesn't mean that fans necessarily sit and do nothing but listen to the music; several reported singing along, dancing, or "playing air guitar." But fans all saw the event as "pure," something private and not to be disturbed. For many fans, this meant listening through a headset while working out or listening alone in the car. As David Mocko explained:

I do listen to his music a bit more frequently while driving around in my car. Kind of makes sense, what with all the car references in Bruce's music, huh? :-) Although I don't think the car connection is why I listen to it in the car—rather I like to play it while I'm undisturbed during driving. (interview, June 2, 1993)

For others, the purity of the event meant listening while not doing anything taxing. College student Andrew Laurence said:

I've found that I focus on the lyrics, and for that reason I don't usually play Bruce's music while doing homework (that is, while reading or writing). Reason is, I focus too much on the lyrics, singing along under my breath, etc., and therefore find it difficult to follow what I'm doing; the music is *too* familiar to me. I therefore listen to Bruce when I'm actively doing something that is more of an activity that, while complex and involved, doesn't require as much active concentration: dressing in the morning, doing laundry, washing dishes, washing the car, telecommunicating (comp.sys.mac. is much more fun with Bruce), tracking down the latest bug in my computer's configuration, developing a FileMaker database, etc., etc. (interview, October 6, 1993).

Summarizing the Music

Fans, perhaps more than ordinary listeners, have a strong sense of Springsteen's work as a whole and are constantly identifying and measuring how different stylistic motifs and lyrical expressions across songs fit together. For some fans, this means conducting statistical analyses of the music. One fan posted an analysis to *Backstreets Digest,* which, based on a computer software program he had found, counted the number of times Bruce Springsteen used specific words in the lyrics to his recorded songs. The results revealed the obvious—such as that Springsteen uses the word "the" 2,092 times—but also some more promising and interesting facts, like Springsteen's clear proclivity for words like "sin," "street," and "tonight." He called the analysis a "preliminary run" and said that he wanted to "do a more thorough analysis using as many lyrics as possible" (Louis 1993).

Other fans talk about the evolution of the various characters and themes in Springsteen's work. For instance, Laurie McLain told me about tracing the theme of "father-son relationships" through Springsteen's work over the years, beginning with "Independence Day" (1980) and "My Father's House" (1982) and moving through "My Hometown" (1984) and "Walk Like a Man" (1987). In particular, she contrasted Springsteen's playing a cover of the Animals' angry "It's My Life" early on in his career to the more subdued and wistful "Independence Day" from *The River* as evidence of the drastic change in Springsteen's views (interview, March 28, 1993). Andrew Laurence wrote about the "meaning of the music" in terms of forming a single world, a kind of musical version of William Faulkner's Yoknapatawpha County:

We're all searching for the Answer as we bumble, stumble, and crumble our way through life. Furthermore, the Answer is never easy in coming, if it comes at all. Let's face it, do *any* of Bruce's songs have a purely happy topic? (OK, "happy" is rather vague, but bear with me, here). I think not. Rather his characters are unfulfilled; if you look at the lyrics of his songs, even the most banal and "happy" rockers, most of them have sad topics:

"Cadillac Ranch" The guy's girlfriend/wife just died; the happiness and rebellion of going down to CR has for him become a nostalgic symbol of earlier happiness. Hence, his desire to be buried there.

"Working on the Highway" Guy goes to jail for nailing and transporting a minor across state lines.

"Born in the USA." One of the most misunderstood songs *ever*. I'll leave it to that.

"No Surrender." See the *live* version. Damn near brings tears to my eyes.

Tunnel of Love. The whole album is filled with doubt.

Nebraska. Except for "Open All Night," a depressing (but brilliant) array of shattered dreams, bringing me to . . .

"Born to Run." He's young, he's virile, he drives a hot rod. "Pullin' out of here to win"? Not according to . . .

"Factory" (interview, September 4, 1993)

In the end, this interest in the music as a whole means that fans probably find it difficult to hear a song really "fresh"; one of the main things they do whenever they encounter a new Springsteen song is compare and contrast it with other Springsteen songs they know and think about how it fits into their knowledge of Springsteen's work as a whole. Thus, my discussions with fans about *Human Touch* and *Lucky Town,* works Springsteen released in 1992 without the E Street Band, often focused not on the merits of the songs themselves but rather on how Springsteen's new sound and emphasis on marriage and family fit within his overall art. Likewise, the 1995 release of *The Ghost of Tom Joad,* ostensibly a folk album in the tradition of Woody Guthrie, prompted similar discussions about, for instance, whether Springsteen had "broken with his rock'n'roll past" or was continuing old themes.

Making Aesthetic Associations

Fans understand Springsteen's music not only as an evolving body of work in itself but also as a form of expression situated in a much larger arena of the arts. Thus fans often interpret the meaning of a Springsteen work in terms of how it fits with certain conventions of style and structure in other expressive forms, such as classical music, jazz music, poetry, literature, and movies. For example, some fans form associations which focus on a particular sound quality in the music, usually due to the use of particular instruments. Al Khorasani told me about his initial reaction to "I Wish I Were Blind," a song Springsteen recorded on *Human Touch* in 1992 without the E Street Band and, particularly, saxophonist Clarence Clemons:

> There is a part where he played the guitar. The first time that I heard that song, I felt so bad that that needed Clarence's tenor sax that it just tore me up! I still have that feeling when I hear that song—that he had to have the sax for that. I don't know. I'm not going to *argue* the arrangement, but it was just something about it. I just said, "That song needed the sax. The guitar just doesn't *do* it." I mean, you're into jazz. I just love horn. That's why I like Southside Johnny [and the Asbury Jukes] and everything, because of the horn section. . . . I think tenor sax, I don't know, they should outlaw it sometimes. That's one of the most beautiful-sounding instruments that there is. (interview, March 23, 1993).

For other fans, the music has meaning in terms of its representation of particular musical styles. For instance, as I have mentioned, I often hear Springsteen in terms of my interest in jazz; indeed, his first few albums, which contained longer and more improvisatory songs with many horns, are among my favorites. Other fans, however, make associations between Springsteen and country or folk music. For Alan Stein, an amateur guitarist who listens to many different kinds of music, Springsteen's stylistic *combinations* are what strike him. As he said about Springsteen's work before 1978: "I love that era, because there's so many different music influences coming together—R and B, jazz, rock—there was so much going on that I just wanted to hear more" (interview, May 24, 1993).

Still other fans relate the music not to musical styles but rather to forms of literary and pictorial art. John O'Brien summarized the songs in terms of their narrative construction, characterizing the plot of every song as "guy caught in a situation, trying to get out, expressing anger." Others, like Alan Stein, likened the music to movies and savored its drama or ability to produce lasting images: "It seems to me that the early stuff told tales that were very vivid. You could see them; you could picture them; movies, kind of. You could see what he was talking about." Indeed, many fans talked about the "poetic" qualities of the language used in Springsteen's songs and derived meaning from the songs' unique word choices, metaphors, and phrasing. As Linda Warner said about Springsteen's songwriting:

> He says it with a real economy of words. He picks exactly the right words to describe what he's trying to say. It's amazing. He's really come a long way. His lyrics have gotten more sophisticated, and he's really grown as a person. He's really—for someone with no education, basically, it's pretty interesting what he's been able to do. (interview, March 23, 1993)

Making Political Associations

Another way in which many fans approach the interpretation of the music is to think about it in terms of a certain political ideology. Springsteen's music has rarely taken a direct political stance (see Cullen 1992), but it often focuses attention on social injustice, whether it is the reception of returning Vietnam veterans in "Born in the USA" (1984) or the sympathetic portrayals of the underclass in songs like "Factory" (1978), "The River" (1980), and "Youngstown" (1995). For many fans, this social concern is central to understanding the meaning of the music.

Paul Fischer, for example, thinking about his Springsteen fandom and his experiences while teaching rock'n'roll to undergraduates as a graduate student, emphasized the music's "political" meaning:

> One of the dimensions of it that I was thinking about . . . was way back in the days when the music had a certain sociopolitical meaning that it doesn't always have today. When I talk to my undergraduate students about popular music, and I try to explain how important the Beatles were or how people hung on waiting for the next release to find out what John Lennon thought this year, they say, "Well, but they just sell shoes." [laughter] You know, they're not wrong. The whole commercialization of the music that has happened since then makes it a lot harder, I think, to make the kind of connection that I feel from Bruce Springsteen and his work over time for young people today. (interview, May 25, 1993)

Mary Krause, a graduate of Cornell University's School of Industrial and Labor Relations, found the music less overtly political yet found meaning in Springsteen's work on *Nebraska* (1982) because it dealt with social issues. She even focused on Springsteen's song "Factory" (1978) in a term paper she had to write:

> I took a sociology course on the sociology of work. And so I did all kinds of like work songs. I used Bruce; I used Woody Guthrie. So, I do like that. Again, a kind of social issue in some ways, the way he describes factory life. Although he describes it without making it political. (interview, April 30, 1993)

Al Khorasani concurred. As an active member of Amnesty International, he admired Springsteen's participation in the Amnesty International tour in 1988, yet he was disappointed about the *lack* of politics in Springsteen's recent music:

> I felt that in his earlier albums—*Born to Run* and *Born in the USA*—he started making some very important points, you know, socially speaking. And I feel that those are the points that still need to be made. I don't in any way feel that it's his duty to do it. As I said, I like the fact that he writes what he feels. But I think that it's good that, say, someone in his position, or anyone at that position, when they write a line on a piece of paper, millions of people get to hear it, as opposed to when I write something only I get to hear it. I think there are points that need to be made. And I felt that he should have maybe continued on with some of the quote-unquote protest stuff that he was talking about. About the social situations and the stories that he used to tell in his concerts. (interview, March 23, 1993)

Along the same lines, many fans and critics welcomed 1995's *The Ghost of Tom Joad*—a work which dealt openly with issues like homelessness, illegal immigration, racism, and joblessness—as Springsteen's "rediscovery" of a political voice.

Making Biographical Associations

As I have mentioned, fans often see Springsteen's music as quite personal, a form of communication about his experiences, feelings, and thoughts. Springsteen's references to actual places and people in his songs and especially his long, rambling introductions about growing up and his feelings about the state of the country during live performances have only reinforced this perception. Appropriately, many fans interpret Springsteen's music in terms of how it relates to what they know about the circumstances of Springsteen's life.

For example, Gene Chyzowych, when talking with me about the meaning of Springsteen's music, focused on what it told him about Springsteen's values:

> From what little I can relate to, you can see that he's made it. But he almost lost everything. I'm not talking about his money, but everything else. He had money, was a superstar, and people adored him, but he didn't have things that were important to him. His family was in a shambles; he was in a great transitional period. He's always—at least the way his lyrics portrayed him—he's always concerned about the most important things: his friends, his family. The things you can't buy with money. That's why he hasn't really changed for me, now that he's this megastar. I know he's got money and all, and that's always going to change a person, but I don't think it's going to change the values he's grown up with. (interview, April 21, 1993)

In one of our conversations, Russ Curley analyzed the changes Springsteen made in recent performances of 1978's "Darkness on the Edge of Town" in terms of Springsteen's growth as a human being:

> CURLEY: The song has become less a fighting song and more this loud, look-at-my-life—the strain and pain is gone, but it's still there and it's more of a—he's got backup singers now and it's more like, "The pain is here, it's been fifteen years since it's been there, and I'm living with it." That comes about in the song, and you hear the way it changes.
>
> CAVICCHI: I never thought of it that way, yeah.
>
> CURLEY: I mean, hearing that live when I saw him in Jersey, the first night I saw him at the Meadowlands—I heard about the arrangements with the backup singers, but when I heard it, I said, "That is a different song, now!" The themes are there, but this is now a forty-three—well, forty-two, then—year-old man singing it, and it's not when he was twenty-eight, when he wrote the song. It's so reflective of his life, now. He lost his wife and—[laughs] he didn't lose his wife, but [pause] he's changed.

CAVICCHI: He might have lost something.

CURLEY: Yeah, ten million with her. But he says, "I lost my . . ." but now he changes the lines: "I lost my faith when I lost my wife." I think that's reflective of his whole period after *Tunnel of Love* and the breakup, and when he went into seclusion to a certain extent. So, he's changing, too, and we all change as we grow up. (interview, April 20, 1993)

Linda Warner likewise talked about Springsteen's 1992 albums, *Human Touch* and *Lucky Town*, in terms of what she knew about his personal life while he was recording them:

I think the only time that I've been a little confused by him was after *Tunnel of Love* when nothing was happening. I mean, he went to L.A., and nobody knew what was going on. I had this—I wasn't doubting him so much, but I was concerned. It was like, "Something's going on." And I have a real close friend who lives in Prescott [Arizona]. During this time, just before he got really seriously working on the albums, and just before Patti got pregnant, he did a long trip through the desert. On a motorcycle. And he appeared one day in Prescott. He was really out there, talking to people. He said he was looking for biker chicks. He was going to biker bars! It was very odd behavior. It was clear that he was looking for something. Images from that trip have appeared in the two new albums. I mean, I can tell there are times when he's talking about this trip. Because right after the trip, Patti got pregnant. It was clear that he was trying to make some kind of decision. And was acting wacko, I mean, he was up in the mountains, up at Jerome, hanging out in those bars up there, and it was wild. I arrived in town like a week after he left. And the town was just buzzing about his behavior and what was going on with him. And I had a few moments, kind of thinking, "He's in some trouble." (interview, March 25, 1993)

Making Personal Associations

Springsteen is important to fans primarily because, as I have discussed, his music "touched" them in some lasting way; this personal connection to his music greatly influences the way in which fans interpret its meaning. Thus, while fans may see Springsteen's work in terms of his own life, they also relate the mood or content of a work to the circumstances of their *own* lives. Mary Krause, for instance, talked about the songs on *Darkness on the Edge of Town* (1978) as having very personal and changeable meanings:

I really relate to this album, although I'm starting to outgrow it, I think. See, college—until kind of getting some professional settling down—really is *Darkness on the Edge of Town*. I'll tell you what I don't like on this album because I like most of the album. "Badlands" is one of my all-time favorite Bruce songs. "Adam Raised a Cain" I could live without. I think it's because I'm a feminist, now, and it's just too many—too much male focus. I can't relate to it as much. "Something in the Night" is okay. "Candy's Room": another very good dance song, party involvement song. "Racin' in the Street": very good. Although, the car thing, also, has started to wane for me. It was fine, I guess, when we were in college, when we didn't have our own vehicles. But Bruce sings a lot about cars, and I've kind of lost that focus. It's gone now; it's just a fact in my life. (interview, April 30, 1993).

Russ Curley explained:

Bruce has said, "People come to my music to find out more about themselves. They listen to my music to understand themselves better." I don't think that could be truer. Just the themes in all the albums. *Born to Run* had a very streamlined character to it, you know: let's run away together. There's themes of running away. Then it continues. Then it changes when it gets to *Darkness*. It's more like those dreams of running away have been changed. It's been disillusioned to an extent, and harrowing and pared-down images are now what the album's about. And that continues for a while through *The River* and through *Nebraska*. And then they change. As he comes all the way through, those are definitely personal things that you go through. He went through them at those points in his life: when he was twenty-eight it was *Darkness*; when he was thirty, it was *The River*. And I think I experienced those things on my own; I internalized them later. It's harder for a twelve- or thirteen-year-old to do it. But I'm twenty-one now, and I can definitely see where he's coming from. (interview, April 29, 1993)

John O'Brien echoed:

I guess this is what really good artists do—he expresses something to me that I've been thinking all along but haven't really known how to say it, you know? I mean, "Human Touch," as a song. Initially it's like, "God, this is so cheesy," but then I listened more and it was like, "You know, that's true!" I've been thinking about that: relationships with people are probably the most important thing in life. When all else fails, you can hold on to that. I was like, "God, that's pretty!" [laughs] Not that he was the first one to think of it, but maybe somehow, to me, that's how I heard it. (interview, March 15, 1993)

On the whole, these six interpretive moves—situating the listening experience in terms of its purity and intensity, summarizing the music in terms of Springsteen's body of work, focusing on the music's aesthetic qualities, focusing on the music's political implications, relating the music to Springsteen's life history, and relating the music to one's own life—all work to constrain the music's meaning for fans. Specifically, the serious and disciplined nature of Springsteen fans' musical encounters tends to favor an understanding of Springsteen's work as fine art rather than as, say, wild celebration.

Of course, when asked about their listening, fans automatically talked about their listening to recordings rather than their concert going, and, as ethnomusicologist Charles Keil has asserted, recordings tend to focus on the individual achievement of perfection, of fixing a certain ideal, rather than on social play and abandon, which are more likely to be found in performance ([1985] 1994, pp. 210–217, 294). However, even fans' discussions of their concert going reflected an appreciative, even studious sensibility. For instance, when I asked fans on my questionnaire about their motivations for attending a Springsteen concert, not a single fan indicated that "partying" was a factor; most, instead, emphasized more serious goals having to do with reverence and acquiring knowledge, like "hearing Bruce's stories" or "hearing the music arranged live." And, on the whole, when discussing with me the meaning of Springsteen's work, fans tended to ignore the more party-oriented songs; blatant rockers with simple lyrics about pleasurable pursuits and standard rock-pop song structures, like "Out in the Street" (1980), "Pink Cadillac" (1984), or "All or Nothing at All" (1992), are appreciated for what they are but are not mentioned much in discussions of meaning. Thus, earlier, Laurie McLain chose to ignore a song like "Pink Cadillac" in her analysis of Springsteen's philosophy of engagement because it didn't address complex life issues. In fact, in most polls of fans' opinions about Springsteen's music, such songs don't usually even rate.

This is not to say, of course, that fans do not find pleasure in the music or see it as fun and celebratory; it is rock'n'roll, after all, and one could certainly point to Springsteen fans' participation in concert performances where they scream, dance, and otherwise "lose themselves." Such feelings, however, are always balanced or held in check by a certain cerebral understanding. While social, celebratory abandon with others is important in fans' encounters with the music, it is always secondary, whereas individual, critical appreciation is primary.

In the end, fans' listening raises issues of class identity and power. As mostly well-educated, middle-class American listeners, the fans to whom I spoke probably were taught in school that "high culture"—whether literature, music, or painting—is positively associated with qualities like complexity, organization, clarity, and seriousness, while "popular culture," or entertainment, is negatively associated with qualities like simplicity, sloppiness, repetitiveness, and superficiality (see Levine 1988). For Springsteen's music to be good or legitimate in such an aesthetic framework, it would have to have some of the qualities of high culture. Not only that, but within the Springsteen fan community such values may work to separate fans from ordinary audience members; by asserting a high culture–related, serious appreciation of Springsteen's music, fans invoke powerful assumptions about class hierarchy in the United States and can assert themselves over others with "low culture" views of what the music is about (see Keil [1985] 1994).

Now, the high culture approach of Springsteen fans to Springsteen's music does not mean that they all agree about what the music means. Despite shared interpretive conventions, Springsteen's music can still mean different things to different people and be the site of highly contested debates and disagreements. Take, for example, a recent debate on *Luckytown Digest* about "Born in the USA" (1984). "Born in the USA" tells the story of a Vietnam veteran who comes back home and finds nothing but rejection and betrayal. While it was sometimes interpreted as "patriotic" (see Marsh 1987, pp. 254–266), during the *Ghost of Tom Joad* tour in 1995–1996, Springsteen jokingly mocked people for getting the "wrong message." When a fan complained that Springsteen was being too harsh since it was easy to misinterpret the song, given its anthemic arrangement, another fan responded by writing:

> I find the often mentioned misinterpretation of BitUSA a very tiring, beaten-to-death subject. The fact is simple: the song is an entirely ironic, bitter and angry deposition; perhaps the most ironic song I've ever heard. The anthem-like tune, the lyrics and even the "patriotic" chorus are deliberately such, constantly mocking the proud, never-ending American Dream. It is crystal clear! No other way would have passed the message. (Aristidis 1995)

This message touched off a firestorm of responses to the *Digest*. What was interesting, though, was not the variety of opinions but the ways in which differing opinions drew on different interpretive moves.

One fan, for instance, drew upon other songs on the *Born in the USA* album, as well as from literary associations, to say that the song was, indeed, a condemnation of the American dream:

> A lot of the songs on *Born in the USA* deal with pretty naive folks, folks who are chasing phantom dreams: "Darlington County," "Working on the Highway," "Glory Days." These are characters who have faith, but faith in the wrong sorts of things. They're made sadder by their dreams, not happier. These people aren't stupid for keeping faith, just naive. This isn't to say that I think Bruce is looking down on his characters; it seems pretty obvious that he has a lot of sympathy for them. *BitUSA* reminds me in a lot of ways of another Steinbeck novel, *Of Mice and Men*. It's an album about dreams deferred, and dreams derailed. (Yamashita 1995)

Other fans concurred but did so by citing the song's likeness to the Police's "Every Breath You Take," a hit of the eighties that was widely misinterpreted as a romantic love song, even though its lyrics describe a jilted lover's angry and pathological obsession (Bulger 1995). Others referred to Springsteen's stated intentions about the song as the basis for their opinion. One fan simply characterized the images presented in the lyrics:

> "Born in the USA" is *not*, in my opinion, a patriotic song. It is not even close. One listen to the lyrics makes it clear to me—images of a dead man's town, being beaten like a dog by society, being treated like a second-class citizen upon return from combat, and having absolutely no sanctuary to flee to. . . . Well, it seems that love for one's country is not something the narrator wishes to express. (Lipsky 1995)

However, other fans, making different interpretive moves, saw the song as having a more positive meaning. One fan compared the song to "I Am a Patriot" by Springsteen's friend and former bandmate, Little Steven Van Zandt (1984):

> In that song, Steven sings: "I am a patriot and I love my country, but my country,
> it don't love me." [*sic*] He goes on to sing, "Ain't no Republican, I ain't no Demo-
> crat, I ain't no communist either—I am a patriot." [*sic*] I think the guy in BitUSA
> loves his country, but that he also feels betrayed by his country. (Mc 1995)

Another fan interpreted the song in terms of his understanding of American
history:

> I see patriotism in BitUSA, but it's an ironic blend of hurt and yearning for the
> ideals that this country stands for, not those that sent him "off to a foreign land."
> Despite—in fact, because of—the unfairness with which our leaders have treated
> this country's young, the speaker still proclaims he was born in the USA. That
> should count for something. It's something we lost during the Viet Nam War era.
> The speaker seems to be bringing the point back home. It's not just anti-war, it's
> anti-vet trashing. I reserve the hatred and venom in this song for the Americans
> who greeted returning servicemen at airstrips with spittle and ridicule. Those who
> wouldn't hire the vet, those who still joke about drug addicts of a certain age.
> Those people don't understand what being born in this country means. And of
> course don't forget Johnson, Nixon, and McNamara.

He then went on to talk about the song's different contexts of presentation:

> I do find it a little disconcerting that Bruce has only now really begun to object to
> the anthemizing of this tune. I agree with the [person] who states that he gingerly
> walked around the Reagan thing back in '84. The images of that tour are still fresh
> in my mind: all red white and blue, flags at the shows, and let's face it, a song
> arrangement that lends itself very well to rock's anthems. I only hope his protes-
> tations now are reactions to the fact that the Reagan Revolution For Selfishness is
> alive and well with Newt [Gingrich]. (Burke 1995)

I was involved in a similar debate a couple years earlier on *Backstreets Digest,* in
which differences arose because people employed different combinations of interpretive moves to make meaning from the music. Fans were discussing the
song "Reason to Believe" (1982), which offers a series of vignettes of people who,
despite obvious pain and suffering, still find reason to go on each day. The stance
of narrator is ambiguous, however; it is unclear whether he is appalled or envi-
ous. When one fan, David, said that he was "bemused" by audiences applauding
the performance of "Reason to Believe," because "we're talking nihilism here"
(Kieltyka 1993a), I responded by comparing the meaning of the song to Albert
Camus's philosophy of the absurd:

> I think that people certainly miss the irony of the song, but I don't agree that the
> song is simply nihilistic. To me, the narrator in the song moves back and forth
> from a distanced critical doubt to a dumbfounded wonder, even a sort of admira-
> tion, at the tenacity of people's belief. The negative rap the song gets is like the
> negative rap existentialists used to get: Camus would say that the universe is ab-

surd and meaningless, and people would stop inviting him to parties. But he also
asserted that because the universe is absurd, we must *create* meaning. That's similar to what Bruce is saying, in my opinion. (Cavicchi 1993)

That prompted another fan to post a message in which he derived the meaning
of "Reason to Believe" by making connections between it and the Bible, as well
as alternative arrangements and other Springsteen songs:

I am really not good in the religious terminology, but ["Reason to Believe"] gives
me the feeling that is also in the Bible in a way, that the ones who are "mentally
poor" are always happy. I mean, the ones without knowledge are happy. And this
could be in that song in a way. But I don't think that there is any basis to make the
conclusion from the irony of the song: the ones who know a lot are always bitter.
Another point of view is if I listen to the version of the song from the *Live* album,
it gives a feeling of safety, mostly after the verses are over, and the band goes on.
You feel like you can fall asleep during the song, because whatever happens outside, these chords and this song gives you shelter. It is very calm. There is not a
minute of irony in there, except the lyrics. I think there is a contradiction between
the refrain and the verses, because if "Still at the end of every hard-earned day /
People find some reason to believe," well, it's not a bad thing at all. But what those
guys find in the verses is not what one would really call "reason to believe." And
also, what grows from their reasons is not faith, but rather like blind faith—this
might be the thing he makes fun of here, the same thing that he has raised his
voice against, for example, in the introduction to "War" so many times.[3] (Palasti
1993a)

After a discussion about differing definitions of faith, it turned out that while
originally I was making meaning of the song by drawing parallels with existen-
tialist philosophy, David was drawing, instead, on personal experience:

I'm not a religious person myself, though I once was. *Nebraska* came along at a time
when I was examining, questioning, and discarding a lot of what I'd formerly taken
for granted or even believed strongly in. That album kept me going in a very real
way. . . . It was my lifeline. Listening to it, I felt I wasn't alone. . . . Here was
someone else who knew what it was like to live in hell. (Figuratively speaking, of
course!) I still feel real close to those songs; I guess that's why I get steamed when
I hear people . . . react to "Reason to Believe" in such a shallow way. I kinda feel
like they're violating my relationship to the song. (Kieltyka 1993b)

Such debates clearly reveal the different ways in which individual fans con-
textualize Springsteen's songs. It should be mentioned that differences occur not
only *between* individuals but also *within* individual lives, as people change their
minds about what songs mean. The idea of interpretive moves also helps make
sense of such changes; the meaning of a song depends on one's cumulative understanding of it, and that meaning may change as one draws on new experiences

and new insights. David Merrill has even come to expect and enjoy such changes in meaning:

> I derive great pleasure in re-discovering Bruce songs. By this, I mean that I can go back and listen to his albums and perhaps find a song that I had never paid much attention to in the past (maybe I was still caught up in the glow, or trying to figure out the meaning behind a previous song, or maybe just distracted by something else going on at the time, etc.), and suddenly I'll hear the song as if for the first time (although I may have actually heard it many, many times) and it will click! "Wow—how did I ever miss such a *great* song? Those are *great* lyrics. I can't believe I never got this song before." . . . I guess that a lot of it might depend on the listener's current state of mind, as well as their expectations of Bruce. A song (or album) which you can't relate to at one point in your life might just be the one to kick you in the face the next time you hear it! That's what I love about Bruce. (interview, May 6, 1993)

In the end, what's important to understand in applying Feld's model to Springsteen fans' experience is that the meaning they perceive in the music is historically and socially situated but also fluid. Listening to the music is not a simple process; fans must sift through all sorts of different layers of meaning—some of which they share as members of a group with specific interpretive conventions and some of which they uniquely hold as individuals with particular and differing life experiences—and select those which, for them, cohere and ring true in that moment. Sometimes social and individual meanings overlap, sometimes they do not, and they are always liable to change.

*L*istening to Experience

The experience of listening which I have described really focuses on how fans participate in and make sense of a musical event, such as a concert or the playing of a CD. But, as I explained in chapter 4, fandom is really about moving *beyond* the musical event and continuing one's role as an audience member in everyday life. Fans' engagement with the music is not simply restricted to participation in musical events and also includes participation in situations and experiences that may be commonly characterized as "nonmusical." During the commute, at work, at school, while making supper, while playing with one's children or visiting friends or getting ready for bed, most fans are still "listening"—that is, still constructing meaning by making associations between perceived musical structures, potential messages, and the contexts of their experiences. They may turn to the actual music and put on a CD, creating a musical encounter like that just discussed. But in such cases of listening, interpretation is initiated not by the experience of musical sound but rather by the experience of a situation, thought, or feeling. Thus, while any discussion of the interpretation of music must include what happens when a listener hears a piece of music, in the case of fans, it also must include what that hearing *makes happen*.[4]

For example, many fans described their listening as enabling them to better manage their emotions and moods. Such a use of music is not uncommon; the research of the Music in Daily Life Project at SUNY Buffalo revealed that people are constantly using music in this way (Crafts, Cavicchi, and Keil 1993). But while most people use different musical styles to manage their moods—rock in the morning, classical late at night, for instance—fans have located the gamut of their emotions in the music of a single artist. In particular, fans talked about either matching or enhancing particular moods by thinking about or listening to certain Springsteen songs or albums. For instance, John O'Brien reported using *Tunnel of Love* (1987) to mirror his emotions during a relationship:

> I remember listening to that in the fall of freshman year in high school, when I first ever had a girlfriend. That's what I was listening to. It was weird. [laughs] And not that all the songs were—most of the songs are about how love doesn't work out. But as far as listening to that and remembering that, using that—[it was about] listening to a song expressing how you are feeling. (interview, March 15, 1993)

Mary Krause explained more generally:

> Well, in a given week, any Bruce album can speak to your mood that week. Like *Darkness* is much more of a rebel album for him and spoke to a difficult time in his life when he was turning things around. And *The River* was his first real money-making album, and it has that—some of the songs have that—party-type happy beat to them. *Born in the USA* was certainly his glory days, and it has that to it. So, it depends what you need—and the new stuff, *Lucky Town* and *Human Touch*—it's happy, it's settled, shall we say. So, you know, it depends on the kind of week you're having at work. You want to be young again, you want to be a rebel again, you go home and put on "Badlands" [from *Darkness*] and you just spit in the face of it all, you know? But, if it's just kind of an okay perky day, you go home and put on "Out in the Street" [from *The River*] and you just kind of dance around and have a great time, everything's just kind of copacetic. Then, if you have a real exciting day, like if you've really achieved something, you put on *Born in the USA*. I'm not settled yet, so I don't listen to the new albums much! (interview, April 30, 1993)

Other fans talked specifically about using Springsteen's music to try to get out of a bad or unwanted mood. One fan explained:

> Generally, his music crawls under my mood and lifts me up. Right now I am listening to a boot from a *BitUSA* show in Cincinnati. The power of the show, the energy takes me away from the mundane world of answering a phone, or the sorrow of breaking up with a girlfriend. I hear so much of my world in the words, feel liberated by the fury or the intensity of the band's playing.

LeAnne Olderman similarly found the music inspiring:

I remember one time, a couple of months ago, I was in the grocery store, and I was in a really bad mood. I was mad at everybody. And a Springsteen song came on, and it was instantaneous: I was happy. "Oh! Okay!" It was just a complete change. . . . When I was growing up, it was—adolescence is difficult, to say the least. For me, [his music] became an outlet. When I would get upset, I would always go and listen to some of his music. The thing is that the people in his songs were always worse off than me. [laughs] And they always managed to do okay. It always makes me feel better. Even now, I'll go and listen. (interview, May 13, 1993)

On a different, more specific level, fans talked about their listening as helpful in "getting through" certain problems and situations. Such problems may be as mundane as a traffic cop. As Paul Fischer explained:

I do have one particular memory of driving the New Jersey Turnpike and intentionally putting Bruce on the box. I had flown into Philadelphia from Los Angeles to do a charity event in New York. I was working for a company that had booked a celebrity to show up at this event. The nuts and bolts of the event are kind of immaterial. But I left Manhattan at like 12:15–12:30 to drive the two hours back to Philadelphia. And I had a tape of *Nebraska* and some old live cuts, and it was kind of like "Mr. State Trooper" was my mantra. It was like, "Please don't stop me, please don't stop me" [the refrain to the song]. And I had this very conscious idea that putting that particular music on the tape player at that particular time would make me invisible to the state police. And I got home in an hour and a half, and it should have taken two hours. It worked beautifully. . . . So that was kind of a particular everyday life usage of the music. (interview, May 25, 1993)

Sometimes the problems may be more serious, in which case fans see the music as teaching or reminding them of certain values, experiences, or commitments. For example, one fan explained in a letter that Springsteen's music got her through years of abuse:

Through my childhood, I was sexually abused by my own father. I began listening to Bruce's music when I was 13. It really got me rockin'. I also liked the lyrics. I would go to my bedroom for hours with my headphones on and just blast the volume. The music took me where I wanted to be, running from the pain in the world. As I grew older, and got married and had children, I realized that running isn't the answer, that the pain follows you. Bruce's music gave me the courage to face my past and deal with the future. It gave me strength to tell my husband and family of the abuse. My so-called "father" was an alcoholic and he died when I was 17. Whenever I need strength or the pain removed or even just a good time, I put a Bruce tape on.

Carrie Gabriel explained how she has always turned to the song "Thunder Road" (1975) during difficult moments in her life:

That is the song that gives meaning to my life. That song is the blood that runs through my veins. It gives me hope when all of my hope is gone. I remember finding out about the death of my grandpa, at age nine. This was the first death I witnessed in my family. The only way I could cope was by shutting myself in my room, turning off the lights, crawling into bed, burying my head in my pillow, and playing "Thunder Road" loud enough to drown out my tears. It was the perfect medicine as the wailing and whining harmonica echoed my wails and whines, and the soft piano, like a warm embrace, eased me into this other world—Bruce's haven built especially for me. This is the ritual I go through whenever anything goes wrong in my life. The way he moves me through the song to the invigorating pounding ending has a mystical quality of leaving me feeling better about my situation. Of course, I don't just save this song for sad times. I play it during times of celebration or when nothing extremely great or horrible is happening, allowing me to say to each day, [quoting from "Thunder Road"] "I'm pullin' outta here to win!" (personal correspondence, March 22, 1995)

On a more general and abstract level, fans talked about using Springsteen songs to come to conclusions about the potential circumstances of their lives, to map out where their current life course might take them and whether they wanted that future. Paul Fischer, for example, explained how his thinking about marriage and family was in part influenced by Springsteen's later work:

He is coming from a place similar to where I am, and I am relating to his view of the world and culture because, in some ways, he's a little bit ahead of me and providing me with some important information. . . . He lost some of his appeal with the mass audience he had with *Born in the USA* with the most recent releases, *Lucky Town* and *Human Touch,* because younger people are not dealing with the issues of a failed marriage, getting married, having kids. But I am. And, in that sense, although we are a couple of years apart in age and he started dealing with the trials and tribulations of marriage and family a number of years before me, that sort of maintained the pattern. You know, he's got these experiences that teach him lessons about life that he puts into songs, and then he records them, and it's like, "Oh, gee, that's very interesting." I remember when *Tunnel of Love* came out. It was much sooner than I was expecting another record from him, and I hadn't heard a thing about it. It was like, all of a sudden, I was driving around in the car in L.A., and it's like, "Here's the new Bruce Springsteen single, 'Brilliant Disguise.'" I was like, "Bruce Springsteen single? What the hell's going on?" And I said to myself, "He must have really had something that he wanted to say." And that song pretty much told the whole story: he's in this marriage that's not really working out, and the rest of the album sort of confirms that. And this was even, I think, before I met my wife. Just hearing all of that taught me a lot of some of the pitfalls that I ought to be looking out for. But, also, having seen him go through the whole marriage thing very publicly and very traditionally and all of that kind of opened that door to me a little bit more, where perhaps I had been resistant to that kind of commitment before. (interview, May 25, 1993)

Susan West, a self-employed fan in her thirties from Pennsylvania, told me specifically how her life was changed by the song "Factory" (1978):

Like everybody else, I had *Born to Run* and liked it OK, but it wasn't till *Darkness* that Bruce really hit a nerve. One song in particular, hit me right between the eyes and caused an epiphany that changed the course of my life. That was "Factory."

At the time (I was 18) I had just started dating my husband, an auto worker who steam cleaned and shoveled metal into a furnace all day. He'd come home so covered in grease and bits of metal that he had to roll up his pants to walk into the house. My husband (boyfriend) *hated* it there. It was hot, dirty work, and about the best he could expect, having dropped out of school (I think he lied about that to get the job). I hated watching him go there every day.

My grandfather had worked at the same place since he came back from WWII. He'd never say a bad word about the place. He was a toolmaker, and as a skilled worker had it a little better. The factory had enabled him to support his family his whole life and having lived through the Depression, he didn't expect anything more.

I dated my husband for four years while he worked there and "Factory" clearly prophesied his future if he stayed there hating every minute of his job. The image invoked by the song was all too real. Anyway, when my husband (fiancé) confided that he wanted to be a cop, I decided we'd do whatever it took to get him out of that hellhole. And that's what we did. I helped him study for his GED and get through the police academy (four nights a week for our newlywed year). And then through the lean years of working two or three part-time jobs at a time before he latched onto a full-time police job. Now he's a sergeant and loves what he does.

"End of the day, factory whistle cries,
Men walk through these gates with death in their eyes.
And you just better believe, boy, somebody's gonna get hurt tonight.
It's the working, the working, just the working life."[5] (interview, May 12, 1993)

As I have mentioned, the idea that artistic expression might educate and serve as a guide for making sense of the world is, historically, associated with the tradition of high culture in the West. While institutionalized arts like classical music, opera, painting, and literature tend to represent values like order, refinement, and hierarchy, rock music is sloppy, energetic, rough, and socially desegregated. Indeed, it is best known for taking a stand against "high culture." For this reason, rock critics like Chuck Eddy have railed against "meaningful" rock music like Springsteen's:

Intellectual sophistication, poetic artifice, "flair for language," all that Cole Porter nonsense, is what rock reacted *against*. So, as far as I'm concerned, what Bruce Springsteen does has very little to do with rock'n'roll. He plays art-rock. Like Rick Wakeman (or, okay, Pete Townshend—same dif) before him, his muse can't be separated from his ego; he's too palpably concerned with how he'll be documented in the history books. Rock doesn't work that way. If post-conscious rock has visionaries, they're guys like James Brown, Marvin Gaye, George Clinton, probably Steve Wonder, possibly Neil Young—guys who don't spend their whole careers trying to *prove* it, guys who never seem vainglorious, no matter how much ground they're breaking. And, needless to say, they break lots more than Springsteen. (Eddy 1988, pp. 10–11)

Springsteen does reflect a more contemplative tradition in rock music. While dedicated to the energy and feeling of early rock'n'roll, he really came to public view in a folk-rock guise, drawing on the lyrical sophistication of Van Morrison and Bob Dylan in his early years and then adding a bit of Woody Guthrie and sixties soul later on. But I would argue that Eddy is too wrapped up in the music's power rather than listeners' power. The seriousness of fans' view of the music, I think, comes not so much from the style or history of the music as from their own kind of commitment and investment in it. In the end, the music is meaningful for fans because they use it meaningfully.

This is not as easy as it sounds. Not all fans are entirely comfortable with using popular music to manage and guide their daily lives. Alan Levine, for instance, resisted my questions about using Springsteen's music according to mood:

> You know, Dan, I never really use music to pull me in and out of moods. Actually, I'm a runner, or at least on and off a runner, and when *Lucky Town* was released, the first thing I did was tape it off the CD and use that as my running tape. So, there's a little bit of motivation there for me. But to be honest, I never really used it to pull me in and out of moods that much. Every now and then, when I was down and needed to blare some tunes, I'd go in that direction. (interview, April 2, 1993)

John O'Brien explained to me that he was suspicious of too close an involvement with popular music and personal feelings:

> I remember Michael—there was this interview with Michael Stipe where he was saying that that's kind of why he doesn't go for that anymore. You know the song "Radio Song" by R.E.M.? He was saying he wrote that as a response to how he remembers being in high school and turning on the radio station on and saying, "Wow, that's exactly how I feel." And then like turning the station and saying, "No, *that's* it." And then turning it and saying, "No, *this* is exactly the way I feel." And that's so stupid, you know? I think I agree with that on a certain level. That's what I wonder: do you do that with songs? Should you? I guess that's why you have to say, "I'm taking this out of the song, but it isn't exactly . . ."—you know. Which in a way is good because it's like some universal thing, not the actual "Let me see if I can match up my situation to this exact song. I just broke up with my girlfriend, oh this song says that, therefore"—you know? (interview, March 15, 1993)

At the same time, however, these same fans who worried about using music as a source of meaning nevertheless pointed to ways in which Springsteen was meaningful for them. Alan admitted that, while he may not use Springsteen's music to manage his moods, "there's a special feeling there" whenever he hears the music on the radio. While John worried that using popular music to feel emotions was wrong, he also admitted that the music helped him think about his life:

It's just like another text that I cite, informing whatever kind of philosophy I'm coming up with. So I think I kind of think about it in that way. I guess—it may seem to a lot of people a dumb vehicle for it—but for some reason that's the vehicle I get it out of. I could do it with Shakespeare, I could do it with . . . I think a lot of people do it with different things. (interview, March 15, 1993)

Music, like any performance, can serve to heighten and open up experience so that people may engage and contemplate it. As Steven Feld claims, music's "generality and multiplicity of possible messages and interpretations brings out a special kind of 'feelingful' activity and engagement on the part of the listener" ([1984] 1994, pp. 90–91). In the case of fans, however, such meaning is often gained in the face of competing notions about the value of rock'n'roll and about where people should turn for guidance in their lives. I do not wish to deny fans' worries or portray them as contradictory, but rather I want to highlight the fact that fans are not *simply* using the music meaningfully; fans must work hard to keep such a practice alive.

*U*ncanniness

During my fieldwork, several fans expressed some confusion about whether their views of the world came from Springsteen's music or whether their views were what drew them to the music in the first place. As Laurie McLain said:

I learned a lot from Bruce! I think I probably—I don't know which came first: maybe I had this philosophy and I didn't know about it and that's why I liked Bruce. But it could be the other way, that my philosophy came from Bruce. Which is certainly possible. I don't want to give him too much credit for my entire existence. I'm sure my parents have something to do with it. (interview, March 28, 1993)

In addition, a large number of fans told me, again and again, that as they encountered songs, they always found them remarkably uncanny, seeming to fit perfectly with the circumstances of their lives. As Linda Warner said about her experience of *Tunnel of Love* (1987):

It's really a wild—I mean, something happened to me that made me doubt something that was really part of my identity, and it happened right when that song came out. I was in the kitchen, baking cookies, and crying about what was going on in my life—that was the first single from the album—and I brought home the single, and I put it on the stereo, and I listened to it, and I lost it. It was like, "He's been reading my mind." It still affects me that way. (interview, March 25, 1993).

John O'Brien explained about Springsteen's benefit performance at the Christic Institute in California in 1990[6]:

He played the song "Real World," which is on *Human Touch* but I don't really like. But he played it just on the piano with him singing. And it was really good. That was all about not having any illusions at all and not looking to this idealistic thing. And it was at a time in my life when I was having all these illusions, and I was like, "Wow!" There's another thing like I was saying with *Human Touch:* it hits you at a time when you really need to hear it or something. And that completely did, and I was like, "Wow," you know. (interview, March 15, 1993)

Russ Curley said about *Human Touch* and *Lucky Town*:

I remember when I first day listened to . . . "I Wish I Were Blind." I mean, I just was going through that with a woman that way, too! I said, "Oh, that's my theme song!" I mean, that's—you couldn't have written a more perfect song. I had heard "Real World"—the acoustic version of "Real World" from the Christic Institute. I said, "Wow, that's exactly where I'm at right now." Like the chorus, he says, "Ain't no church bells ringing, ain't no flags unfurled." I had a problem in my life and I'm moving on with it now. At that time, things weren't working out or whatever in your life, and I go through the same things with him. How did he know I was thinking that? (interview, March 15, 1993)

Such feelings of connection and uncanniness are important to understanding how fans make meaning from Springsteen's music. Feld asserted that "each listening is not just the juxtaposition of a musical object and a listener. It is a juxtaposition—in fact an entangling—of a dialectical object and a situated interlocutor" ([1984] 1994, p. 84). For fans, however, this "entangling" never really ends. While I have presented fans' listening and interpretation of music in two parts—as a musical encounter and as a turning to the music during nonmusical events—reality is far more complex, and it is, at times, difficult to tell where the music ends and fans' experiences begin.

Of course, fans do not really lose their sense of reality; they are always aware that the music is played by Springsteen, another person, and that they are only listening to his work. However, fans' descriptions of their listening indicate that the significance of the music is not limited to the musical encounter but resonates long thereafter. Fans' "listening," then, is not simply hearing and interpreting a song but an ongoing process of deepening the connection between their hearing and their lives.

Fans always have the feeling that Bruce is reading their minds because "their minds" are active elements in constructing and interpreting the music. Springsteen's music always heightens their awareness of what is going on elsewhere in the general circumstances of their lives because the general circumstances of their lives are always framed and shaped by their listening. Here, fans constantly move between, and connect, seeming opposites: form and experience, the individual and the social, the musical and nonmusical. Springsteen fans' listening is not simply about making sense of music; it is about making sense of the world in which music is created and shared.

6 *Musically Shaping the Self*

In the beginning of my fieldwork, I started interviews with fans by asking them to tell me a little about themselves. While I was acquainted with several of the people with whom I spoke, most were strangers who had simply answered an advertisement, and I intended the question as a way both to break the ice and, more important, to allow me to learn about who they were. Such an approach was fairly effective; while some people seemed uncomfortable with the question, most answered it good-naturedly, talking about age and occupation and engaging in guarded small talk about their aspirations. I knew the question put them in an awkward position, but it was a start. I assumed getting to know them personally would take some time, that I would learn more as I met with them again and worked to gain their trust.

However, to my surprise, as soon as I turned conversations toward the topic of fandom, almost all the fans with whom I spoke suddenly began to share all kinds of things about their personal identities that they had withheld only minutes earlier: they told stories about themselves in different situations; they reminisced about their pasts, their families, and their friends; they offered cogent self-analyses about their likes and dislikes, habits, and attachments; and they took great pains to articulate how they thought they were similar to or different from others they knew. In fact, in discussing fandom I learned much about people that may have otherwise taken a lengthy friendship; while they may have just warmed up to me after the first question, it seemed more as if fandom suddenly and actively enabled them to share what they could not in ordinary discourse.

There is something about fandom that quickly leads people into the realm of the private, that focuses their discussion and thinking on their personal experiences and thoughts. As I showed in the last chapter, listening involves creating associations between the music and experience; in fandom, the two become so entangled that it is difficult to locate the music's meaning without talking about

fans' personal lives. I've already argued in previous chapters that concert going is
as much about *being seen* as about *seeing* a performance; it involves forming a view
of oneself as similar to other fans and as different from ordinary audience members. I might also talk about fans' public discussions and debates, which are always, in part, about displaying individual tastes and experiences. In particular,
polls about favorite albums and songs, which appear regularly in *Backstreets* and
computer discussion groups, are not so much about evaluating Springsteen's
work as about representing oneself. Not surprisingly, fans labor over them as if
they were résumés.

Indeed, by studying fandom, I have, in many ways, been studying people and
who they think they are. Fans talked to me frequently about using fandom to
signify and think about their personal identity. For some people, the music was
more like a mirror, enabling them to recognize themselves in either Springsteen
or the characters in his songs. As Andrew Laurence explained, "I think my fandom of Bruce's music basically boils down to one thing: it speaks to me. I identify with a lot of his characters' thoughts, ideas, and dreams. I put on a record and
pieces of me come out" (interview, September 28, 1993). For other fans, the music
was a photo album of sorts, organizing the passage of time and helping them create a linear narrative of their lives. As one fan told me:

> I often use the music to see how I've grown or changed. It's not really a conscious
> effort—just something I discovered a few years ago. On occasion I'll hear some-
> thing in a song that was always there yet I hadn't heard it or interpreted it that way.
> It lets me see things in myself that I hadn't seen before. Or I'll hear something and
> remember thinking or feeling a certain way about a song. And it helps me re-
> member what I was like at that particular time and to see how I've changed.

On the whole, for many fans, talking about fandom was tantamount to talking
about themselves. Andy Sirk, who grew up in Massachusetts, said:

> I'm the kind of person that is very—things that I like, I'm attached to. Like the
> sports teams, here [in New England]. Like Fenway Park. Like the Celtics. I mean, I
> feel the same way about them as I do about Bruce Springsteen. It's something that
> I'll never change; it will always be part of my makeup, a part of what I'm about a
> little bit. So, that's the way I feel about that. Now, that's just the way I am. People
> around me—I might not let on. I'm not an overt, you know—people may not
> know unless they know me really well. And if they know me really well, they'll
> understand why because that's the way I am. (interview, March 5, 1993)

What exactly is the connection between self and fandom? Scholars in anthropology have raised significant questions about the very idea of "the self" because
it relies on a concept of individuality that is absent in many of the world's cultures (e.g., Marsella, DeVos, and Hsu 1985; White and Kirkpatrick 1985; Carbaugh
1988; Kondo 1990; Battaglia 1995a; Biolsi 1995). And even if one recognizes that
fans use specifically Western ideas of personal identity, those ideas are numerous

and varied, changing across racial and ethnic groups and drawing on such disparate sources as religion, politics, work, and popular culture. Indeed, definitions of self in the West tend to hinge on very different sets of issues, depending on the situation and one's particular agenda. The self may be biologically determined, mystically given, or socially constructed; singular or multiple; static or in flux; or made up of various combinations of these characteristics (see Gergen 1993; Battaglia 1995b).

The most widespread view of the self in the West, commonly associated with psychoanalyst Sigmund Freud, is that of an inner psychic structure which develops when a young child, in a process called "identification," internalizes the experiences, values, or personality of another. Actually, Freud rarely used the term "self," but his notion of "identification" nevertheless emphasized the shaping of a fixed personality early in life (Gay 1989; Modell 1993). The influence of Freud on people's understanding of who they are has been immense; fans often talk about "unconscious" motivations or the consequences of unhappy childhoods, for instance. And American studies scholar Barry Shank (1994), using revisions of Freudian theory by French psychoanalyst Jacques Lacan, has analyzed fans' construction of personal identity by identification with local music scenes and bands.

However, I have found that Springsteen fans' discussions of personal identity fit better with the psychological theories of nineteenth-century philosopher William James. James rejected the Freudian notion of an inner psychic structure developed in childhood and instead saw the self as a matter of ongoing perception. In fact, he simply defined the self of each person as "all that he is tempted to call by the name of *me,*" explaining:

> In its widest sense . . . a man's self is the sum total of all that he can call his, not only his body and his psychic powers, but his clothes and his house, his wife and children, his ancestors and friends, his reputation and works, his lands and horses, and yacht and bank-account. All these things give him the same emotions. ([1890] 1981, p. 279)

In particular, James stated that this sense of "me" is created in two ways. First, he talked about shaping self-awareness—that is, seeing oneself as an object, from the outside looking in, as it were. As he said, even considering the self in the first place means "abandoning the outward-looking point of view and of our having become able to think of subjectivity . . . to think ourselves as thinkers" ([1890] 1981, p. 284). Second, James talked about a process of creating self-continuity, a recognition of the same "me" over time even as one's social roles or values change. He saw this continuity as a process of selecting and connecting present and past selves as a rancher might brand his cattle ([1890] 1981, p. 317).

When fans talk about recognizing themselves in the songs or using the music as a photo album that maps their life histories, they are engaged in an ongoing process of self-discovery, shaping a sense of "me" in James's terms. In fact, fans' musical activities seem to do exactly what James describes: various kinds of collecting and listening enable fans to think about themselves objectively and to consciously shape a sense of who they are over time. While fans are not simply constructing themselves through music—most fans insisted that their lives were more than fandom—musical practices seem to have an especially powerful function in the construction of personal identity.

Shaping Self-Awareness

For James, the process of shaping self-awareness has solely to do with the inner workings of cognition itself. But fans indicate that their fandom can act as an important tool for that thinking. As I have argued, fandom is about being touched by Springsteen and his music, making a personal connection between oneself and something outside oneself. However, fans' becoming-a-fan stories show that while fans fans feel a unity with another and, to some extent, lose themselves in Springsteen's performances, that feeling of unity is paradoxically accompanied by intense self-awareness, a detailed accounting of exactly how he changed their lives. This heightened self-awareness is not something that simply disappears after the first blush of connection; it is manifested in various ways throughout a person's fandom.

One source of fans' self-awareness is their collecting. Although not all Springsteen fans would define themselves as "collectors," a large majority at least do collect items related to Bruce Springsteen. *Backstreets* has published an "A to Z" list of Springsteen collectibles, pointing out that "with the exception of the Beatles and Elvis Presley, Springsteen is the most collected [music] artist" (Cross et al. 1989, pp. 133–143). And in my survey, fans indicated that their collections included CDs, books, news clippings, set lists, ticket stubs, fanzines, import singles, photographs, pins, posters, T-shirts, videos, dice, license plates, Asbury Park memorabilia, tour books, key chains, mugs, autographs, commissioned paintings, and even "grass from his front lawn."

One of the most important types of collecting is what Susan Pearce has called "the fetish," in which people remove objects from their original context of meaning and give them new uses and meanings (1992, pp. 68–88). Springsteen fan Anna Selden's collection of Springsteen photo mugs is a prime example:

> I worked for a photo store for a handful of years in high school and during college in the summers, and they made mugs. There's a guy out of Philly who took shots of a lot of Bruce concerts. And I sent to him for free samples under a couple of different names. [laughs] So I got a couple of them, and I got one of them put on a mug. Which is great. But someone got coffee stains in it; I was pissed. [laughter] I was like [in an exasperated voice], "What were you thinking of? You can't use it!" (interview, January 12, 1994)

While a collector may give fetishized objects any number of new uses and meanings, most collectors use them to "extend the self," as Pearce puts it, or "act as reminders and confirmers of our identities" (1992, p. 55). Fetishized objects have what literary critic Susan Stewart (1993, p. 158) calls a "metaphorical relationship to the world"; by being arranged and organized in a way valued only by the collector, the subsequent collection represents the collector.[1] In talking about their collecting of Springsteen CDs, posters, ticket stubs, and other items, several fans mentioned that their collections served to display and represent themselves.

For instance, J. D. Rummel talked about how his collection identified him at work:

> I don't have any posters, but my office has a section my coworkers refer to as "The Shrine." It has news clippings and photos, some of which are provided by friends who are aware of my interest in Bruce and are thoughtful enough to bring them to me. (interview, May 20, 1993)

LeAnne Olderman, a college student, explained that displaying a Springsteen poster in her apartment at college was important in letting people know who she was:

> OLDERMAN: Now, I have one poster up in my apartment. Like I said, I live in an efficiency and there's not a lot of walls. It's really cool: I've got the poster with the cover of *Born in the USA*, which is his butt, basically. [laughs] And I've got a T-shirt from the *Born in the USA* tour. It's like the back of the T-shirt. And I've got the T-shirt pinned up so that it's like if the poster continued and it was a real person, it would be like he was wearing the shirt. It's cool! So, it's like where the arms start, that's where the T-shirt sleeves end. And I have all these buttons on the T-shirt. So, that's pretty cool. For me, it's like a territory thing. When I move into an apartment, that's the first thing that goes up. Now, this place is mine.
>
> CAVICCHI: It marks the room.
>
> OLDERMAN: Right! This is mine. I live here. This is it. And that's a tradition; I always do that. (interview, May 17, 1993)

The collection as a representation of self was also manifested in fans' feelings of attachment to it; many talked about how disturbing or disrupting their tapes created a strong sense of personal violation. As Jackie Gillis explained about her fiancé's collection:

> He has a fireproof safe that Chris keeps everything in for protection. It's funny that when I get a CD, I keep it out and listen to it for a while and am pretty laid back about how I store it (e.g., what's wrong with it staying in the CD player for 3 weeks?) However, when Chris gets hold of them, he becomes paranoid that someone will break in ("they"—who, aliens?—know I have a new Bruce CD). Anyway,

he is very protective of our collection and I anticipate that we will have a locking file cabinet or safe at some point. (interview, June 10, 1993)

The collection as a representation of self was also manifested in fans' worry about not being able to display it properly; such a problem often made people feel out of sorts. As Al Khorasani lamented:

KHORASANI: I used to have my tickets all over the room, stuck everywhere; my Bruce poster; my fishnet on the ceiling; my black light—then I got married.

CAVICCHI: Can't do that anymore when you get married. You have to decorate.

KHORASANI: Right! I couldn't put my—I had a mirror "Boss" thing on top of the waterbed that I had bought. All of that . . . had to go. Now we have to wait to get a— she said, "When we get a house, you can have your own room." (interview, March 23, 1993)

In addition to collecting, fans' listening also significantly contributes to their self-awareness. One of the things I heard again and again as I talked to fans about their listening was that they recognized themselves, or parts of themselves, in Springsteen or his music. This awareness can even be seen linguistically: most fans to whom I spoke, when recognizing a parallel, did not say "I'm just like him," moving from their own subjective position to empathy for another, but rather they said "he's just like me," moving from empathy for another to an objective understanding of themselves.

Al Khorasani, for instance, said: "He's a father and has two kids. He talks about those things eloquently. And I, myself, have gotten married. I can relate to some of that." Mary Krause told me about recognizing herself in Springsteen's ambivalence about his Catholicism, particularly on his first album, *Greetings from Asbury Park* (1973):

KRAUSE: "Lost in the Flood," "It's Hard to Be a Saint in the City"—I like his Catholic stuff. Catholic symbols—because he obviously grew up Catholic, as I did. But he's very lapsed. And I always find it—even in the new albums, he continues to use Catholic symbols, or Christian symbols, too, as well.

CAVICCHI: Once a Catholic, always a Catholic.

KRAUSE: You just can't escape it. But he tries, like the best of us. (interview, April 30, 1993)

Other fans, like LeAnne Olderman, saw themselves specifically in the characters of Springsteen's songs:

It's just that the characters in the songs speak to me. Even down to—the one about the used car, the "brand new used car" ["Used Cars" from *Nebraska*]. That's so true! [laughs] That happened to me when I was growing up, when my parents bought a new used car. And he was a loner and maybe a rebel. And I was always perceived to be sort of a loner when I was growing up; that's changed now to an extent. So, I identified with that, too. I think that's like the overall theme, here. I really identified with it, the music spoke to me, and that's why it stuck. That's why I'm *still* a fan. That's why he doesn't come out with music for three years and I'm *still* anxiously awaiting. (interview, May 17, 1993)

Of course, the process of recognizing oneself in Springsteen or in his songs is not entirely unproblematic. First, some fans refer to the recognition of themselves in the music as "identification," a term which can mean many things, including both equation and association. As I have explained, identification in Freudian theory refers to an internalization of the traits of another—usually a parent—into one's psyche. And several media scholars have followed Freud's lead to show how people internalize the behavior of certain stars. Thus film scholar Jib Fowles explains:

> The spectator identifies with the player and, by an act of the imagination such as only humans are capable of, is temporarily able to take on the role and to act as the performer acts. The audience member "becomes" Jane Fonda or O. J. Simpson, and empathetically shares the star's experience. (1992, p. 157)

Judy and Fred Vermorel, in *Fandemonium* (1989, pp. 68–70), likewise featured people who believed they were "controlled by the spirit" of a performer or who sought to impersonate certain stars.

I do not doubt that people are internalizing the traits and behaviors of media figures; however, as psychologists Robert M. Galatzer-Levy and Bertram J. Cohler have argued (1993, pp. 31–32), such an idea seems to state what's happening too literally, relying on a cannibalistic metaphor that can lead to dangerous distortions and unnecessary alarm on the behalf of psychologists and media critics. And Freud's theory does not quite describe fans' accounts of their identifications with Springsteen or his characters. On the whole, fans seem to be speaking of a process closer to what James called "self-seeking," or the way in which people hold "ideal" or "potential" selves in their minds as a way to guide their actions and steady their sense of who they are and want to be. As he explained, "Our self-feeling in this world depends entirely on what we *back* ourselves to be and do. It is determined by the ratio of our actualities to our supposed potentialities" ([1890] 1981, p. 296).[2]

When fans talk about wanting to play guitar like Springsteen, they are not talking about a wholesale internalization of Springsteen, actually becoming him, but rather using him as an ideal to guide their sense of who they might be. Louis Lucullo explained:

> I guess part of being a fan is that the musician is either being someone you want to be or saying something you want to say, but you are not able to. So you follow this person and identify with the person. Growin' up, there aren't that many kids that

don't dream about being a rock star. As a Jersey kid growing up, he became someone I wanted to be. Now that I'm older, I appreciate the music more than the
myth. (interview, March 28, 1993)

Al Khorasani joked about his own identification, explaining that, while he uses
Springsteen's nickname, "The Boss," on the Internet at work, he could never actually *be* the Boss:

> I send notes to some people who don't know me because of work things, and they
> think that they got a note from John Akers, the chief executive officer of IBM,
> who's going to quit in a couple of weeks. It scares the hell out of them! [laughter]
> Because they get a thing on the reader: "the Boss." You know, it's like [imitating a
> frightened worker], "Oh, God! Something from Akers!" So, I told them, "No, he's
> *a* boss. There's only one *the* boss." When you say "the boss," there's only one. Ac-
> tually, we were talking with my friends, and we said we gotta get Bruce on the Net!
> And then we said then I would have to change my user-ID because he'll probably
> want to have his ID as "the boss." I've had that for a *long time*. Actually, I went to
> New Jersey—I lived in New Jersey for a while—and I wanted to get that for my
> plate numbers. And they said that it was taken. I wonder who has that plate?
> Hmm. (interview, March 23, 1993)

Indeed, for many Springsteen fans, the entire idea of Freudian identification is a
sign of some sort of pathology. John O'Brien explained:

> I don't think I'd really like to be him. I don't think everything about him—you
> know, as far as the thirty-million-dollar house—sometimes when I hear him talk
> it doesn't sound like me. I don't think I would agree with everything. But there's
> something about certain ideas that he's come up with that I've really linked into,
> and that, I think, is the good thing. And if you can do that with a writer or a movie
> director or whatever, I think that's good. As long as you keep it in perspective. It's
> the idea, it's not *him*. (interview, March 15, 1993)

This point was further outlined for me by J. D. Rummel. As I said in chapter
2, J. D. once explained his identification with Springsteen by saying, "Part of me
wanted to be that guy up there, part of me wanted to be the star. There is a certain aspect of vicarious living involved here. He is doing something that I would
like to do." But when I asked him whether "vicarious living" meant that he was
replacing his own identity with Bruce's, he responded:

> Although I certainly understand the negative perception that some people have of
> fandom (I have talked to glassy-eyed adults who have seen *Star Wars* over a hundred
> times, or who have wept furiously over the suggestion that Elvis would ever use
> drugs) my own enjoyment of Bruce's music stops far short of fanaticism as I un-
> derstand it. At any rate, I don't believe I obsess about him. My life is fairly well-
> rounded and my interests extend beyond my appreciation of Bruce Springsteen.
> One link that I feel with Bruce is my sense of self as an artist. I write short stories,
> and though I have had the usual starting-out, low-rent exposure through local

papers, journals, etc., any commercial success I have experienced has been non-existent. My own "vicarious thrill" is seeing someone who took his passion and made it work. Bruce's dedication to his art has strongly influenced my own outlook on my writing.

Occasionally I will play the air guitar while listening to a record, though.

My friends accept my affection for Bruce's work and my interest in his life. They know I have other interests and my world in no way revolves around the life of a popular musician I have never met. My coworkers know that he is my "hero" in many respects, and they accept "The Shrine" as part of the "Far Side" cartoons, *Star Trek* trinkets, and pithy quotations that decorate my work space. All are means by which I express myself, and a healthy self I think it is.

As far as others are concerned, I would first say that I am sure there are many in the world with a similar stance to my own. These others are equally healthy, though perhaps coming from a separate approach. Springsteen the artist has touched them where they live and they are better for this.

There are of course some who do have what I would deem to be a disproportionate interest in Bruce (or Madonna, or whoever) over their own development as human beings. I think such individuals may use celebrities as an escape from whatever uncomfortable circumstances they find themselves in. If they do not have a life they are satisfied with, they may find vicarious comfort in the perceived success of others. This may be why we see young people with still nascent personalities making up large percentages of fandom. As they grow older, mature in their interests, and become more centered, their fan involvement decreases. (interview, May 28, 1993)

Here, J. D. recognizes those who use a media star to singularly form their personal identity along Freudian lines and those, like him, who are more concerned with potentially doing what Springsteen does than with actually becoming a replica of him.

A second issue involved in fans' recognition of themselves in the music is whether everyone is equally able to see themselves in Springsteen or the characters in songs. In general, fans see the process of identification as universal; they believe that all fans can *potentially* recognize themselves in the music. Thirty-four-year-old retail manager Amy Thom, for instance, while admitting that she couldn't relate to everything about Springsteen, did identify more abstractly with the growth represented in Springsteen's songs:

He's definitely been in a process, as we all are in our lives, of growth. It's like every time a new album comes out it just rings so true to me. You know what I mean? He's older than I am, he's from a different socioeconomic background than I am, and he's certainly in a different one now, in many ways, but nonetheless there's this connection. The last couple of albums, although there was a lot of stuff that came from having a family and finding true—you know, what I would describe as truly finding love finally for himself—there were certain aspects of that that maybe I couldn't relate to personally, but there was so much, so many overtones of growth, other types of growth mentioned in the songs. That's just always the case. (interview, April 1, 1993)

John O'Brien wrestled with the fact that he wasn't from the working-class neighborhoods of New Jersey:

I didn't grow up in like Freehold, New Jersey. But I wonder—that's another issue. Do people who grow up in Freehold listen to Bruce? 'Cause it's kind of about what they're going through. Maybe not, maybe it's a luxury of kind of like middle-class people, vicariously. I don't know. I do know that the reason it works is that he's dealing with something that—there's some kind of anger, some kind of emotion that people have that he's connecting to—it's kind of universal. . . . Actually, I have a quote that I wrote down. [tape ends while he searches for the quote in his bookbag] I was reading this stuff on James Baldwin for a paper I'm doing. And I just found this quote; it was from *Sonny's Blues*. [reads from piece of paper] He says, "For while the tale of how we suffer and how we are delighted and how we may triumph is never new, it must always be heard. There isn't any other tale to tell. It is the only light we've got in this darkness. And this tale, according to that faith, that body, those strong hands on those strings, has another aspect in every country and a new depth in every generation." (interview, March 15, 1993)

However, many fans see the identification process as based less on one's flexibility and imaginative ability to empathize emotionally and more on a structural correspondence between one's gender, nationality, race, and class and that of Springsteen or his characters. In fact, some fans believe that such categories of social experience enable them to identify more easily with Springsteen or the music than others.

For instance, some fans and nonfans claim that Springsteen's music appeals mostly to men. Amy Thom explained to me, "It seems to me Bruce attracts similar—if not larger—numbers of male fans as female fans. Unscientifically, this appears unusual to me as, typically, females are more "fanatic" about male rock stars than males are" (personal correspondence, November 26, 1995). Many Springsteen songs are told from the point of view of a male protagonist and detail the traditionally "masculine" concerns of cars and girls. As one woman, a feminist historian, once told me when I explained this project to her, "Springsteen is the last great, white, male hero."

Whether men actually outnumber women among Springsteen fans I cannot say conclusively. During my fieldwork, however, I did encounter almost twice as many men as women. At first, while reaching fans through the Internet, I thought the skewed proportion may have been due to American gender divisions around the use of technology, but my later attempts to reach fans through *Backstreets* produced similar results. This imbalance has also come up in other contexts, such as the annual subscriber poll on *Luckytown Digest* (e.g., Stockinger 1996). At any rate, the idea that Springsteen appeals mostly to men has led to important debates about identification; namely, female fans have reported that men often see them as second-class fans because of an inability to really relate to the music and have protested such stereotypes.

Mary Krause explained: "See, guys don't like to know you're a Bruce fan. Because they know that, primarily, the first thing on the list you like Bruce for is buns. Can I say that on tape? [laughs] That's number one, you see. But it's kind of tied in with the music and the concerts and the whole thing" (interview, April 30, 1993). After hearing rock'n'roll singer Melissa Etheridge talk about identifying with Bruce, one woman named Jen explained on *Luckytown Digest* that she cried:

> So why did realizing Melissa also identified with Bruce cause such an emotional storm? Well, several times on this digest lately I've read "Maybe someday women will connect with Bruce's music the way that we men always have. . . ." I read a similar assertion in the last issue of *Backstreets* and came damn close to ripping it up. Why does the assumption that women don't connect with Bruce's music bug me? Maybe because it implies women don't really think about the music, or are skipping the lyrics or are just somehow deficient? I have *always* connected emotionally with Bruce's music. My dream wouldn't be to date Bruce; it would be to do what he does! (Kilmer 1995)

Another woman concurred:

> I just read the message on being a woman and identifying with Bruce. I've always identified with him—that was what really got me hooked on him, much more so than the fact that I had a major crush on him as a young teenager. The crush was a whim, but being moved by his message and his music was the root of my infatuation. As Jen says, I'm not a man, but I wanted to be Bruce, too. I wanted to experience what he did. In many ways, he provided a window to a world of excitement, energy, and life that I did not have access to as a kid. This was why, when I played *Greatest Hits* I had a really intense "Proustian" experience. I wound up sobbing too—some part of me exists within the framework of his music. I never could explain it to my friends, who were more into punk at the time. (Detweiler 1995)

However, beliefs about differences in identification along gender lines persist. When Springsteen released a new song called "Secret Garden" on his 1995 *Greatest Hits* CD, about a woman with a hidden, inaccessible part of herself, many male fans on *Luckytown Digest* identified with the song from the perspective of a man. As one person wrote, "I agree with the interpretation that the woman being spoken about as having a wall to prevent becoming intimate. I've been in the singer's shoes; it's not fun, trust me" (McLean 1995a). Another, while deferring to the possibility that women might see themselves in the song, nevertheless talked about a specifically male view:

> To me, "Secret Garden" is about failed relationships. You (as a man, invert this if you're a woman; I'm sure it's about the same) go up to a woman, and that's OK: yeah, she'll go out with you. You go to see her at her house, that's OK, too. She'll

let you kiss her too . . . and if the relationship goes on long enough, you can have sex too. But that doesn't mean you own her, or that she'll open up completely. (Powell 1995)

In contrast, many women identified with the woman being sung about: One person wrote:

I love this song. Right now, it's my favorite of the new ones. Mostly because I can really relate to this woman, since there's a part of me that no one really ever sees, not even my husband. And that fact has been troubling me lately. Shouldn't I be totally honest and open with him? Or is it alright for me to keep my Secret Garden? I don't know, but I think it's wonderful that an artist whose lyrics have always spoken to me is talking about an issue that is so personal to me right now. (Andrulis 1995)

Another even claimed it as a "woman's song":

Quite frankly I think you have to be a woman to fully understand it—or at least in close touch with one. The fact that Bruce writes a song that comes that close to our souls is . . . well, it's downright scary and it strikes hard. Play this one right next to Patti [Scialfa]'s "Spanish Dancer" and it says a lot about . . . women and men. . . . I'm just glad "Murder Incorporated" kicks in right after this one on the *Greatest Hits*. While that sweet sweet sax is still fading and tears are streaming, in the next second I'm dancing around the house in my underwear! Leave it to Bruce. We're crying and laughing at the same time. (Duerr 1995)

Even those who didn't find the song's appeal to be absolutely limited to either men or women still pointed out the differences in the ways in which men and women might understand the music. As one woman wrote:

It's not surprising that the lyrics are striking many of us differently; we are a diverse group after all. I've never found any of Bruce's lyrics distasteful in any way. His treatment of women over the years have always seemed a combination of fun and tenderness. A nice mixture. Yeah, he was *always* trying to get those girls in those backseats, he was *always* promising to love someone forever, but who ever got the impression this was a guy who would hold himself responsible for his actions. . . . So all you guys out there who have been wondering where all the women on the Net are, well, we're here, smiling softly as you talk about your cars and stuff, knowing that Bruce always liked *us* best. . . . :-) (Wilkie 1995)

Discussions about "Secret Garden" and women's identification with the music sparked similar discussions about national identity on *Luckytown Digest*. For instance, one fan wondered how international fans understood the music:

While I know that "music is universal," etc., etc., to me, so much of Bruce's work is, um, what's the word . . . "American"? I mean, he deals with a lot of local issues, things going on in our society and culture, our economic system, our participation in world conflicts, etc. And just a lot of things that I don't think you could "get" unless you know exactly what he's talking about. (Cecchini 1995a)

A fan from London responded by talking about the universality of the music and how it related to his own life:

> The issues he writes about concern us all; as I've posted before, "The River"'s line, ". . . though I know the river is dry . . ." spoke to me as a reflection of the status of my relationship at that time. My girlfriend of six years left me for another guy two weeks after we saw him sing that. Don't tell me marital/relationship problems are an American monopoly (although, come to think of it :)). As to American involvement in world conflicts—what, don't those conflicts affect the rest of us, too? We also know what goes on, you know; we've got TV and radio over here as well. Bruce sings "Better Days"—we, too, can have good times in our life. . . . I don't think there is a single Bruce Springsteen song that I cannot relate to in some way. (Carl 1995)

However, the American persisted, acknowledging that international fans could *understand* the music but maintaining that they could not have the same quality of identification with it: "I guess what I'm getting at is: I can't imagine what goes through someone else's head (a non-American) when they hear something like, say, 'Darlington County.' I mean, I've driven thru Darlington County and spent some time in the deep South. I *know* what it's like there" (Cecchini 1995b)

This statement touched off numerous postings from fans around the world about whether one needs to have actually experienced the locations in the songs to identify with the characters or situations. A fan from Hungary wrote that it was a matter of imagination:

> There are some songs (a relatively large part of Bruce's work) by Bruce that are universal. Some of them are felt to be universal without any references to certain U.S. places or names. Some of them may really have U.S. references, but only to an extent, and it could be any place in the world with the same cultural background (if it's Saint Mary's gate in "Independence Day" or a small town in my country—it delivers the emotions behind). I guess a lot of references to places in the U.S. are not even clear to all of you Americans. Like, off the top of your head, where is St. Mary's gate? Ever been there? You know what it's like? And if all your answers are "not," does this create an obstacle for you to get the song? Nor does it to me here on the other side of the Ocean.

Yet he did admit, "Yes, there are some songs that are hard if not impossible to relate to. Take 'Born in the USA.' For me, this song only works in the third person" (Palasti 1995b).

Another fan from South Africa wrote that identification for him involved translation:

> The words in "My Hometown" symbolize a lot of things that have been going on around here. We had our own Vietnam in Angola a few years ago. Starkweather homicide = Barend Strijdom shooting 15 black people in Pretoria a few years back.

I could go on in this way for ever. I can even relate to a lot of concert stories that could arguably only have relevance to life in the USA. (Moolman 1995)

Yet another American pointed out that identification requires only being able to relate *emotionally* to the music:

What draws us all to Bruce's music is the feeling, the emotional power of the lyrics, not the specific images in the song. If we go by being able to relate to the specific images, how many fans, American or not, have been to Route 88, Darlington County, Kingsley Ave., or Highway 9 [places mentioned in Springsteen's songs]? While many people have, most people have seen similar roads or been through similar areas, and can visualize the image in the song based on what they see around them. And while this was probably discussed a while ago, how many of us can identify with the feelings of the singer in "Streets of Philly?" [a Springsteen song about an AIDS victim]. Hundreds, probably, many without HIV/AIDS. If you go by the rationale behind the "how can non-U.S. residents understand Bruce's music," then only persons living with HIV/AIDS could identify with "Streets of Philadelphia." (McLean 1995b)

One of the most interesting challenges to ideas about the universal appeal of the music was a discussion on *Luckytown Digest* about race. Around the time that people were discussing women and national identity, someone wondered about the lack of African Americans in Springsteen's audience and what that said about people's ability to identify with the music:

At both of the concerts that I attended and even the ones I've watched on video, Bruce's audience has predominantly been white. Even Clarence made a reference to that fact when he was talking about performing during the Amnesty [International] tour [1988] and how great it was to see so many black faces in the audience at some of the concerts in Europe. So even though I've always gotten the impression that evidently Bruce's music did not appeal to blacks, I've also seen several black TV journalists throughout the years who seemed to be strong followers of Bruce's music, i.e. Al Roker, Mark McEwen, J. J. Jackson, and others. I guess my question is . . . does Bruce have a black audience and if the answer is no—why not? (Beth 1995)

Springsteen biographer and rock critic Dave Marsh responded by pointing out the divergence of black and white rock in the late sixties and early seventies, when "the black audience focused heavily on elements that are the least interesting in Bruce Springsteen's music: namely, the bottom and the beat." He later added:

So why do people like [Leonard] Pitts, Jr., McEwen, Roker, Jackson, etc. find themselves interested in Bruce?[3] Well, for one thing, because no culture is monolithic— just like I have been the only white face at many black shows in my life, and stuck out because of it. Second, though, I think there is a class element at work here; black middle class kids of Bruce's generation relate to the specifics of what he has to say (as Leonard does in what sounds like one of his really fine personal essays—

Pitts is one of the most under-rated music writers) to a greater extent than some of their less-advantaged brethren, and perhaps to the form as well. (Marsh 1995)

While the discussion about race veered into a long and contentious debate about whether Springsteen fans have an antipathy to "black music," discussion about the lack of a black Springsteen audience continued. For instance, one fan found Marsh's answer not entirely adequate and wondered why Springsteen's audience wouldn't mirror the composition of his band:

> It seems that Bruce's music can cross racial lines among performers, but not in his audience. Listen to this quote from Bruce in 1978: "Clarence and I are like that (crosses his fingers tightly). His music and my music are ideally suited. We breathe the same thing." (*Bruce Springsteen, In His Own Words*) If black musicians can appreciate, perform, and in fact "breathe the same thing," where are the blacks in the audience? (Steve Shaw 1995)

Some fans agreed with Marsh's analysis of race and class:

> This is something that I've wondered about for years; at the many shows I've had the pleasure of seeing over the years, I've seen a total of maybe 20 African-Americans. . . . But Bruce is not really unique in this aspect; I find pretty much the same situation at most rock'n'roll and blues concerts I've been to. I've always found it curious that, although so much of our music owes to black culture and music, black youth today seem to prefer rap and dance almost to the exclusion of these other genres they helped to create (i.e. rock, blues). An all-black rock group today is almost more of a rarity than an all-female band (one thing that set Living Colour apart from so many other bands was that they were an all-black *rock* group in an age when black kids didn't listen to or play rock anymore). I think for the most part that Dave's on the money in terms of why Bruce's audience is so monochromatic, and how class probably plays a role in explaining why some African Americans do appreciate Bruce's music. (Papleonardos 1995)

Another fan, though, wanted to collapse discussions of race into the larger issue of class, seeing identification, on the whole, as a kind of liberal empathy:

> Over the last several years I've read numerous published comments on the nature of Bruce's audience being incongruous with the music he sings about. We tend to be mostly upper middle class and above. We are people who aspired to "pulling out to win" [a line from 1975's "Thunder Road"]. A friend once questioned how I had ever suffered in order to understand Bruce's music? The people Bruce wrote about early on were my family, the people in my town, but they weren't me. What Bruce did for me was to articulate my aspirations as I looked around, trying to understand how they lived their lives, and where they may be headed. I do not believe the people who truly understand and enjoy Bruce's talents live those lives. Quite frankly, if I was "laid off because of the economy" [from "My Hometown 1984], I don't want to sing about it. I've also seen comments on the absence of a black audience, particularly during the *BitUSA* tour. I've always felt debates on racism

should really focus on the class issue. I think you could look across the audiences of our favorite singer/songwriters (BS, Petty, Seger, Mellencamp) and see a remarkable economic and social homogeneity to the audience. . . . I would like someone to explain to me why the 200 million plus American who live the life Bruce sings about haven't bought the albums. (Maynard 1995)

Fans do not share any sort of consensus about the place and scope of gender, nationality, race, and class in one's identifications while listening. Many fans still cling to the idea that potentially everyone can identify with the music; indeed, they point to the persistent diversity of fans in terms of gender, age, and nationality to support such a claim. Yet, for some fans, the lack of a black audience is an undeniable sign that not *everyone* can identify with the music. As one person commented: "Does it strike anyone else as ironic that the conversations about how Bruce's music *doesn't* reach the African-American community are occurring at the same time as many on *Luckytown Digest* are proclaiming the *universality* of his music?" (McCann 1995).

In the end, the process of identification discussed by fans reflects significant issues about the self. Social categories of gender, nationality, race, and class represent one of the primary modes of objectifying oneself. When I, for example, think of myself as a man, or an American, or white, or middle class, I am moving out of my subjective experience and thinking about how I am constituted as an object in social life; I see myself in terms of other people. However, not everyone agrees how such categories form one's sense of self. Some fans believe that categories like, say, race or gender, are primary in their senses of self, particularly in a society which is predicated on such divisions. Others believe that such categories are only *parts* of their senses of self, which may or may not be highlighted in particular situations. In many ways, such discussion among fans represents a microcosm of current cultural debates in the West, particularly in the United States, about whether identity is shaped solely by social and cultural factors or whether identity also involves other shared, universal, or human qualities.

What's important in the context of this chapter, however, is that fans' listening should even lead to debates about identification and identity. Whether fans agree that everyone or only a limited number of people can recognize themselves in Springsteen's music, they nevertheless agree that such a process potentially exists. Fans see their participation in the music as an act that ideally enables them to shape their sense of "me," to work through the complexities of who they are.

Shaping Self-Continuity

While fans may develop self-awareness through fan activities like collecting or listening, no one remains exactly the same year after year. For instance, many of the fans I interviewed over the course of my research changed where they lived, with whom they lived, and how they lived; they also changed more mundane aspects of their lives like their clothing and hairstyles. Yet, despite such changes, fans did not take on entirely new identities. For the most part, they still thought of themselves as the same persons. William James thought that this feeling of continuity—being able to think, "I am the same self that I was yesterday"—represents a second important way of constituting the self. And again, while James saw it as a process of consciousness itself, fans indicated that fandom plays an important role. In particular, fandom shapes and maintains a continuous self by acting as a map or overlay with which to mark the passage of time and organize one's perception of oneself in it. This process is especially evident in both the activities of collecting and listening.

I have already mentioned that one prominent type of collecting among fans is based on the fetish. Another type, however, is based on what Susan Pearce would call "the souvenir" (1992, pp. 68–88). In this type of collecting, objects are removed from their original contexts but given meanings that remain connected to those contexts; in fact, the objects represent those contexts in ways particular to the collector. In Susan Stewart's terms, while collections based on the fetish have a metaphorical relationship to the world, collections based on the souvenir have a metonymical relationship to the world; they "stand for" events in the collector's past (Stewart 1993, p. 151). Pearce has explained that souvenirs' relationship to the past is important for shaping an idea of self:

> [Souvenirs] are an important part of our attempt to make sense of our personal histories, happy or unhappy, to create an essential personal and social self centred in its own unique life story, and to impose this vision on an alien world. They relate to the construction of a romantically integrated personal self, in which the objects are subordinated into a secondary role.[4] (1992, p. 72)

Fans frequently told me about collecting Springsteen items in order to remember their experiences and map themselves through time. For instance, many fans to whom I spoke talked about keeping files or notebooks filled with newspaper and magazine clippings having to do with Springsteen and regularly looking through them. For most fans, the clippings represented their attempt to somehow "capture" Springsteen or surround themselves with information about him, but such collecting also always had a personal, temporal element. As Russ Curley explained:

> I guess I do go back. I don't want to disrupt a lot of it, because it's kind of fragile. The newspaper's going yellow. If nothing else, I guess it serves to show a progression. I can look back and read old stuff and say, "I remember when I liked him here." I can gauge how far I've come. But I like the pictures, too. I think he's a cool guy, I think he's a cool-looking guy, the way he dresses and stuff like that. (interview, April 20, 1993)

Other fans explained to me that such articles helped to organize their sense of the past. Anna Selden, who explained that she has "numerous, numerous magazines; anytime he was on the cover, I went and picked it up," specifically talked about reflecting on clippings as one might look at old photographs: "At one point, I took a whole bunch of stuff I had and put it in a photo album. That was kind of neat" (interview, January 12, 1994). I, too, collect articles about Springsteen; I file them by year and, every once in a while, look through them with waves of nostalgia, not only remembering specific events or the music but also reminiscing about what I was doing in the mideighties or the early nineties and thinking about how Springsteen has been there the whole time. The process of collecting and looking at such things is, for me, about creating some sort of temporal consistency; I can survey myself.

In addition to collecting newspaper clippings, others talked about collecting tapes and specific souvenirs of concerts. Much concert tape collecting is really what Pearce calls "systematic collecting"—that is, the classification and sorting of items according to a particular ideology (1992, pp. 68–88). For instance, several fans told me about either collecting every single concert Springsteen ever played, creating a complete series, or collecting "highly regarded concerts from various tours in order to put together a well-rounded representation of Bruce's concerts over the years." However, many of the fans to whom I spoke linked concert tapes to their own experiences and used the tapes to remember those experiences. As one tape collector explained:

> I became a fan on 10-25-80. That was when a friend originally from the East Coast said he had an extra ticket to the show in Portland. I said sure, I kinda like that "Born to Run" song, and I'm not doing anything tonight. We went up to the show and Springsteen *blew me away!* I started seeking out live tapes immediately after.

Another explained that concert tapes really interest him only if he had attended the concerts: "The boot that's known as *This Gun's for Hire*—well, that was one of the shows at the Spectrum that I attended. So, that was kind of, 'Oh, I remember this!' . . . So, that's kind of a nice experience."

Other fans explained that they collected other kinds of concert souvenirs. Mary Krause, for instance, shared with me a huge "Bruce bag" of items, ranging from buttons to videos, which served to remind her of her fan experiences. During one of our meetings, she mentioned that she had added a few new items recently after attending a concert in Syracuse:

> KRAUSE: I must say someone was thinking of me, because it turns out that Betsy, who was one of my apartment mates—her father drove limo for Bruce and the guys when they were at the Carrier Dome for the *Human Touch* tour [in 1992]. So, he got a towel that Bruce used at the concert. It's very interesting to own, I must say. I had never ever dreamed of owning a sweaty towel from a Bruce concert. And I got the lit-

tle patch that went on the jackets from the limo driver. And drank the Evian water, as well. There was an extra bottle of Evian that they had left behind. But it did travel with them for quite a while, while they were in Syracuse.

CAVICCHI: So where's the towel, now?

KRAUSE: It's at home. In the Bruce bag.

CAVICCHI: Do you ever take out the Bruce stuff, at all?

KRAUSE: Once in a while. The towel, most recently. When I got it I wanted to preserve it, so I put it in a plastic bag. Now, you take it out once in a while.

CAVICCHI: Does it still have that sweaty smell?

KRAUSE: No, it doesn't smell. My mother asked if I was going to wash it. I said absolutely not! "That would take the value out of it, Mother." (interview, April 30, 1993)

Jackie Gillis likewise told me about giving her fiancé a souvenir of a recent concert they had attended together:

For my fiancé's birthday, I had a color picture of Bruce from the new *Backstreets* book framed with our Indy concert ticket stubs and a single red rose placed on top. . . . In Indy, I brought Bruce a dozen red roses and *no one* else did, so they caught his attention when I threw them during "Leap of Faith" [quoting a line from the song] ("I . . . slipped into a bed of roses"). We were in the second row, so when he wandered over and picked them up, he put them in his mouth and did his old "Rosalita" jump and looked right at me—it made my night. He eventually threw them out to someone else but one fell on the stage and a roadie let me get it during the break. (interview, June 4, 1993)

While fans tend to embody and signify their pasts in lasting objects through collecting, the activity of listening actually heightens their sense of time. Few scholars have addressed the importance of listening to popular music in marking time in people's lives, though such a function is commonly acknowledged in well-known phrases like "they're playing our song." On the whole, there seems to be something about the process of producing commercial music, with its continuing emphasis on new releases and the updating of hit charts, which serves to publicly document the passage of time; people's emotional attachments to present and past songs allow them to situate themselves personally in that public document. Springsteen fans, in particular, use both their abstract knowledge of the progress of Springsteen's music over time and their concrete memories of listening to the music to think about and cohere who they are and who they have been. As John O'Brien explained:

I guess part of it is that people have a lot of music that brings you back to where you were when you first heard it and it's kind of part of your history. That's just a good reliable thing to have. And just 'cause it still kind of affects me; I still get really excited by it. But it's strange because it seems like a certain song can really excite you and be emotional to you, and then it won't. It's kind of interesting. And then maybe you listen to it a year or a few months later and it does it again! It's just strange. (interview, March 15, 1993)

Such a linkage between listening and the past is not always intentional; when Springsteen's *Greatest Hits* CD was released in 1995, several fans reported suddenly realizing such a link and experiencing waves of nostalgia. One wrote in *Luckytown Digest*:

> Hearing familiar songs in a new, but roughly chronological, order gave me a sense of my adult life passing before my eyes, only in fast forward, the classic near-death experience. ("No! Wait! It can't be 1982 already. . . .") It was a series of shocks, and the long intros being truncated just added to the sensation of life rushing by before it can be fully savored. This is the soundtrack of my personal movie, or at least, the short version. (Suzy Shaw 1995)

At any rate, for many fans this linkage between the music and the past helps them to mark or divide their lives into different periods. For example, becoming a fan is, for most fans, a milestone in their lives in which "everything changed"; they tend think about themselves in terms of being a fan and not being a fan. Mary Krause explained that she associated Springsteen with college in her mind, so that high school became a completely different period of her youth:

> I don't know why when I was in high school I didn't pick up on Bruce. That's always been curious to me. Because I didn't like "Hungry Heart." But I guess I never really was a groupie in high school for anybody. Never did the concert scene or really bought a lot of albums or anything. Didn't do my own music; it was more of a radio thing for me when I was in high school. I kind of listened to the radio; whatever was top pop was—there was something I liked there. (interview, April 30, 1993)

Many other fans described their first Springsteen concerts in the same way. As Alan Levine joked: "My first concert I will not forget. It's sort of like the first time I . . . drank a beer! [laughter] We're on tape." Alan later explained more seriously that his first concert defined a period of his life that was wrapped up with high school: "It was a phenomenal time. At this point, I was in high school. And I still—one of the guys who I used to go with, my high school buddy, we're still very close friends. Every now and then, we'll reminisce about that summer" (interview, April 2, 1993).

Beyond these initial Springsteen experiences, almost all fans told me about using different Springsteen albums or tours to mark discrete segments in their lives. Paul Fischer, for instance, in describing one of Springsteen's albums, said:

> *Darkness on the Edge of Town* is one that I will listen to all the way through. I still like that a lot. I like its moodiness, and I like the songs. "Badlands," "Prove It All Night," that sort of stuff. It speaks to me of a time in my life when I was starting to get a greater sense of control or mastery over certain things. That's when I was really

getting into the concert business and thinking that that was something that I wanted to do and all of that. (interview, May 25, 1993)

In fact, many fans to whom I spoke, including Paul, were able to go through *all* of Springsteen's albums and, as if they were looking at a photo album, discuss where they were and what they were doing at the time such albums came out. Others just as readily listed all of the Springsteen concerts they had been to over the years and talked about the circumstances of their lives around each one.

Related to this use of the music to mark periods of their lives, fans reported that their listening helped them to map out specifically how they had changed or not changed. Several fans, for example, recognized that the waning of their fandom indicated that they had changed over the years. However, such fans talked about continuing to use the music for the specific purpose of capturing and maintaining their sense of who they used to be; it served to, as Mary Krause put it, "keep the history alive." One fan explained in a letter to me:

> I think of Bruce very much like an old school friend. We don't have much in common anymore and we don't talk quite as often, but from time to time I still hear from him and whenever he comes to town, we try to get together. Many of the other friends that I still keep in touch with from those days are people I met because of our love for Bruce!

Andy Sirk likewise told me that he listened to Springsteen primarily to remember or capture something about his teenage years: "Nowadays I listen when I get in a little bit of a nostalgic mood or whatever. It just feels good and puts you in a good mood to throw on some of the old songs, stuff like that" (interview, March 5, 1993).

Other fans, feeling themselves changing, used their fandom to think through that process. Alan Levine, who had thought much about his fandom over time, recognized significant differences between his being a fan in the past and his being a fan today:

> There is a difference. One, I am older. Not that same adolescent enthusiasm. And the music's different. Although, I tell you, I went to one of the Meadowlands shows—when he kicked off the *Human Touch* tour—and I still had to go an hour early and have beer in the parking lot. [laughter] At the time, I went with my wife; she was pregnant at the time. So things are different, you know what I'm saying? (interview, April 2, 1993)

Yet, at the same time, he recognized that some things never change, like his father's antipathy to his fandom: "Even now, when I went to the show recently, my father was like, 'You're thirty. You're still going to rock concerts?' 'But Dad, it's Bruce.' You know?" Alan Stein said that his dislike of Springsteen's recent music was a sign of age:

I think it just lost that intimacy there, or something. I just don't feel it. It's good rock'n'roll, but it's not special to me like the early stuff is. And maybe that's also because I started listening to that stuff when I was very young, and it just reminds me of that era. I'm hitting that thirty-year midlife crisis thing, I don't know [laughs]. (interview, May 24, 1993)

Several fans even mentioned about how their entire Springsteen fandom itself was a sign to them that they were getting older. Alan Levine, for instance, summed up his reflections by mentioning an encounter with a boy during a trip:

It's funny. I took an airplane ride—God, probably a couple years ago—and I was sitting next to this little boy. And he had this Discman or Walkman on, and I asked, "What kind of music do you have?" He said, "Well, I got Duran Duran" and this and that. He was like, "What kind of music do you listen to?" He must have been eleven or something. I was like, "The Rolling Stones." He's like, "I think I've heard of them." I was like, "Have you ever heard of the Who?" "Yeah!" "Led Zeppelin?" So much was lost on him. He actually heard of Springsteen. He was like, "Yeah, *Born in the USA!*" I'm like, "Have you heard any other albums that he did?" He was like, "No." "Have you heard of *Born to Run?*" He was like, "No." I was totally feeling my age. I felt like jumping out of the airplane. (interview, April 2, 1993)

Al Khorasani explained:

KHORASANI: Actually, the newer generation, the younger—I hate to say this, I feel so old!

CAVICCHI: Isn't that awful?

KHORASANI: Yeah, when you get to the point—you listen to someone and talk to high school kids and they haven't heard of him? That's when you say, "Aw, I gotta go to Florida, now." Gotta go to Florida and wear one of these pants that comes up to— like that commercial, you know—wear pants that come up to your chest and complain about government.

CAVICCHI: [laughing] That Burger King commercial.

KHORASANI: That's right. So . . . the newer, younger crowd, the high school crowd, listens to the kind of music that we used to listen to when we were in high school. I don't like that. I think kids should listen to music that the older generation absolutely despises! (interview, March 25, 1993)

Many scholars have pointed out the importance of creating a narrative of one's life and of seeing it as a continuous stream. As psychoanalyst Robert Jay Lifton has said, "The symbolizing self centers on its own narrative, on a life story that is itself created and constantly re-created" (1993, p. 30). This process is, of course, central to psychoanalysis, in which one's life is constructed and then reconstructed in the form of a story (Spence 1982; Sarbin 1986; Shafer 1992), and is assumed by James in his use of first-person autobiographical accounts in his discussions of the self (James [1890] 1981, pp. 352–378; [1902] 1925). Fans' collecting and listening help to shape such coherent narratives. Such activities allow fans to "brand" and gather together their previous selves and to evaluate, interpret, and organize their personal histories.

*T*he Modern Self

The majority of works on the self say little about participation in popular culture. Indeed, most psychological theories about the self narrowly focus on face-to-face social relations among family members or friends as the only factors that shape personal identity. Reading books, listening to music, going to movies or plays, and watching television shows—acts that can be deeply moving for many people and can occupy an important place in their lives—do not exist or, at least, have little or no role in processes of self-formation.

The few psychologists who have focused on popular culture in self-formation have focused almost exclusively on the power of twentieth-century electronic mass media. For such scholars, mass media like television, radio, and computers have created a new, historic environment which has completely transformed the self into something it has never been previously. Robert Jay Lifton, for instance, drawing on the media theorist Marshall McLuhan, has recognized the enormous importance of the media in creating what he calls the "protean self," an ever-changing, many-sided individual. In particular, he argues:

> The phenomenon of worldwide media saturation is both new and crucial to the late-twentieth-century self. While that self invokes defenses of withdrawal and numbing, it remains continuously bombarded by ideas and images and is in some measure recast by them, made more fluid in response to the surrounding fluidity. (1993, p. 21)

Kenneth Gergen (1993), in arguing that "media figures . . . enter significantly into people's personal lives," has outlined how the media "saturate" people with myriad new social relationships, eventually creating a "populated self" which has no coherence but rather is multiple and constantly changing from situation to situation. Likewise, psychologist and philosopher Raymond Barglow (1993) has echoed such an argument by claiming that new technologies and their development of a modern, rationalistic bureaucracy have created the "selfless individual," who functions like information-processing devices in a larger network.

Certainly, what we mean by the "self" has become more flexible and complex in recent years because of new kinds of social relationships engendered by electronic communication, but it seems to me that these theories overstate the importance of the mass media in the twentieth century and its power over people's lives. For one thing, Springsteen fans indicate that participation in popular culture is not solely about mass media technologies; while listening to the radio, watching videos, and logging onto the Internet are important elements in fandom, listening to records with friends, collecting various items, participating in concerts, and making pilgrimages—acts that do not emphasize new means of electronic social interaction—are just as important. In addition, Springsteen fans' conscious discussions of self making do not indicate that popular culture is shaping their identity but rather that they are shaping their identity with popular culture. Fans talk about recognizing themselves in the music, about using the music to shape a sense of themselves over time, but are careful to see themselves as independent of the music, as having, in J. D. Rummel's terms, "a well-rounded life" filled with other interests and influences.

In fact, theories of the "mediated self" draw on an old philosophical tradition, beginning with the work of David Hume ([1739] 1961), which denies the validity of an autonomous individual and, instead, sees the self as a set of social relationships. According to such a view, when the social environment changes, as it did in the twentieth century with the advent of the mass media, then the very structure of the self changes, too. However, fans' discussions of self fit more with a different philosophical tradition, stemming from the work of William James, which privileges individual autonomy and sees the self as a perception of unity and coherence. In this view, the different environment created by the mass media simply offers individuals new tools with which to shape personal identity; the necessary act of perceiving remains unchanged.

On the whole, Springsteen fans' collecting and listening indicate that the importance of fandom for personal identity is not so much about the disorder caused by the mass media as it is about the order found in devotion. To form a sustained attachment to Springsteen and his music does not unhinge the self, making people more "protean" or "populated" or "selfless," but rather anchors the self, allowing people to shape a coherent idea of their individuality. Collecting and displaying Springsteen-related artifacts and listening and identifying with Springsteen or the characters in his music heighten self-awareness and help fans see themselves objectively. Collecting newspaper clippings about Springsteen or concert tapes and listening to how the music has changed over the years heighten a sense of self-continuity and help fans map where they've been and where they are going as they construct a personal history. Neither of these activities is without problems. Identification with characters in the music, for instance, raises questions for some fans about how to define identity itself. But in the end, for fans, participating in the world of popular music serves rather than destroys, enhances rather than diminishes, their perceptions of themselves as unique individuals.

7 Belonging Together

Fandom, Community, and Connection

At first glance, Springsteen fans seem an unlikely group. When I distributed questionnaires to fans through an ad in *Backstreets*, I received answers from more than fifty people, aged fifteen to fifty-seven, with widely varied educational levels and occupations, from all over the United States and Canada. While meeting and talking with specific fans, I have likewise encountered people with many different backgrounds and concerns—professors, insurance clerks, part-time cashiers, housewives, students, musicians, the unemployed, men and women, teenagers and golden-aged adults, citizens of many states and countries—most of whom have not met and probably never will.

However, despite this diversity, all the Springsteen fans to whom I've spoken have expressed to me a strong affinity for one another and a sense of belonging together. Many have mentioned the "invisible magnet" which draws them to other fans or the "instant connection and knowing" which occurs between fans meeting for the first time. Indeed, as a Springsteen fan myself, I have felt an immediate familiarity and friendship during interviews with complete strangers. As Alan Levine explains:

> There's like this fraternity of people out there who are like us. When you talk to someone who's like you—and I'm in sales; I talk to millions of people—it's amazing, if they have the same connection, how nice it is. I mean, you can spend hours on the phone with someone! I've got a guy, one of my clients, who's like right up there. He's a fanatic. You know, we'll swap tapes. But he's a client of mine. It's just wonderful. We were at the same show at the Meadowlands together, and I went up and met him and his wife at their seats. And he's a business client of mine, but there was no business associated with this. It was Bruce. And the next day, we would get on the phone, and it was like, "Oh, yeah! How'd you like the way he did 'Thunder Road'? 'Born to Run' was kinda great. What about the crowd? Wasn't the crowd

great? Talking during some of the songs. . . ." There's like this connection. (interview, April 2, 1993)

Most people would expect such a sense of belonging in a small community, like a neighborhood or town, where residents interact with each other daily, obey the same laws and leaders, share the same institutions, environment, problems—in short, intertwine their lives and experiences in a certain place. But how does one explain such a solidarity in the "Bruce world," whose members neither live in any one place nor necessarily share similar experience? Do Bruce fans constitute a community?

Many people continue to follow the lead of nineteenth-century sociologist Ferdinand Tönnies, who used the word "community" or "gemeinschaft" to refer to the types of human relationships found in rural life, characterized by sentiment, tradition, and common bonds based in family or "soil." He opposed this type to society or "gesellschaft," which he used to refer to the types of human relationships in modern, industrial states, characterized by individualism and shaped by lack of emotion, little or no identification with a group, and codes of duty and law (1973). However, while Springsteen fans share a number of gemeinschaft-like ties such as adherence to specific traditions or strong identification as a group, their membership in many diverse cultures from around the world and enthusiasm for the mass media obviously do not correspond to this sort of face-to-face community.

In addition to the notion of a geographical community, people often talk of a "scientific community," an "international community," or a "student community." The word in these cases works metaphorically. The "community" is not a geographical one, but people still share their lives in so many ways other than face-to-face communication that the term "community" seems applicable. The metaphor is used as a way to describe the presence of a loose relational network between people who share a common interest.

Springsteen fans share a common interest, but the bonds created between them are not as loose and ephemeral as those implied in the metaphorical use of "community." Many fans believe that they are part of a real, living group; this social identity is something tangible and serious, important to their fandom and sense of well-being. As Laurie McLain explains:

> I guess for me the main changes that have taken place during the almost eight years I've been doing this have to do with the community aspect. I've always seen Bruce fandom as a community with a common language, mythology, basic value base. It may be stretching it a bit, but it seems that the network of fans is much more elaborate for Bruce than it is for most other performers (there are definite exceptions—the Dead, for instance). For most of the people I've talked to about it, Bruce Tramps have some sort of a need to communicate with other Bruce Tramps,

on a wider scale than I've seen elsewhere. When my first [Springsteen] pen-pal friend and I first met, he said something like, "Wow. I've never seen a Bruce fan in person before." It was a big deal to him. (interview, March 11, 1993)

In fact, Springsteen fans suggest that the absence of geographical ties, rather than leading to a loose association based on common interest, causes fans to develop even closer social ties than they would ordinarily. For example, Judi Johnson, a Bruce Springsteen fan from Michigan, proudly told me that she has developed close friendships with other fans *despite* clear disparities of region and age:

I would probably say that most of my closest friends I have met through the Bruce world. I have a very close friend in Chicago. I have a very close friend in Los Angeles, a very close friend in New York, and a very close friend in Sudbury, Ontario. These are all my closest friends. . . . I have a lot of other friends and acquaintances—people I talk to regularly, men and women. I'm the oldest of all of us. [laughs] The matriarch. Our ages vary from mine down to—I correspond with a guy in Italy who's now eighteen. When he first wrote me, he said [imitating him], "I hope you're not disappoint for my age. I'm only seventeen." [laughter] So I wrote back, "Well, I hope you're not disappointed with mine! My children are way older than you are." [laughter] So, it's such a bridge. There's no generation gap when we're talking about Bruce's music. (interview, January 13, 1994)

If Springsteen fans do not form a group based on shared region, and if they do not simply form an association based on common interest, how do we account for—and talk about—their strong sense of group identity? Several scholars have addressed such a problem by arguing for the validity of nongeographic community, for the ways in which disparate individuals may develop solidarity in modern industrial societies (e.g., Durkheim 1964; Weber 1968; Sapir 1985; Anderson 1991). In particular, sociologist Max Weber directly revised Tönnies's theories, stating that relationships between people may be, on the one hand, communal and characterized by a subjective "sense of belonging together" or, on the other hand, associative and characterized by "a rationally motivated adjustment of interests or a similarly motivated agreement." Unlike Tönnies, Weber makes no mention of rural or urban factors or their value and recognizes that communal and associative relationships are only "ideal types," which may exist together in any sort of environment (1968, p. 41).

Weber's idea of community as a subjective "sense of belonging together" and his recognition of the ways in which it is intertwined with more economic kinds of association involving conflict and difference are most important for understanding the Springsteen fan community. First, Weber's idea moves beyond an understanding of community as a pure, face-to-face phenomenon in a particular place to something that can exist in a complex modern world. In fact, he mentions various forms of modern community, including "a religious brotherhood, an erotic relationship, a relation of personal loyalty, a national community, or the *esprit de corps* of a military unit." Second, Weber emphasizes that community cannot be based on common interest only but rather requires a "mutual orientation of [people's] behavior to each other." By rejecting the idea that community is simply something to which people belong by accident of birth or residence, as is often the case in face-to-face community, he recognizes that it may be *created* in different ways by different groups of people.

The Bruce fan community is not a village, it's not on a street, it's not affiliated with an institution or organization, but it brings people together with a remarkably strong commitment and goodwill. Fans create community or a "sense of belonging together" not with actual shared experience but with the *expectation* of shared experience. It begins the moment a person reaches out to Springsteen as he or she becomes a fan and reaches fruition in the ways in which they reach out to each other for good conversation and debate. In the end, this sense of belonging together is part and parcel of fans' social world. It shapes the tenor and quality of fans' interactions not only with each other but also with other nonfans like family members, friends, and coworkers.

*D*eveloping Association

A major factor in community development is whether the members of a group *intend* to create a community (Moore and Myerhoff 1975). As anthropologist Jennie Keith writes:

> Factors which affect the developmental aspects of community formation . . . can be divided into those which are present or not present among a collection of individuals at the beginning of the process, and those which may or may not develop over time. When the individuals involved are not intentionally trying to create community, the process of community formation begins when they find themselves living together in a shared territory. Background factors can then be observed from the beginning of their common occupation of this territory; the other factors may or may not appear as they continue to live together. (1982, p. 7)

Springsteen fans' group identity begins not with a conscious attempt to create a group but rather with fans' general feeling of isolation from nonfans. When asked on the questionnaire I circulated "How do non-fans view your fandom in general?" a clear majority of fans replied that other people "think it's strange" or "they don't care." Almost all fans to whom I spoke felt misunderstood or unwelcome in the eyes of those around them. Such isolation ranged from toleration to downright hostility. When talking to Linda Warner, for instance, she explained:

> WARNER: People find it very amusing. Because here I am—you know, I'm not a young person anymore—and I have these really eccentric sort of things that I do. And

it's one more eccentric thing that Linda does. I mean, I have very odd hobbies and this is just one. People find it charming and amusing but a little odd. [laughs]

CAVICCHI: Yeah, that's a widespread reaction to being a fan. I don't know, sometimes I get the feeling that fandom is supposed to be something that you do in your teenage years and that you're supposed to grow out of it.

WARNER: That's what most people think. Because my mother will say it. She'll go, "Well, do you still like Bruce?" And I want to say to her, "Mom, I'm not gonna grow out of it. Please stop asking me that question!" [laughs] But she still is like, I'm going to come to my senses eventually. She doesn't get it. (interview, March 25, 1993)

Like most human beings who congregate with others like them, fans combat feelings of loneliness and find validation by seeking out others with the same experiences and feelings. While not unintentionally finding themselves living in shared geographical territory, as Keith suggests, fans do unintentionally find themselves sharing the same *social* territory, separate from that of nonfans, as they seek out each other and develop knowledge of each other. The lack of acceptance from members of a fan's immediate social world and the intolerance and distortion of much of the media function as "background factors" which create an association and help to set the stage for community.

Fans find one another through several different avenues. Some fans actively set out to do some detective work. For example, LeAnne Olderman, a college student living in Texas, told me of one time when she was at the library: "You know, they have those little slips that they stamp that show . . . when the book has been checked out. So, here I am looking at these books on Springsteen. And these books have been checked out! So, somebody here likes him. [laughs]" (interview, May 13, 1993). However, most fans find each other through more established avenues.

Fanzines

Fanzines are publications written and produced by fans for other fans. Like record company hype about a star, fanzines are hype about being a fan. They usually contain the latest "inside" news leaked from the record company, letters, articles and analyses, fan fantasies, concert announcements, personal and merchandise ads, and announcements of fan conventions and contests. They vary wildly in content and production quality. Some are professionally done and approved by the artist (called a "fan magazine"); others are done by and for a small group of fans out of someone's basement, often at a financial loss (referred to as a "fanzine" or "'zine"). Fanzines come and go at the whim of the finances and interests of fans; in the words of rock bibliographer Paul Taylor, "There are no general collections of this literature, and one must attempt to discover the current fan-club secretary: itself a difficult task" (1985, p. 473).

While there have been no Springsteen fan magazines, there have been several Springsteen fanzines over the years. As of June 1994, there were nine publications, including one in Switzerland, one in England, two in Spain, and two in Italy, as well as several in the United States. As I have mentioned, one of the most popular and long-lasting is called *Backstreets*. In fact, many fans talk about *Backstreets* as one of the important places where they seek each other out and develop a sense of belonging to a group. Laurie McLain explains:

> I subscribed to *Backstreets* magazine and found that there was a community of fans out there. I didn't answer any of those ads for penpals and actually join the community until about two and half years ago. [One] guy I met was the same age as me, lived in the same area, and had an extensive tape collection which he was gracious enough to share with me. While he and I have never become really good friends, we've spent hours and hours talking about Bruce and related topics. He had met someone else in the area through the ad and the three of us saw shows in Tacoma and Vancouver, B. C. this tour. (We live in Portland, Oregon). That third person and I have become very good friends and he's the one that told me to get e-mail and got me on [*Backstreets Digest*]. (interview, March 11, 1993)

Likewise, Judi Johnson told me that *Backstreets* allowed her to meet other fans:

> I subscribed to *Backstreets;* that's how I found you. And everyone else. That's how I got—I, eventually, in '88, found all these people in the Bruce world, we refer to it as. And this is how my life completely changed, because I would say that the majority of the people I now know, am friends with, converse with, talk to constantly, are all Bruce fans. During this last tour, we all got together and went from city to city. It's just—it's made the whole . . . subculture. I find Bruce fans to be—we're all very different in some ways, but there seems to be a common bond. (interview, January 13, 1994)

Computer Discussion Groups

A computer discussion group is any electronic mail service to which people publicly post messages and news to each other about a specific topic. On both the nonprofit computer network known as the Internet and commercial networks like Prodigy and America Online, discussion groups exist for many topics—everything from folk art to skateboarding to library science—and are usually run by an "administrator," who handles incoming messages and sometimes organizes them into a magazine-like or "digestified" format, called a "mailing list," which is regularly sent to "subscribers."

There are several Springsteen fan computer discussion groups; as I have mentioned, the one in which I participated and know the most about is on the Internet and is called *Luckytown Digest* (formerly *Backstreets Digest*). Like *Backstreets*, *Luckytown Digest* is important to fans seeking each other out. It contains heated debates over the meaning of certain songs, announcements of Bruce's whereabouts and latest activities, detailed discussions of how to get tickets for concerts, concert set lists, and concert reviews. Often, new subscribers post their first message by mentioning their isolation and how astonished they are at all the people participating. Alan Stein told me about losing interest in Springsteen during his college years and reviving his interest in part through participation on the *Digest*:

> I'm trying to think when I got back into Bruce. Getting on the list, the e-mail list, made a big difference in how much I was listening to him. . . . I was amazed at the tapes and collections that people have and how much Bruce is a part of these people's lives, still, in their thirties and stuff. You know, I'm coming on thirty, now, and its like. . . . [smiles] You get back into it. It sort of keeps you young. It's really funny because I've become electronic pen pals with people. (interview, May 24, 1993)

Otherwise, regular participation on the mailing list allows fans to maintain a strong sense of commonality, particularly when they are isolated at home. As David Merrill told me in an e-mail message:

> As far as Brucemania in my daily life, I'm a loner out here!!!!!! My wife tolerates my playing Bruce (she just doesn't get it, ya know?). . . . I have quite a few Deadhead friends (co-workers who actually turned me on to the Dead) but no Bruce friends other than people I know via e-mail from the *Backstreets Digest*. It's nice to know that there are other folks out there who are as absorbed by Bruce's music as I am. (interview, May 25, 1993)

Concert Events

By "concert events," I mean all of the formal and informal fan activities related to the appearance of Bruce Springsteen in a locality during a concert tour. Such activities may include waiting in lines to purchase tickets for a show, hanging out in the parking lot before a show begins, attending a concert itself, and waiting backstage or at the stage door to meet Springsteen as he leaves for the night. Springsteen is notorious for waiting years between albums and between concert tours, so such an avenue for fan meetings is not as frequent as, say, fanzines or a computer discussion group may be; however, the concert event is one of the most anticipated and talked-about events among Springsteen fans. Between tours, fans continually speculate about the date of the next Springsteen record release and tour; during tours, fans go to great lengths to attend as many concerts as they can. In fact, in the questionnaire I used in this project, every fan who responded indicated that they had attended a concert, most having attended two or three and several having seen more than fifty.

A concert is obviously a chance for fans to see Springsteen live but it also provides a rare opportunity for large numbers of fans to congregate, meet, and interact face-to-face. Many fans describe finding fellow fans during concert events. Anna Selden explains:

> The weird thing is most of my friends—I'm trying to think—most of them don't like Bruce. So, it comes on the radio and I'm like [sternly], "Put that back on!" And they're like, "Yeah, yeah." And they know now; they know not to mess with the radio stations. And I'm slowly teaching people here that if they don't put Bruce back on, their driver *will* hit the embankment. [laughter] But I haven't run into a lot of people that are big fans. Of course, when tickets go on sale—it's funny, I see people with T-shirts on—like someone had a *Human Touch* T-shirt—and I just want to go up and talk to them. [laughs; then, warmly] "Hi," you know, "my name's . . ." and start talking to them. It's funny; for me, I didn't run into a lot of fans until concert time. (interview, January 12, 1994)

Not only do fans meet but also they have the opportunity to see themselves physically—in line for tickets, in the parking lot, or all seated before a stage in a stadium—as a group. Gene Chyzowych told me about the time when he brought a friend to a Springsteen show:

> This was his first show, and it was just—his excitement really rubbed off on me. It was like, "Wow, this is incredible. He is so psyched to go see Bruce." I'm like, "This is a great experience." We actually were hanging out at a place, having a bite to eat before the show, and it was just packed with Bruce fans who were all going to go to the Garden in about an hour or so. And all of a sudden, just randomly, the place started chanting, "Bruce . . . Bruce . . . Bruce!" I mean, over dinner! It was fantastic. My friend, Joey, was just totally awed. He was like, "This is incredible!" He was like such a little kid, he was so excited. And going to see the show, there was such a sense of like—everyone was there to see a common thing, have a common experience. (interview, April 21, 1993)

Other Social Events

The final major avenue for fans seeking out other fans is the various parties and informal gatherings which, whether directly related to Springsteen or not, tend to attract fans. For instance, from time to time, participants on *Luckytown Digest* have a party and invite anyone on the list who wishes (and can afford) to attend. Several people in New Jersey held such a gathering on July 4, 1993, and more than fifty people from across the nation showed up. Sometimes, various fanzines hold a get-together. *Backstreets* is known for holding social events in Seattle; the editors have also toyed with idea of a more official "Bruce fan convention," like those successfully held for artists like Madonna and Kate Bush.

Besides parties, Springsteen fans also go to other concerts by Springsteen-related artists in order to meet one another. On any given night, there are always a number of Springsteen fans at the Stone Pony, the Asbury Park, New Jersey, bar where Springsteen got his start and sometimes appears when warming up for a tour. Likewise, Springsteen fans invariably appear at concerts for other New Jersey Shore musicians, like Southside Johnny and the Asbury Jukes, Clarence Clemons, or Little Steven Van Zandt. On September 2, 1993, I attended a free concert by Southside Johnny at the Hatch Shell in Boston. There, I found not only a fan with whom I had met a couple of times earlier but also several other Springsteen fans whose names I recognized from the fan computer mailing list. In fact, I saw many people in the crowd, wearing Bruce Springsteen concert T-shirts and hats, all singing along to the Springsteen songs Southside Johnny chose to include in his set.

While Weber rejects the idea that the mere existence of common qualities constitutes a community, he does cite the importance of such qualities in the development of communal relationships. Like the shared territory of a geographical community, fanzines, computer discussion groups, concert events, and other social events provide a common, shared social space in which fans, often feeling isolated or misunderstood, interact. When fans first meet in these avenues, they have what Weber might call an "associative" relationship, that is, they are connected by the fact that they share a certain position or interest. To develop "communal relationships," however, they must achieve a "feeling of belonging together," which requires a concerted, intentional effort to generate and maintain a "mutual orientation of their behavior toward each other."

Creating Community

Most Springsteen fans explain that Springsteen's music is the force that unites them. As Judy Johnson remarked:

> I find Bruce fans to be—we're all very different in some ways, but there seems to be a common bond. We all respond—well, obviously, we all respond to the same music. That's how we got where we are. [laughs] We may veer off on other artists, but when it comes to Bruce, we all feel as passionately and strongly about his music as the others. (interview, January 13, 1994)

I would agree that Springsteen's music is certainly a unifying force among Springsteen fans. Many musicologists have discussed the ways in which the experience of music may create unity among listeners. Ray Pratt, for instance, has outlined the ways in which the experience of sound creates a new "social space" for listeners in which they may feel temporarily empowered and unified (1990, pp. 21–45). However, simply sharing the experience of the same music does not completely explain the strong relationships between Springsteen fans. Many people hear the same radio programming, for instance, but not all radio listeners feel a strong bond with each other. And, as we have seen, not all Springsteen fans interpret and understand Springsteen's music in the same way. Although fans may feel the same kind of affinity for the music, something more must be involved in creating the strong feeling of affinity and belonging they feel toward *each other*.

Many scholars have recognized the importance of various kinds of discourse in creating communal relationships. Weber, for instance, recognized that "a common language, which arises from a similarity of tradition through the family and the surrounding social environment, facilitates mutual understanding, and thus the formation of all types of social relationships, in the highest degree" (1968, p. 42). Sociolinguists have focused on "speech communities," debating whether shared language practice can act as a unifying aspect of social groups (Bloomfield 1933; Gumperz 1971; Gumperz and Hymes 1972; Hymes 1974). Recently, with the increasing popularity of computer networking and discussion groups, several people have sought to explain how specific language practice on electronic mailing lists creates communal feeling (see Baym 1993; Perrolle 1991; Stone 1991). And historian Benedict Anderson, drawing on the work of the Annales school, has shown the ways in which the nineteenth-century state, through the rise of commercial printing, created "an image of communion" for its citizens through naming all the parts of the nation's territory, mapping and creating a territorial symbol of the nation, imposing language laws, and creating national "biographies" or historical "narratives of identity" (Anderson 1991; see also Kammen 1991). I have located a similar function of discourse in my fieldwork with fans.

From Bruce Springsteen's beginnings in the early seventies as a local performer with a cult following to his current international stardom, a continuing and important element of his appeal has been his ability to captivate his audience through storytelling. During performances, before songs, or sometimes in the middle of songs, Springsteen often tells spontaneous, long, rambling stories about his experiences: growing up, meeting other band members, or participating in current events. The stories always serve to place songs in particularly meaningful frames and establish an important connection between Springsteen and those listening. Concert goers often cite "hearing stories" as one of the main reasons for attending a Springsteen concert, and many claim that part of the attraction of collecting concert tapes is to hear Springsteen's various stories. As one collector said: "One of my favorite things is when he talks, when he tells stories. . . . That's what I want to hear: the whole lead-in, the transitions, the segues between songs. I love that! That's really when his creativity comes out."

Springsteen fans' attraction to his stories parallels an intense interest in, and sharing of, their own personal stories about being a fan, which they call "Bruce stories."[1] *Backstreets* always contains letters from fans talking about their experiences, for instance, visiting New Jersey or attending concerts. *Luckytown Digest* regularly features the stories of fans who are first discovering Springsteen, making "road trips" to concerts, or meeting Springsteen in the street. Bruce stories are even more prevalent in the face-to-face encounters between fans at concert events. As Judi Johnson said about waiting in line for concert tickets: "You all talk in line, and it's a very fun bonding experience. Everybody tells their Bruce stories and talks about the music" (interview, January 13, 1994). When attending Springsteen concerts during his 1992–1993 tour, I noted again and again in my field journal that the people around me, often strangers to each other, were continually striking up conversations about attending past concerts or getting tickets. Just as Springsteen makes connections with his audience through telling stories, members of his audience make connections with others through similar behavior.

Fans consider Bruce stories vital for basic social interaction and for establishing a social bond between strangers. As Alan Levine explained:

> It's nice when you meet up with some people who are as lunatic like you, and you can share these war stories with them. "Oh, yeah, I drove to Syracuse in a blizzard to see two shows." "Wasn't that the show he was sick?" "Yeah, yeah!" "He closed the show with 'I'm on Fire?'" "Yeah, I remember that! I remember that!" [laughter] It's like getting into this tangent. You can talk for hours about their concert experiences and what they were doing during it. (interview, April 2, 1993)

Indeed, the absence of storytelling among fans is recognized as a serious problem. For instance, in November 1993, the volume of *Backstreets Digest* increased significantly because of new subscribers. Digests were appearing three times a day and contained all sorts of lengthy and contentious debates about the details of lyrics and concert bootleg tapes, but few stories. Finally, a fan who had been a participant in the discussion group for a long time responded with a message which said in part:

> To everybody . . . especially the (apparent) mass of new people reading, please share your Bruce stories. Many of us have already revealed our well-worn mushy "how I came to love Bruce" stories and have gone on to nitpicking. New Blood: Save us from ourselves, please! . . . P. S. Did I ever tell you about the time Mon & I met Bruce at Count Basie? Oh, you heard that one? Never mind. (West 1994)

The message is an attempt by a more experienced fan subscriber of the *Digest* to instruct the uninitiated and remind the more experienced about its proper use and purpose. Experienced subscribers have forgotten the stories they used to tell each other; to "save" the experienced fans from themselves, to maintain the community, newer fans must get them back to what's central and important to the mailing list's congregation of fans: sharing stories.

In each of these instances, telling Bruce stories is inclusive. As Judi Johnson said, "Everybody tells their Bruce stories." It is important that *everybody* participate, that a swapping take place. Threads of storytelling on the mailing list can go on for weeks in order to accommodate everyone; when someone started a "How I Came to Love Bruce" theme on April 30, 1993, the exchange of stories continued daily until the end of May. Competence is not an issue. While some people worry about the depth of their experience—in my fieldwork, for instance, I heard apologies like, "Other than getting skunked out of tickets, I really don't have any stories"—making a bond with others is considered more important. As Mary Beth Wilson said in a letter to me, responding to an ad I had put in *Backstreets* to solicit participants for my research:

> I'm sure I don't have the war stories and Bruce encounters to tell you about that some other people might, but I am passionate about the subject of Bruce Springsteen. I'd be happy to share my personal experiences with you, especially knowing that you are a fan! I'm always looking for new people to discuss him with until the wee hours of the morning! (personal correspondence, November 15, 1993)

The sharing of Bruce stories among fans creates community in several ways. Psychologists have shown the way in which narrative functions to organize human cognition (Sarbin 1986; Polkinghorne 1988); Bruce stories similarly construct fans' understanding of their experience. In particular, they order and define fans' personal experiences according to socially derived categories and thus enable fans to understand their experiences as shared.

A Bruce story is a person's story of his or her personal experience as a Springsteen fan. In one sense, it is a form of what folklorists call the "personal experience narrative," fitting the general definition of Sandra Stahl (1989, p. 15): it has a dramatic narrative structure, a consistently implied assertion that the narrative is true, and a correspondence between the identity of the teller of the story and the story's main character. However, because folklorists wish to distinguish personal experience stories from other kinds of folk narrative that are collective, widely known, and formalized, they tend to emphasize the idiosyncrasy of personal narratives' form and content. Sandra Stahl, for instance, claims that personal narratives are "items that serve primarily to express and maintain the stability of an individual personality rather than an entire culture" (1989, p. 21). This division between the individual and the social is unclear in Bruce stories: fans are recognized as individuals, each with idiosyncratic personal experience, but the experiences about which they choose to talk closely parallel those of other fans and derive their meaning from a shared fan identity. What is created in Bruce stories is not simply a conception of self but rather a conception of self as a member of a specific group.

In this way, Bruce stories resemble other personal narratives that operate in specific group contexts. In Susan Kalčik's study (1975) of the personal narratives shared in women's discussion groups, in James Leary's study (1977) of white toughs' stories about adventure and risk on the street, or in Jeff Titon's study (1988, pp. 260–276) of the religious testimony of Appalachian Baptists, personal narratives are not solely about personality. Experiences recognized as idiosyncratic are simultaneously shaped by social conventions of form or content, and the sharing of personal narratives has meaning both for the identity of the individual teller and for the identity of the group in which the telling takes place.

Fans understand their personal experiences in terms of several separate, socially derived categories of storytelling, most of which I have already presented in previous chapters: becoming-a-fan, pilgrimages, getting tickets, concert going, and meeting Bruce. In addition to shaping fans' understanding of their personal experiences as shared, these types of Bruce stories also shape expectations of group behavior. They identify general values important to being a fan and, in the cases of certain types of stories, serve as models for thinking and acting in specific situations in which fans might find themselves. Thus, as in philosopher Michel Foucault's idea of discourse (1986), Bruce stories define a group of people through exclusion, through limiting the possibilities of acceptable behavior.

An example of stories that identify general fan values is the pilgrimage story. As the name suggests, a pilgrimage story tells of fans' travels to, and experience of, certain sites important in Springsteen's life and work. The sites are typically located in the state of New Jersey, although some fans have made pilgrimages to other places mentioned in Springsteen's songs, such as the Badlands. Pilgrimage stories are always about achieving a goal and emphasize both the commitment of fans in the face of adversity and their special status as pilgrims.

Many stories dramatize the action of travel. Framed as quests, they often detail fans' experiences on the road: getting lost, breaking down, dealing with the unexpected. For example, Linda Warner told me about her pilgrimages to New Jersey with a friend:

> We have these really strange experiences. We had this clue that he lived across the street from a school. But that's all we knew! So, we're driving around, and we passed the Rumson Country Day School. And Amy was like, "This is it. This is the house." And we had nothing to base it on other than the fact that it was across the street from a school! And the mailman was coming down the street. So I got out of the car, and I walked up to his car, and he said, "Before you say anything, I'm not supposed to tell you." He knew that was what I wanted to know! Because without either of us saying his name, he goes, "Yes, this is his house." And we had this long talk about taking mail up to the door and what a nice guy Bruce was. Things like that would happen to us all the time. (interview, March 25, 1993)

Other pilgrimage stories mention travel but emphasize the experience of a place once it has been reached. Often fans describe the excitement they feel on coming across places mentioned in Springsteen's songs or their disappointment of finding that their imaginations are grander than reality. One fan told a story of traveling far out of his way to Asbury Park, New Jersey, eager to see where Springsteen was part of a vibrant music scene and where he set many of his character-filled songs, only to find an economically depressed and empty boardwalk. "Now I know what civilization will look like after the neutron bombs hit," he said (Eric 1993). Even though evaluations can be positive or negative, such stories nevertheless emphasize the authenticity of Springsteen as a person. As Alan Levine explains:

> Just recently I drove by his house in Rumson, New Jersey. Friends of ours live close by, and we went to visit them, and they were like, "What do you want to do?" I said, "The first thing I want to do is drive by his house." And sure enough they knew where it was, of course. So, they drove us by, and I got to see his house in New Jersey. No big deal, you know. Could have been anyone's house. (pause) But it was Bruce's house. (interview, April 2, 1993)

On the whole, both types of pilgrimage stories emphasize the importance of fans' making a pilgrimage. It is portrayed as an ordeal, an activity which sets true fans apart from mere audience members. Many fans plan for years to go to Asbury Park, New Jersey; since many Springsteen pilgrimage sites are located on the East Coast, pilgrimages take on an even greater importance for fans living in the Midwest or West. As LeAnne Olderman, a student in Texas, said determinedly:

> I still want to go to New Jersey and make a pilgrimage. . . . They tore down all the stuff on the boardwalk, supposedly. You know, and when they were telling us that this was fixing to happen, I really wanted to go but I wasn't old enough. Now, if I said, "Okay, Mom and Dad, I'm twenty-one, and if I want to take my car and drive to New Jersey, I can go!" I wasn't old enough to do that. And I really was upset about not getting to go before they tore everything down. But, now I'd like to go to the Stone Pony, which reopened; and they have that little museum up there . . . I still want to go. I will eventually. (interview, May 13, 1993)

Another example of Bruce stories that promote specific values and serve as models for thinking and acting is the ticket story. Most ticket stories deal with the post–*Born to Run* era, after Springsteen had become a star and after the reorganization of ticket sales in the eighties to handle the demands of stadium rock tours. While early fans often have a few stories to tell about camping out overnight to get a good position in line at a local box office, most fans have many stories about the failure of computers, the inadequacy of the telephone system, and the bureaucracy of ticket agencies. Nevertheless, plots of ticket stories over the years have been essentially the same: fans' desire to see a Springsteen show is pitted against the ineptitude and corruption of the music business. In this scenario, fans are honest, try to do the right thing, and abide by the rules, while the business is greedy and works against such good intentions.

The primary representative of music business corruption—and often the antagonist of ticket stories—is the scalper, who buys up many tickets and then sells them at a profit to desperate fans. Often the scalper hovers in ticket stories as a kind of devil, tricking or tempting fans to participate in corrupting or immoral activity. My wife and our friend Mary often tell a story about the time they met a man looking for Springsteen tickets and offered to give him a ride to an agency out of town; however, they soon realized that he was not what he seemed:

> He had to pick up his stuff at the University Sheraton, so we drive up on the bricks, sit in front of the front door. I just can't believe we're doing this. We talked about how much money we had in our pockets—just a couple hundred bucks—and he's got like thousands. And we're sitting in the front going, "Did you hear how much money he said he's got?" I said, "Yes, I heard how money he said he's got." [laughter]

Mary explained to me that after dropping my wife and the man off at the ticket agency and returning later, she found my wife rather confused:

> She stops me and says, "He's been changing shirts." [laughter] He was giving money to people in line, because there was an eight ticket limit or something. And they'd buy him tickets. He didn't want to get caught. He wouldn't want somebody to say, "Yeah, that guy in the blue shirt had me do this." So, he was changing his clothes every so often. [laughter] So, by the time he was done, he was in a Hawaiian shirt. We had our tickets; that's all I cared about. (interview, April 30, 1993)

In the end, ticket stories are about the organization and commitment of fans to Springsteen and to each other. To actually get tickets after all kinds of preparation, work, problems, adventures, and longing, to overcome the obstacles of the ticket process, is what is important, as Judi Johnson's story shows:

> We were the first ones in line, and we were there for eighteen hours. People came all through the night, and you know, you all talk in line, and it's a very fun bonding experience. Everybody tells their Bruce stories and talks about the music. . . . We were so anxious to get good seats. We wanted good seats. We really *really* didn't want to pay a scalper. [laughs] So, we get up, and we're sort of pacing around, and we're nervous because we're first in line—David and I are. We went in, once they opened it; we get in, and we're there with our money and, you know, hearts in throat. And everybody at this point's laughing 'cause they knew—we were there so many hours before anyone else ever showed up. The guy starts clicking in, you know, right before the tickets go on sale. And he says, "All right, I've got a connection." The tickets came up—and they were front row center. You know, like a "Rocky" movie. Everybody in line cheered! [laughs] There *was* a guy in line who offered us five hundred dollars for them, and I know he was a scalper. He was enough people back that I knew he was. "You can get five hundred dollars for those!" I said, "Uh uh! Nope, they're mine." So I just think that's a good thing to know: you *can* get front row center seats to go see Bruce. (interview, January 13, 1994)

Fans actively invoke these values by sharing ticket stories during ticket-related events. As I explained in chapter 1, when I went to my local ticket agency to get in line according to the number on a wristband I had received days earlier, before the line even formed, I overheard people sharing stories about previously getting tickets by using the wristband process. When the ticket official ordered us according to number, people reminisced about their placement in line on previous occasions. When the ticket computer system failed, and we had to wait fifteen minutes until it was fixed, people nervously exchanged stories about previous ticket computer failures and about the probabilities of getting good seats at concerts. This storytelling helped to ease the tension of the ticket process by marking the situation as typical and providing models about what to expect and how fans should behave.

Finally, while Bruce stories act as a discourse which socially constructs experience and controls behavior, they also function as communication between fans, allowing fans to learn about each other and map out what is idiosyncratic and what is shared. As Russ Curley explained about his experience of the Springsteen fan computer mailing list:

> I was happy because I figured, first, I'm normal. [laughs] And secondly, that there are people who believe what I'm believing, that there's this power that's coming from the music that people are saying, "Hey, he's affected me." I thought I was the only one, but then I realized people were affected very deeply. That's something that's interesting on the computer, where people tell stories about meeting him or stories about how their lives have changed. There was a whole sequence last spring where people were talking about it. A girl was going to commit suicide. I don't think I was ever that . . . depressed, but still, the point remains that he's had this effect on people, and it's very comfortable realizing that the feeling that you're feeling is definitely tangible; other people are going through it, too. (interview, November 2, 1993)

J. D. Rummel echoed this sentiment while discussing his experience of the mailing list:

> My interest in *Backstreets Digest* is the satisfaction in finding people on a common ground. It makes one feel less alone in the world, less separate from fellow travelers. So many wonderful things can happen when people can come together in one purpose. I'm not concerned with recording tips or suggestions on chord changes, but I love the stories of meeting Bruce, of stories relating how someone else perceives the music, how it impacts others I have never met. I find both common ground and stimulating differences. (interview, May 20, 1993)

One of the first things I noticed when I started meeting other Springsteen fans and analyzing our conversations was fans' frequent and varied use of the word "story." While fans limit the meaning of the word to some sort of narrative, they use it to identify a variety of referents: accounts of Springsteen's life, Springsteen's monologues between songs at a concert, his songs themselves, and their own discussions about being a fan.

The wide use of the word "story" in the Springsteen fan community is no accident. As words like "spirit" and "message," for instance, have a special, extraordinary meaning to members of a religious community (Titon 1988, p. 195), the word "story" among Springsteen fans resonates in powerful ways. While the conventional meaning of a story is an account of an event, for Springsteen fans the word refers to a particular means of understanding the world. It is not simply a closed text which represents a factual or fictional occurrence but a *process* of organizing, interpreting, and enhancing experience.

Thus it plays an important part in the creation of fan community. Springsteen fans do not all share a way of life in a certain place; they simply share a mode of participation in the world of popular music. Telling stories about that participation enables fans to understand their experiences as shared, to behave with relative uniformity, and to learn about one another. By telling Bruce stories, fans move from abstract similarity to Weber's "mutual orientation," to a feeling of belonging together.

Personal Relations

While the Springsteen fan community may not be geographical and is, to some extent, imagined—that is, existing as a subjective feeling—that does not mean that such a community is not influential in fans' face-to-face social relations. In fact, the mutual orientation of fans' behavior toward one another often leads to significant and lasting personal relationships which go beyond the group identity created by the communal relationship. While one might logically assume that fans would build a feeling of group identity from their face-to-face interaction with other fans, I found that the opposite takes place: fans build face-to-face interaction with other fans from their sense of group identity.

Again and again in my conversations with fans, I was told that the shared experience of fandom provided the common ground for closer one-on-one encounters, a way for individuals to "connect." As John O'Brien told me: "Just this semester, I met a guy in my hall who's a really big fan. I guess it was a few nights ago that we just sat around and started talking. It [fandom] just gives you this whole dialogue instantly about each album. We just connected right off on that" (interview, March 15, 1993). Mary Krause talked about hitting it off with another fan, Stacy, in college:

> She was from New Jersey, Parsipanny, New Jersey. One thing led to another. You know, you meet someone who's a Bruce fan, so you talk a lot about Bruce. She was in my classes, so I'd see her around. We'd see her—she seemed to live around us. Anyway, because of that, when we went to the *Born in the USA* shows at the Meadowlands, she went with us to one of the shows. It was very cool. I mean, it was a stadium show, but we had plenty of dance space. We were just having a good time, being together, being at a Bruce show. (interview, April 30, 1993)

While not all fans are friends, and some encounters between fans serve only to remind them of their communal bond, the shared experience of fandom often provides the basis for a deeper friendship. Amy Thom, for instance, talked about meeting fellow fan Linda Warner at a concert:

> Initially—it's funny, I don't think we initially talked about Bruce, but we were both going to a Tom Petty concert or something like that. Not together, but we both had tickets. And I'm supposing that maybe that conversation led to some other musical conversations. Like, "Oh, who else do you like?" or whatever. Because I really don't have a strong memory on exactly what it was, but I'm guessing that it came from that. We did go to the—the first time either one of us saw him in concert, we went to that concert together. That was in Phoenix in '84. (interview, April 1, 1993)

Linda explained that after meeting they started to participate in fan activities together:

> In '84 *Born in the USA* came out. That summer my husband did a sabbatical at Princeton. And Amy came back for two weeks of the sabbatical, and we decided we were going to learn about the Shore and learn about where Bruce came from. So we got in the car and went to all the places that we could find. Went to Freehold, went to Asbury Park, you know, went to the Stone Pony, did that whole thing. And *then* we became obsessed. That was the beginning of the hard-core . . . problem. [laughs] That's how we refer to it. When we moved back here [New Jersey], Amy's business brought her back here every couple of months, and we started to get really serious about this. You know, we found the house in Rumson, and we found the gym, and we kept running into him. We kept seeing him all over. And we really are obsessed now. (interview, March 25, 1993)

On the whole, Amy explained that her friendship with Linda is based, in part, on their shared fandom:

> I know another guy who's a Bruce fan, but he was somebody that I just, you know, met socially. He used to go on and on about Bruce. [laughs] The *Greetings* album. This was early on, too. This was quite a long time ago. But for the most part, my only true Bruce fan friend is Linda. And it's funny because all of my friends know how serious I am about him, and half of them think I'm nuts. But I can see how it probably appeared that way. [laughs] But I don't think anybody understands it as well as Linda does. That's something that's really neat about our friendship. Something you can really share that we both have an understanding of. (interview, April 1, 1993)

Linda echoed this, adding that her friendship intensified her fandom:

> I think if I hadn't met Amy, I probably would've remained a fairly casual fan. I would have really liked his music and really admired him. But my relationship with Amy really centers around—we love the music but we also—both—are just infatuated with the man. When it went from the music to the man was when my

behavior changed. And the two of us sort of feed each other. It's like one of us will come up with this idea: "I know, let's go find his high school." So, we'll go, you know, to St. Rose of Lima. "Let's go"—he went to community college for a while. We went to the community college. I mean, we've been *everywhere*. And we have a great time doing it! And it's really a big part of our friendship. It's this activity that we do. So, it's all tied up with friendship and feeling. (interview, March 25, 1993)

Mary Beth Wilson similarly talked about her friends Joe and Dave, whom she met after one of them saw her Springsteen calendar hanging outside her cubicle at work. Their interaction often involves fan activities; besides going to concerts, they listen to music together. As she explained:

Frequently, I'll answer my phone and I hear [laughs] Springsteen on the other end. Because my friend Dave will call me up and just—like if he's listening to something—like he just got the "Bomb Scare Show" [a concert bootleg] so, of course, the second he comes home he puts it in and calls me and just puts the phone to the speaker. And then he'll just let it go on for a couple minutes and then, "So, what do you think?" [laughter] (interview, January 17, 1994)

In addition to developing friendships between fans, the shared experience of fandom can lead to romance. Indeed, several fans hoped that they would have a romantic relationship with another fan. As LeAnne Olderman worried: "I wonder how it's going to be? What happens if I fall in love with a guy and he can't stand Springsteen? What am I going to do? [laughs] It would be the most awful thing in the world! Maybe that should be a criteria, I don't know" (interview, May 13, 1993). Several fans told me about using shared fandom as an aid in dating. Al Khorasani, for example, explained:

Well, every girl that I've known in New Jersey has, at one point or another, been in love with Bruce Springsteen. I just, I was like—that was a big—Oh! Here's a funny one. There was this one girl in college. God, she was nice! I asked her to go out on a date; she wouldn't go out with me. I was in a fraternity; she was in a sorority next door to us. And she wouldn't want to go out. Finally, Bruce came to Albany—that was *The River* tour. We got tickets. So, I got an extra ticket, and I waved it in front of her. And, God, I have a lot to thank Bruce for! Besides all those inspirational lyrics, I have a person—[laughter] If I ever meet him, I'm gonna say, "Bruce, I owe you one." If there's some way I could return the favor, I don't know. (interview, March 23, 1993)

Others have had more serious and lasting relationships. Several fans on the computer mailing list have posted messages about having a "Bruce wedding" and asking for suggestions for Springsteen songs to be played at the reception. I have already mentioned Jackie Gillis story about becoming a fan in chapter 2; in it she talks about the ways in which her relationship with her husband was closely intertwined with his (and later her) fandom. And, as I have already discussed, again in chapter 2, my own relationship with my wife began at a Springsteen concert.

Of course, the linking of Springsteen and romance is not always happy. As Mary Beth Wilson explained, referring to a former boyfriend, "You start identifying this music with different things, and sometimes that's good and sometimes it's not." Nevertheless, fans expect that the shared experience of fandom will lead to meaningful, romantic relationships.

Fans also attested that their feeling of belonging together not only leads to new relationships but can be used to maintain or strengthen existing relationships. For some fans, fandom was a new, shared experience for old friends. Mary Krause, for instance, consistently described her fandom while using the pronoun "we," indicating the involvement of her roommate from the beginning:

KRAUSE: We started stocking up on Bruce albums. And then we started stocking up on Bruce singles. And then we started stocking up on Bruce books! [laughs]

CAVICCHI: What did you do with all this stuff you were stocking up? Did you just keep it on a shelf? Did you listen—

KRAUSE: We listened to it. We read the books. We listened to the music. [pause] And then we had a TV in our room, you see. So, we watched the videos on MTV as they came out. (interview, April 30, 1993)

Alan Levine likewise described his fandom as something he and his high school friends used to bond with one another:

LEVINE: In the high school years, in the earlier tours, there were two other guys, who were friends of mine from high school. They were very similar to me in their love of his music and concerts. We must have gone to fifteen shows. And the enthusiasm that they had was similar to mine, which was, you know, if you go to a show now, is similar to most of the fans in the building. It's this almost spooky ritualistic approach to him. Again, more so in the older days. *Born to Run, Darkness* tour, *The River* tour. My friends, yes, they shared the same enthusiasm for him as I did.

CAVICCHI: There was probably a lot of bonding going on at the fifteen concerts. I mean, you shared this experience that not many people did.

LEVINE: Absolutely. Like I said, one of the guys I'm still very close to. He was the best man at my wedding four years ago. We still talk about it to this day. The other guy, unfortunately, we've sort of lost touch with, as happens during those years. But yes, it was a great experience to go through, and I did feel closer to these guys. You know, that was my high school years. These were my buds! That's what we did. (interview, April 2, 1993)

The strengthening of relationships through fan activity was particularly apparent in fans' descriptions of their families' involvement in fandom. Participation in rock'n'roll is commonly thought to be an avenue for teenagers to rebel against the staid ways of their parents, which continues to be true for several fans. Most fans, however, explained that their fandom was a family affair; they used it to bond with, not alienate, their parents, and often siblings and children got involved. Several fans talked happily about their parents' participation in activities like getting tickets or collecting. Mary Beth Wilson, for instance, talked about her mother as a source for concert information:

> It's fun; it's a lot of fun. Actually, when he just did those two benefit shows last summer, I was at work one day—and I get to work at about seven o'clock in the morning—and at about five after seven my phone rang. It was my Mom. I was like, "What's the matter?" She doesn't call me that early in the morning. And she was like, "I've got an update for you!" I'm like, "What?" "There's *Boss* news." She loves to call him the Boss; she thinks that's the greatest. [laughs] She says [imitating her mother's voice], "There's a thing in the *Star-Ledger*"—which is the New Jersey paper. "He's doing two benefit shows on these dates in the Meadowlands and Madison Square Garden. . . ." She's reading the whole article to me at five after seven in the morning! So, from my mother's mouth it went out to my whole network of friends, and we were all informed by about seven-twenty in the morning. [laughter] We were already plotting out how we were getting tickets and who was going when, you know. (interview, January 17, 1994)

Mary Krause talked about going to a concert with her sister:

> My middle sister is very much into Bruce, as well. Lenore. She was a budding Bruce fan. She followed us everywhere like our shadow. We took her to the New Jersey shows; she had a great time. We kidnapped her; it was great. We didn't tell my mother where we were taking her. . . . So, she's a Bruce fan. And my little sister, Jennifer, she tried not to be a Bruce fan. And she doesn't really like his voice or his music, but in high school she did a Bruce Springsteen collage and gave it to me. The whole family has kind of partaken in the whole Bruce thing. (interview, April 30, 1993)

Russ Curley explained that his parents now recognize Springsteen:

> When I listen to him, they know who he is. I remember when I was home this summer, the night of the show, I was getting dressed, and my mother yelled, "Hey, hey! He's on TV!" And I flipped it on, and they showed him rehearsing with Southside. So, I knew it was going to be a special night. But she knew who he was. (interview, November 2, 1993)

If family members were not participating in fan activities, many fans told me that they nevertheless attempted to educate them about fandom. Several fans I met, for instance, told me about sending their parents to a Springsteen concert. Laurie McLain even made a "training tape" for her parents so they'd know what to expect. Others tried to educate their parents by playing the music frequently. LeAnne Olderman said: "They tolerate it. They're not—I mean, I've made my parents listen. All I remember is that at one point my sister and I got into playing music on my parents' stereo while we were eating breakfast. We would make everybody listen to it" (interview, May 13, 1993). Still others have recruited their parents in activities like getting tickets. Even though Mary Beth describes her father as "not too interested," she said:

> I do have to say he would call me, or he would let somebody know, if he heard something about him. . . . And he did—I actually put him on phone duty last time, calling Ticketmaster. [laughs] He didn't get through, but he sat there and gave it a good try. He doesn't understand, but for whatever reason, he'll do it for me. (interview, January 17, 1994)

Sometimes, fans even "convert" their parents or siblings. Judi Johnson, for instance, told me a humorous story of how her daughters introduced her to Bruce Springsteen's music:

> Well, I came to Bruce very late. Considering my age. It was in '84, when naturally the whole world was there. [laughs] I knew who he was; I knew "Hungry Heart." And that was probably the extent of it. I mean, I just knew who he was. I did not own any of his records. It wasn't for any particular reason that I didn't. It wasn't that I listened to him and disliked him—I remember I really liked "Hungry Heart" when it was on the radio. I suppose it was where my head was at that time: I still was real busy raising my children, and my life was just overcrowded. So, in '84—they call it the day of infamy in our house [laughter]—my middle child, my youngest daughter, was watching MTV. And I was in the kitchen, and she called me. She said, "Hey, Ma, come here and look at Bruce Springsteen." So I came into the television room, and "Dancing in the Dark" was on. I said, "Oh, wow, he's really changed." . . . I think it was in September when she called me in to see the video. And he had already been here, and at some point, maybe after Christmas, I bought the *Born in the USA* album. I really, *really* liked it. I was listening to it going, "Oh, wow! Oh wow!" And then I remember *We Are the World* came out and "Oh! This is just. . . ." Then I became really interested, and I started reading about him and trying to find out everything I could about him. And I remember telling my daughters, "You know, I want to go see him." And they said, "He's already been here." I said, "No! You can't be telling me that! [laughs] No, I want to go see him." "No, Mom, he was here last summer." I said, "No!" I was devastated.

Later, when Judi did see a Springsteen concert, the daughters couldn't believe what they had done. As Judi explained:

> I was rather frantic, at the time, to see him. And the show came. It was kind of funny—my daughter went with me, the daughter who blames herself for the change in our lives. [laughter] Because it did. My life changed at this point. [pause] She was with me in the second row. My other daughter was also at the show, but she was with her husband and they were seated elsewhere. It was very funny, because she had a friend, who she worked with, who was a fairly big Bruce fan, and she was saying, you know, "I'll just be so glad when he comes. She goes to the show and we can get back to a normal life in our house." And her [friend's] reply was, "Oh, Kelly, I'm afraid it could get worse." [laughter] (interview, January 13, 1994)

On the whole, the activities of fandom provide a way for family members to come together; fans frequently described parents who, even if they didn't care for Springsteen themselves, used their son or daughter's fandom as a way to communicate with them. For example, Russ Curley talked about how fandom aided his relationship with his father:

> Well, they never overtly, or outwardly, criticize what I'm doing. I think my mother would probably say, "He spends too much money on this stuff" and that I talk about him all the time. But I think they realize that it's something that I care a lot about, and they respect it. My Dad has, actually, over the years, saved me many newspaper articles, especially when I'm gone at school. I remember in about '87 or '88 we had a big fight about something, and to make up for it, he actually bought these—he got them somewhere pretty cheaply; I guess they were old. This was '88, so . . . he got them—these were *Born in the USA* official tour posters. Big, huge . . . two of them! And I came and saw them in my room, and I was like, "Wow!" Whatever we were fighting about went out the window. [laughter] (interview, November 2, 1993)

Andrew Laurence also described his father, a rock critic, as using fandom to bond with his son:

> I think my dad takes a kind of secret pleasure in the fact that I like a lot of artists that are either from his era of rock'n'roll or ones that he really liked as a critic. He and I (almost) went to a Van Halen concert a couple of years ago, but I think that was more of an offshoot of a parental/quality time thing than any other. . . . He wanted me to come over to his apartment a while back, "to see something I taped off Letterman the other night. It's a surprise." He seemed kinda disappointed to find out that I'd already seen it. ;-) (interview, October 23, 1993)

Fans, too, use their fandom to reach out to family members. Judi Johnson, for instance, talked about taking her daughter, also a fan, to New Jersey:

> In '87, I decided that I wanted to go to New Jersey and see all those places. And I took my oldest daughter, who had, at that point, just divorced and she was kind of going through a rough time. So, the two of us went, in the summer of '87, to New Jersey. We went with the intention of seeing all the places that are in all those songs. And when we got there, it so happened that he was in town. And we went to the Stone Pony on Sunday night, and it so happened that [voice quickens] he showed up and played! (interview, January 13, 1994)

In the Music in Daily Life Project at SUNY Buffalo in which I participated, I found evidence that people were mirroring their relationships with stars in their face-to-face interactions. For instance, while one woman described a "female camaraderie" with Rickie Lee Jones and Joni Mitchell, she also described a similar bond with her sister, who discovered "many of the same musicians around the same time." Another woman described an intense, almost mystical connection with Pink Floyd's Roger Waters, which paralleled her intense relationship with her brother. (Crafts, Cavicchi, and Keil 1993, pp. 69–73, 90–93). The same kind of mirroring may be taking place among some Springsteen fans. But what I've learned in the case of Springsteen fans is that it is difficult to make such a simple parallel because fandom is not only about a relationship with a media figure— many fans would rather talk about their relationship to the music—but also about powerful ideas of community and belonging. In fact, the relationships fans develop with others around them probably parallel their own ideas of what other fans are like, or about how fandom can bring people together, more than their relationships with Springsteen.

Conflict and Community

Traditional studies in social science often portray a social group as a single, homogeneous unit whose members all have a similar degree of commitment to the group and equally share its values and modes of behavior. For instance, anthropologists for the last century have primarily attempted to outline the behaviors or beliefs of single villages or tribes. New ideas of culture, however—particularly those promoted under the banner of cultural studies—have consistently recognized that such homogeneity is an abstraction and something which, in a complex, changing, modern, industrial world, needs to be rethought and revised (Rosaldo, 1989).

The idea of community has undergone a similar transformation. Nineteenth-century comparisons between simple and cohesive rural community and complex and divisive urban society seem oddly out of place in the modern world, where racial, ethnic, religious, class, and sexual differences pervade city and country alike. Instead of portraying a community as a group of people sharing the same beliefs or bound by interdependent roles, many scholars today espouse a view of community that is based in power and conflict, a complex conglomeration of smaller communities and subgroups, continually negotiating the overall community's definition (Rosaldo 1989, pp. 27–28). Even scholars like Jennie Keith, who have defined community rather traditionally in terms of geography, talk about faction and conflict (1982).

There have been clear cases of conflict among Springsteen fans, in which one group of fans has exercised power in order to oust another fan or group of fans who have allegedly violated the rules of the community. For instance, toward the beginning of my fieldwork, one such case involved a Springsteen fan and collector who, after promising to make copies of a concert tape for other fans who sent him five dollars for his expenses and time, allegedly disappeared with people's money. His phone was disconnected, he didn't respond to e-mail postings, and soon speculation about his whereabouts were regular features of the *Digest*. While a few people defended his name, many people were angry.

The collector had clearly violated the trust of many fans and was held up by them as an example of how Springsteen fans ought not to behave. My wife has often commented that "Bruce Springsteen fans are such nice people." I have heard that again and again from the fans with whom I spoke for this project; they all believed that Springsteen fans, since they have a common bond and admire the music of someone who espouses a struggle for a better world, at least will treat each other with respect. In this case, the collector was branded as someone who did not live up to that widespread belief. Six months after the public questioning of the collector started, he posted a brief message of apology to *Backstreets Digest* and has not posted again.

In another instance, a fan who claimed to be the brother of Springsteen's wife joined the *Luckytown Digest* and proceeded to post all sorts of messages that purported to inform the other subscribers of "little-known facts" that any fan would have known, as well as several unsubstantiated rumors about upcoming Springsteen releases. His messages were written in a difficult-to-read, stream-of-consciousness style, with a variety of uppercase and lowercase letters and varied formatting. While some fans welcomed his presence, many others who had been active on the *Digest* complained. After a month or so, the administrator of *Luckytown* made an announcement that Bruce Springsteen's alleged brother-in-law had, through mutual agreement, withdrawn his subscription to the list.

While these instances of conflict were striking—perhaps more so because they were played out in a dramatic narrative over time on a public computer discussion group—conflict is common among fans. As I described in chapter 4, in the Springsteen fan community important social divisions are based on level of experience, age, region, attitude, and behavior. Even the differences in listening styles I mentioned in chapter 5 sometimes create barriers between fans. Who is allowed to use the label of "fan," who is a poseur or "casual fan," and what kinds of activities constitute fandom are, at any given moment, topics for debate and discussion among fans. Such discussion and debate point to a community that is continually trying to define itself and address the experiences of its various members or adapt to those of new members.

I think, however, what's ultimately important in talking about the fan community is not necessarily its divisions or the exercises of power which shape its contours but rather the tenacity of its coherence, the fact that such a diverse and widespread group of people even *have* feelings of belonging and even *come to develop* meaningful social relations in the first place. Unlike geographical communities, where divisions and exercises of power seem to go against the "given" continuity and cultural unity of the land, as it were, in the nongeographical community of Springsteen fans, feelings of unity and continuity seem to go against the "given" divisions and unequal power relations that stem from their diverse geographical and social locations.

What needs to be recognized is that creating a fan community is hard work.

Through storytelling, fans outline who they are and what they share, and they attempt to orient their behavior toward one another. This does not mean that the Springsteen fan community is static or a monolithic entity. Groups of fans are continually debating certain issues and negotiating significant differences in philosophy and behavior. At times, such division has the potential to fracture the large, ideal community presented by Bruce stories into several subgroups. But fans consistently make a conscious effort to return to common ground—to call for more Bruce stories in order to save fans from "nitpicking," for instance, or to remind each other why they became fans in the first place.

Linda Warner once told me, "I think it's really hard to be a Bruce fan by yourself. It's something you really want to share with other people" (interview, March 25, 1993). Although fans in general continue to be stereotyped as isolated, obsessive loners engaging in abnormal, "unhealthy" social relations with imaginary public figures, Springsteen fans' creation and maintenance of community shows that they not only have a connection with Bruce Springsteen but also are struggling to share, connect, and ally with one another.

Conclusion

Toward an Experience-Near Understanding of Popular Music

Early on in graduate school, I wrote a paper for a seminar on popular culture in which I used cultural theory to interpret the activities of Springsteen fans. Specifically, drawing on the work of neo-Marxist theorists of culture like Antonio Gramsci, Stuart Hall, and Frederic Jameson, I argued that Springsteen fans were consumers who, in a certain position of economic power since they were regular and dependable customers, sought to actively resist marketing manipulation by Columbia Records. By analyzing closely record company advertising for each of Springsteen's releases and then also the fan "response" in *Backstreets* magazine, I showed how fans constantly redefined their tastes in order to engage the record company in a process of negotiation about the meaning of Springsteen's image.

Such an interpretation of fandom as social and political "resistance" seemed to fit with the tone of the class I was taking and also with the academic study of popular culture in general. It was (and still is) commonplace to think about popular culture as a tug-of-war between corporations and consumers, to talk about a "star system" and "consumption," about "ideology" and "utopia," and about "negotiation" and the "struggle for hegemony." By speaking such a language and engaging in those theories, I was striving to become a member of a specific interpretive community, to prove myself a "serious" academic scholar of popular culture.

However, while writing such a paper, I became increasingly uncomfortable with my argument. While it made sense to me in an abstract way as an intellectual, I also knew that it did not fit with the way I, as a fan, understood fandom. I had never thought about Springsteen's image or being manipulated or resisting record company hegemony much before writing that paper, nor had any of the fans I knew. In fact, such things seemed quite irrelevant to my experience. At best, I felt that the paper was too strident, wrapped up in a leftist intellectual agenda at which most fans would raise their eyebrows and roll their eyes. At worst, I felt as if it was disrespectful to the people I knew, attributing motives and plots to their behavior without even asking them for their own understanding of what they were doing. In the end, I handed the paper in, but I was so disgusted with it that I didn't even read the professor's comments when I got it back.

This book is, in many ways, a reaction to that paper, an attempt to set the record straight and find a way to be both an intellectual *and* a fan. In particular, I have tried to create a portrayal of fandom that values fans' own ideas and understandings of who they are, what they do, and why. Too many times in the study of popular culture, it seems to me, people's understandings of their actions are revised according to scholars' ideological concerns—that is, either dismissed as "false consciousness" or "pathology" or transformed into "resistance" or "rebellion." Such characterizations completely circumvent the ideas and beliefs of the very people they address and, ultimately, affect. Instead, I have sought to engage fandom as it is experienced. I have repeatedly met and talked with fans, listened to what they have to say about who they are, circulated questionnaires, and analyzed my own experiences both in the field and as a fellow fan.

Of course, I have not abandoned scholarship and simply taken for granted that what audiences and fans say is the absolute and only truth. I am an academic, trained in the conventions of scholarship in the humanities and social sciences, and, to understand fans' activities and motivations, I have employed numerous "academic" theories in the course of the text. But I have attempted to use such theories in a dialogue with fans' own theories, moving from the lived experience of fans, to scholarship that illuminates or challenges that experience, and back again. I have tried to avoid the tendency to see everything as a "text" to be "read," which locates meaning solely in the cleverness of interpretation and which can easily descend into specious armchair theorizing. Instead, I have tried to follow models from folklore and anthropology that locate meaning *in people* and are based on collaboration and dialogue between scholars and those they encounter in "the field."

I hope that this project does at least present a challenge to the studies of fandom (and popular culture more generally) currently in vogue. While media critics tend to value fandom as a model for the dangers of mass consumerism and cultural studies scholars value it as a marginal activity that serves to open up pockets of political resistance, fans value their fandom for the ways it addresses the existential reality of their daily lives, how it creates needed meaning, identity, and community in a world in which such things are absent or ephemeral. Although media critics and cultural studies scholars are often concerned with these issues—particularly identity—such concern is often situated in an abstract context of social institutions and structures of power. Fans are not necessarily thinking about where they stand in an abstract, larger social order or how their fandom can change that order; rather, they are concerned with how to get through each day and how their participation in performance helps them to understand the fluctuating and contradictory experience of daily life and to make connections with other people around them.

In fact, rather than the metaphors of control used by media critics and cultural studies scholars to describe fandom, such as "starstruck," "textual poachers," or "popular productivity," Springsteen fans tend to rely on metaphors of religion for explaining who they are and what they do. Many of the fans to whom I spoke said that seeing Springsteen in concert is "inspirational" or a "religious experience" in which one might have an "epiphany" or be "baptized." One fan said, "A couple friends and I, who were Springsteen fans—we talked about going to a Springsteen show as going to church. You know, 'We're gonna go worship tonight.' In some ways, really, there's an element of truth in that." Several fans talked about "converting" others to Springsteen fandom or "spreading the gospel," as if they were proselytizing; others talked about making "pilgrimages" to the towns where Springsteen grew up or the places he mentions in his songs; still others had walls of Springsteen pictures or shelves of collectibles in their homes or at work that they dubbed "shrines."

As I mentioned in chapter 2, the connection between fandom and religion even goes beyond this metaphorical language; there are several structural parallels between the lives of Christian believers and the lives of fans. Both Christianity and fandom often involve a "turning," the development of a close attachment to an unattainable other; the stories both fans and evangelical Christians tell about such experiences have a similar structure and social importance. Connected to that turning is the fact that Christianity and fandom involve a particular kind of moral orientation in which people derive meaning and value not from direct communication with the other but rather by signs and representations; as Christians' ongoing, daily life of devotion to God involves interpretation of the Bible and thinking about how God's will is revealed in their lives, so fans' ongoing, daily life of devotion to music involves interpretation of Springsteen's songs and puzzling over how the music addresses their experiences. Finally, Christianity and fandom engender similar kinds of community based on the sharing of a specific but largely immeasurable devotion and rituals and traditions that sustain that devotion. One could even draw parallels between divisions in Christianity, based on theological differences about the nature of faith, and the divisions among Springsteen fans over ideals of commitment, attitude, and behavior.

Because of such structural parallels, people have sometimes interpreted fandom literally as a kind of "cult." For instance, in a letter to the editors of *Backstreets* in 1987, a reader wrote:

> I must compliment you on your one-of-a-kind magazine. I too am a Bruce Springsteen fan and respect him in many ways—even though I disagree with several of

his beliefs. Springsteen is a human being just like the rest of us, who happens to have a very special talent. A talent given to him by God and to be used for God. It seems to me that you tend to "worship" Springsteen as if he were some kind of immortal being with no faults. . . . I am not trying to tell you that being a Bruce Springsteen fan is wrong or is a sin. I'm simply trying to have you consider whether you have dedicated your life to God or whether you have dedicated your life to Bruce Springsteen, man. (DiNatale 1987)

Similarly, BBC journalist Ted Harrison wrote a book on Elvis fans in which he argued that Elvis fan culture represents "a religion in embryo." In particular, he outlined the religious aspects of the culture, such as an emphasis on an "Elvis Gospel," the worship of "icons and relics," and the power of the Elvis "resurrection myth" (Harrison 1992).

Such interpretations miss the point. Fans' use of religious language in explaining and thinking about fandom and the clear parallels between their behavior and that of Christian believers do not mean that fandom *is* a religion; rather, they point to the fact that both fandom and religion are addressing similar concerns and engaging people in similar ways. David Merrill explained:

Two weeks ago I was on a trip to visit Civil War Battlefields with a group of mostly older folks, myself being the youngest. I would say that our ages ranged from 37–67. Anyhow, one day while we were driving around in the van (10 of us) one of the younger ladies (closer to my age) and I discovered that we both shared a common interest in Bruce. We began talking about concerts we had seen and various experiences, etc. When I said something to the effect of "after a Springsteen concert you feel like you've been to church" it drew a scoff from one of the older ladies (very active in her local church, choir leader I might add). I did not even try to explain the sort of revival feeling that a Bruce concert provides, since this lady was obviously from a very different musical orientation than myself (she mentioned having seen Glenn Miller), however my younger Bruce compatriot understood exactly what I meant!!

Anyhow, I thought it interesting that this "Bruce as religious experience" came up again, especially in this situation. All sorts of things fill in for religion for people who do not go to church, and music is certainly one of those things for me, and I definitely do feel as if I've been to a "spiritual revival" after a Bruce show, but it is very difficult to explain that to folks who have not experienced that feeling. (personal correspondence, November 8, 1995)

For some fans, like Carrie Gabriel, fandom is similar to religion in that it represents a search for values. "This obsession I have for Bruce is not a sexual thing," she explained, "as I hope you could tell. It's much more of a spiritual thing. I really do see Bruce as my savior. His songs are my bible. His words are just about all the 'truth' I see in this world" (personal correspondence, March 22, 1995). For other fans, like Laurie McLain, fandom simply has the same kind of substance or weight as religion does. She said: "I don't want to be deistic about it. Or theistic.

But there's a certain importance that it has that's aside from the rest of life" (interview, March 28, 1993). On the whole, as religion somehow stands "aside from the rest of life" and represents an alternative society based on the kingdom of God, fandom represents for fans a refuge from the turmoil of everyday life, an institution that exists above the ordinary and provides a steady and continual source of values, identity, and belonging.

Ultimately, the connections between fandom and religion point to the important function and meaning of performance in the daily lives of people living in modern industrial society. Performance which entertains, such as theater and spectacle (rock music may be included in such a category), has been generally characterized as an opportunity for spectators to think through and experiment with roles, behaviors, and meanings important to them. In the words of Richard Schechner (1985), performance is "twice-behaved behavior"; it recasts and heightens accepted models of reality. Thus, anthropologist Clifford Geertz, for instance, talks about the Balinese cockfight as working to "materialize a way of experiencing, bring a particular cast of mind into the world of objects where men can look at it" (1973, p. 443), and Victor Turner (1988, pp. 99–122) talks about how performances enact moments of liminality, where the structure of a society (including its roles, institutions, and divisions) may be suspended temporarily and substituted with a new "antistructure" to help people probe their society's roles, institutions, and divisions. Anthropologist William Beeman has summed up these theories by saying that theater, as a form of entertainment performance, "does even more than engage participants and spectators in the immediate context of the theatrical event. It evokes and solidifies a network of social and cognitive relationships existing in a triangular relationship between performer, spectator, and the world at large" (1993, p. 386; see also Babcock 1980; MacAloon 1984; Barnouw and Kirkland 1992).

Clearly, fandom, as a role born in rock music performance, affirms this sort of "metathinking" on the part of spectators; again and again in this study I have shown how fans are engaged in examining themselves and their place in the world. However, I would argue that fandom goes one step further and represents a heightening of this heightening of reality. As I explained in chapter 4, fandom involves an extension of the performance-based feelings of connection and community into daily life. Such participation beyond the performance frame points to more than a temporary time-out to reaffirm or reshape existential meanings; it is, like religion, a continual *source* of such meaning. Fandom sustains the reflexive properties of performance so that every time one acts as a fan, one is launched into a realm where personal, cultural, and human values are brought into relief and opened to scrutiny. That's why it is important for fans, and that's why it should be of particular interest to scholars.

Anthropologist Clifford Geertz (borrowing terms from psychoanalyst Heinrich Kohut) has talked about two different approaches to cultural life: "experience-distant," which is based on use of concepts which "specialists of one sort or another . . . employ to forward their scientific, philosophical, or practical aims," and "experience-near," which is based on use of concepts which someone "might himself naturally and effortlessly use to define what he or his fellows see, feel, think, imagine, and so on" (Geertz 1984). In this project, I have clearly been arguing for the importance of experience-near concepts. While media critics and cultural studies scholars assume that fans are either duped by the commercial media industry or are so close to their experiences that they are unable to see that they are actually engaging in hegemonic struggle, I have shown that fans have their own ideas about what they are doing, which are different than both of these interpretations.

I do not want to argue that everyone should stop conducting analyses of texts and making abstract generalizations about culture and its institutions. Such experience-distant work has an important and necessary place in scholarship and human understanding. However, if scholars of popular culture are truly interested in creating an informed and useful understanding of the world and in any way having a lasting role in public debate, then they've got to start being more relevant, start engaging the ideas of the people about whom they write, or risk tunneling deeper into caverns of inscrutability and isolating themselves with ineffectual and circular debate. Fandom may figure in the power of the mass culture industry, and it may also be a kind of twentieth-century cult, but for fans, it is about devotion, creating meaning in daily life through sustained attention to musical performance. Without recognizing fans' feelings *in their own terms*, scholars of popular culture engage in the very "colonizing discourse" to which their work is supposed to be an antidote.

Of course, giving fans a voice in their own representations complicates matters of knowledge. Fans and academics, in many ways, speak different languages, and, like academics, not all fans agree on everything. Opening up scholarship to fans also raises vexing questions about ethical responsibility, about who is qualified to speak, and whose knowledge counts and when. Don't academics' years of education and training qualify them to speak about certain subjects with authority? But who are they to say that fans' own understanding of their fandom is wrong or really means something else? Addressing such issues is the only way to achieve knowledge of popular music which is relevant, useful, and ultimately meaningful to both those who find it intellectually important and those who participate in it. In general, there is a need for less scholarly arrogance and more cooperation, less looking and taking and representing and more meeting and sharing and learning, and fewer scholars speaking *for* others and more speaking *with* others. Only then will the study of popular music move toward being what popular music itself is for those who love it: something which excites and angers, motivates and provokes, brings people together, and makes sense of the world.

Postscript

Much has changed since I began this project in the spring of 1993. At that time, Bruce Springsteen was in the middle of a U.S. tour in support of his two simultaneous CDs, *Human Touch* and *Lucky Town,* which he had released a year earlier after a five-year hiatus in recording. Given Springsteen's usual hibernation between album releases, no one much expected any more activity from him until at least 1996. But he proved everyone wrong.

For one thing, after 1993, he became unusually active in recording and releasing works. He started contributing songs to Hollywood films, including "Streets of Philadelphia" for *Philadelphia* in 1993, "Dead Man Walking" for the movie of the same name in 1995, and in 1996 "Missing" for *The Crossing Guard* and "Secret Garden" for *Jerry MacGuire.* He did various tribute performances, including a cover of Curtis Mayfield's "Gypsy Woman" for a 1994 tribute album to Mayfield, and a live set at the opening concert for the Rock and Roll Hall of Fame and Museum in 1995, a recording of which was released in 1997. Finally, he released three major works: a compilation of his songs, *Greatest Hits,* in 1995; a CD of acoustic songs, *The Ghost of Tom Joad,* also in 1995; and a video documentary and CD called *Blood Brothers,* about his reunion with the E Street Band for *Greatest Hits,* in 1996.

In addition to this musical activity, he was given, for the first time in his career, a number of prestigious awards. He won both a Golden Globe and an Academy Award for "Streets of Philadelphia" in 1994. He won four Grammy Awards, including "Song of the Year" for "Streets of Philadelphia," in March 1995. He won another Grammy Award—best folk album—in 1996 for *The Ghost of Tom Joad.* In 1997 he was awarded the Polar Music Prize from the Royal Swedish Academy of Music, and by the time this book is published in 1998, he most likely will have been nominated for the Rock and Roll Hall of Fame.

Even more unprecedented is that Springsteen appeared for the first time on network television. He initially performed on *Saturday Night Live* and then on the last *David Letterman Show* on NBC in 1992. After that (perhaps deciding that television wasn't so bad), he made appearances on *Late Night wth David Letterman, The Tonight Show,* "The Grammy Awards" telecast, and even *60 Minutes.*

Fans have changed, too. Over the years, many of those that I met moved, got new jobs, graduated from school, married, divorced, had children, or lost relatives and friends. After I first spoke with Carrie Gabriel in the spring of 1994, when she told me about her dream of contacting Bruce Springsteen, she finally did just that after a concert in December 1995 and proudly shared with me photographs of her and Springsteen. When I first spoke with LeAnne Olderman in May 1993, she despaired of ever finding a man who liked Springsteen as much as she did; she has since become engaged to be married to a Springsteen fan she met through *Luckytown Digest.*

While many of the quotations and stories in this project stem from fans' fascination and exploration of Springsteen's work during the early nineties, now the same fans are thinking about Springsteen's new work, his new songs, his new direction in the mid nineties. Several fans even discovered Springsteen anew in his 1995 solo acoustic tour; if we talked now, they might have very different things to say about Springsteen and about their fandom. As Russ Curley wrote to me after reading a draft of this book and seeing a recent show:

> While before December 13, 1995, I agreed completely with adjectives such as "energetic" and "exhausting" to describe a Bruce show, since seeing the solo acoustic show in NYC I'd have to say those adjectives describe only one *type* of Bruce show. After seeing him in December I'd have to say "evocative," "emotional," "aching," "earnest," and "heartbreaking" now all fit in the lexicon of adjectives to describe a Bruce show. It was not a rock concert, it was more of a folk performance. The show proved that Springsteen can mesmerize a crowd without breaking a sweat, without yelling at the top of his voice, and without exciting the crowd to a fever pitch—he can do it sitting down, playing an acoustic guitar. You may have to write a whole new section! (personal correspondence, January 19, 1996)

I, too, have changed. For one, in 1996, I became a father for the first time. While I had appreciated Springsteen's take on family life on *Human Touch* (1992) and *Lucky Town* (1992) before, it was only after I started caring for my son during the day that the songs really struck a nerve. Judi Johnson had mentioned to me a few years before about recognizing her own parenthood in Springsteen's song "Living Proof" (1992), particularly the line about a child "crying like he swallowed the fiery moon." I now know exactly what she means.

When I began the project, I didn't know many Springsteen fans, other than my wife and my friend Mary from college; now I've either corresponded with or met about a hundred fans. While I was a latecomer to fandom and not very experienced in terms of concerts or knowledge, I now know a lot more about fandom—mine and others'—than I ever thought possible. I have listened to people's Bruce stories, engaged them in debate about Springsteen's work, and thought deeply about what it means to be a fan. Whereas I had only Springsteen's albums before I started the project, now I have a large collection of fanzines, books, and academic articles on Springsteen, a file cabinet filled with interview transcriptions, comments, and correspondence with fans, and various tapes and souvenirs I have exchanged with people as we met and shared our lives.

Of course, such knowledge has not come without a price. While I have learned a lot, I am not the same kind of fan that I once was. Whereas in the beginning, getting tickets and attending that concert in 1992, I was eager and excited about being a fan and exploring my experiences; now, I am warier, more careful about separating my "fandom" and my "scholarship," so that Bruce Springsteen does not become "work." Indeed, while working on this project gave me the luxury of focusing my personal and professional energies on the world of Bruce Springsteen for most of each day, and it was exhilarating at first, maintaining my relationship with Springsteen has become more of a struggle because of my intense consciousness of it. When I listen to a Springsteen song, I am unable to simply enjoy its energy or emotion or what it tells me about my life; instead, that enjoyment is more complicated by a self-awareness of that enjoyment, by the ways in which the act of listening to Springsteen is wrapped up with my professional identity, and with my experiences with the people I've met.

I'm also tired. When tickets went on sale in Boston for Springsteen's solo acoustic tour in September 1995, I had an important appointment in Providence, but rather than abandoning everything to go get in line, I chose to keep the appointment and let my wife give the tickets a go up in Boston. She waited for an hour but was unable to get a wristband; while I felt bad about the whole thing, at the same time, I found myself curiously unaffected. I suppose I had had my fill of Bruce Springsteen while working on this project day in and day out for three years; somehow missing a concert didn't seem to be as big a deal as I thought it might.

Such changes of feeling are not unique or necessarily connected to academic work. For some people, the familiarity and knowledge created by fan activity eventually leads to burnout. Several of the older fans to whom I spoke talked about having to dig deeper and deeper into Springsteen's performances to find something which interested them. After exhausting the body of Springsteen's recorded work, including concert tapes and bootlegs; reading everything there was about him in books, magazines, and newspapers; participating daily on computer discussion groups; and seeing twenty or more concerts, such fans simply become bored. As one fan admitted when we first spoke:

> In the beginning, I ate up every single live recording I could. I had two real goals: to get the stories and the rare songs. After years of trading, I have met those goals and now have so many of the stories, rare songs, goof-ups, etc., that the thrill of

getting a new one has worn off. So the fun is wearing thin. Couple that with the fact that his set lists are pretty static nowadays, and he's rarely ever telling stories, and there's very little fun left. In addition, my daughters are getting older and I have so many other activities going on that trading is becoming more of a wearisome job than the fun it once was . . . it's time to move onto another hobby. Okay, I've already moved on. I'm now into mountain climbing. That's taking a great amount of time, and I have to find time to do the trading.

These changes are inevitable; people grow, tire, and become affected by the world around them in different ways as time relentlessly moves forward. And, as I said, in this project, I have made it a point to base my discussion on the lives of real people in a specific period of time. Some strengthened their fandom while others seemed to let go of it a bit, moving on to other things. Some people have kept in contact with me, interested in the final draft; others have spoken with me once and then drifted away silently. On the whole, this book is bound to reflect a few contradictions, a few inconsistencies that we all tend to live with in the amorphous flow of everyday reality but recognize only when we are confronted with them in the somewhat harsh and concrete stasis of print.

Nevertheless, I think that the general themes and concerns I have outlined remain accurate and are important to an understanding of what fandom means to fans. I have defined music fandom as a somewhat flexible position created in the relationships involved between people in any musical performance; by doing so, I have emphasized fans' view of themselves as located in a complex modern world of both mediate and immediate others. Fandom is based on a special and lasting attachment to Springsteen but is shaped in the intersection of all sorts of emergent relationships: with Springsteen in and out of performance, with the music business, with ordinary audience members, with other fans. In addition, I have addressed what is at stake in fandom for fans; I have specifically focused on the ways in which people use their fandom to manage daily emotions and values and to create personal and social identity. Fans' listening, collecting, and storytelling are all activities which give them a strong sense of purpose and well-being; their feelings of value, self, and community really matter in their lives and go some way in making them more meaningful.

Not all fans have agreed with every detail of what I've said, of course. Not all fans feel the same way about Springsteen, the music business, or about other audience members, and not all fans equally use the music to make meaning, shape a sense of self, or create community. But, on the whole, most of the fans who read and responded to drafts of this project at least located themselves in it and found it meaningful for them. As Al Khorasani said, "It was like seeing an old friend. Reading your thesis and reading about other fans and his music is like a therapy for me." Mary Beth Wilson explained:

The amazing part of reading these five chapters was having people—total strangers—describe things I have felt or experienced. My feelings about Bruce are so personal and close to me it's truly amazing when you read other people saying the same things. Every Bruce fan comes to the table with different stories, for different reasons, looking for different things, but at the core are the words and music of one man. Some may think it weird. I prefer to call it powerful. (personal correspondence, November 19, 1995)

A project like this one never really ends. Fans' lives are not loose threads to be neatly tied up and summarized so that we may all move on to other concerns or other projects. After this book goes out of print, fans will continue to listen to Springsteen and use their fandom to make and remake meaning in their lives. And I know that we will continue our dialogues, revisiting each other to check on what we are doing and thinking. That "checking in" is a large part of fandom; in writing and reading fanzines, participating on computer lists, attending concerts, sharing Bruce stories, and even buying Springsteen's latest releases, fans find others and learn from them. It is up to scholars to do the same and join the discussion.

Appendix A

Springsteen Fan Questionnaire

This questionnaire is part of a Ph.D. project I am conducting on music fandom. The questions are intended to elicit your experiences as a fan, as well as the role music plays in your daily life. Please return the questionnaire to me in the self-addressed stamped envelope, or to Daniel Cavicchi, Department of American Civilization, Box——, Brown University, Providence, RI 02912. Thanks for your time and cooperation.

1. How long have you been a Springsteen fan?   _____ years

2. Had you heard of Springsteen before you became a fan?   Y   N

3. How did you become a Springsteen fan?

   _____ friends/relatives introduced me   _____ I heard one of his songs
   to the music   on the radio
   _____ happened slowly over time   _____ I saw him perform
   _____ I became friends with a fan   _____ I saw/heard/read about him in
   _____ I bought one of his albums   the media
                                              _____ other:

4. Have you seen Springsteen in concert?   Y   N

5. If yes, when did you see him? (indicate no. of shows per tour, if applicable):

   _____ early appearances (1965–1974)   _____ Born in the USA Tour
   _____ Born to Run Tour (1975–1977)   (1984–1985)
   _____ Darkness Tour (1978–1979)   _____ Amnesty Human Rights Now!
   _____ The River Tour (1980–1981)   Tour (1988)
   _____ Tunnel of Love Express Tour   _____ HT/LT Tour (1992–1993)
   (1988)   _____ Other (club appearances,
                                              benefits, etc.)

6. What was your favorite concert?

7. What is most important to you when attending a Springsteen concert?

    _____ seeing Bruce   _____ being with other fans
    _____ seeing the band   _____ partying
    _____ hearing the music arranged live _____ other:
    _____ hearing Bruce's stories

8. What three adjectives would you use to describe Springsteen in concert?

    _____   _____   _____

9. Do you own all of Springsteen's official recordings?   Y   N

10. Which official recording is your favorite?

11. Do you collect/trade concert tapes?   Y   N

12. Which is your favorite concert tape?

13. On average, how many hours do you listen to music each day? (circle one)

    1   2   3   4   5   6   7   8+

14. On average, what percentage of your overall listening is devoted to Springsteen?
    (circle one)

    10%   20   30   40   50   60   70   80   90   100%

15. What other performers or music do you like?

16. When do you listen to Springsteen? (check all that apply):

    _____ in the car   _____ while doing an activity (cook-
    _____ at work/school   ing, cleaning, running, etc.)
    _____ at home after work/school   _____ occasionally, at no particular
    _____ when I'm getting ready to   time
            go out   _____ other:
    _____ before I go to sleep

17. Complete the following: "In general, I use Springsteen's music to":

    _____ find inspiration   _____ remember the past   _____ work through
    _____ have fun   _____ socialize with others   my moods
    _____ relax   _____ think about life   _____ other:

18. What other Springsteen-related items do you own, if any?

_____ books	_____ import singles	_____ T-shirts
_____ bootleg recordings	_____ photographs	_____ videos
_____ concert ticket stubs	_____ pins	_____ other:
_____ fanzines	_____ posters	

19. Do you know other Springsteen fans?   Y   N

20. How do nonfans (i.e., family members, friends, coworkers) view your fandom in general?

_____ they approve	_____ they don't care
_____ they think it's strange	_____ they aren't interested but understand

21. What would you say to Bruce if you met him?

22. What is your age? _____

23. You are: (circle one)   Male   Female

24. Education completed (circle one):

    A. some high school
    B. high school diploma
    C. some college
    D. college degree

25. Present employment (circle one):

    A. unemployed
    B. part-time
    C. full-time
    Occupation: _____

26. Marital status: (circle one):   single   married   divorced

27. Would you be willing to talk further about your interest in Bruce Springsteen?   Y   N
    If yes, leave name and phone or e-mail address where I might contact you:

If you wish to elaborate on any of your answers above, please feel free to attach an additional sheet of paper.
Thanks!   DRC 10/93

Appendix B

Bruce Springsteen, American Discography
(Major Works)

Greetings from Asbury Park, N.J. 1973. Blinded by the Light; Growin' Up; Mary Queen of Arkansas; Does This Bus Stop at 82nd Street?; Lost in the Flood; The Angel; For You; Spirit in the Night; It's Hard to Be a Saint in the City. CD Columbia CK 31903.

The Wild, the Innocent, and the E Street Shuffle. 1973. The E Street Shuffle; 4th of July, Asbury Park (Sandy); Kitty's Back; Wild Billy's Circus Story; Incident on 57th Street; Rosalita (Come Out Tonight); New York City Serenade. CD Columbia CK 32432.

Born to Run. 1975. Thunder Road; Tenth Avenue Freeze-out; Night; Backstreets; Born to Run; She's the One; Meeting across the River; Jungleland. CD Columbia CK 33795.

Darkness on the Edge of Town. 1978. Badlands; Adam Raised a Cain; Something in the Night; Candy's Room; Racing in the Street; The Promised Land; Factory; Streets of Fire; Prove It All Night; Darkness on the Edge of Town. CD Columbia CK 35318.

The River. 1980. The Ties That Bind; Sherry Darling; Jackson Cage; Two Hearts; Independence Day; Hungry Heart; Out in the Street; Crush on You; You Can Look (But You Better Not Touch); I Wanna Marry You; The River; Point Blank; Cadillac Ranch; I'm a Rocker; Fade Away; Stolen Car; Ramrod; The Price You Pay; Drive All Night; Wreck on the Highway. CD Columbia C2K 36854.

Nebraska. 1982. Nebraska; Atlantic City; Mansion on the Hill; Johnny 99; Highway Patrolman; State Trooper; Used Cars; Open All Night; My Father's House; Reason to Believe. CD Columbia CK 38358.

Born in the USA. 1984. Born in the USA; Cover Me; Darlington County; Working on the Highway; Downbound Train; I'm on Fire; No Surrender; Bobby Jean; I'm Goin' Down; Glory Days; Dancing in the Dark; My Hometown. CD Columbia CK 38653.

Live 1975–85. 1986. Thunder Road; Adam Raised a Cain; Spirit in the Night; 4th of July, Asbury Park (Sandy); Paradise by the "C"; Fire; Growin' Up; It's Hard to be a Saint in the City; Backstreets; Rosalita (Come Out Tonight); Raise Your Hand; Hungry Heart; Two Hearts; Cadillac Ranch; You Can Look (But You Better Not Touch); Independence Day; Badlands; Because the Night; Candy's Room; Darkness on the Edge of Town; Racing in the Street; This Land Is Your Land; Nebraska; Johnny 99; Reason to Believe; Born in the USA; Seeds; The River; War; Darlington County; Working on the Highway; The Promised Land; Cover Me; I'm on Fire; Bobby Jean; My Hometown; Born to Run; No Surrender; Tenth Avenue Freeze-out; Jersey Girl. LP Columbia/CBS CX5 40558.

Tunnel of Love. 1987. Ain't Got You; Tougher Than the Rest; All That Heaven Will Allow; Spare Parts; Cautious Man; Walk Like a Man; Tunnel of Love; Two Faces; Brilliant Disguise; One Step Up; When You're Alone; Valentine's Day. CD Columbia CK 40999.

Human Touch. 1992. Human Touch; Soul Driver; 57 Channels (and Nothin' On); Cross My Heart; Gloria's Eyes; With Every Wish; Roll of the Dice; Real World; All or Nothin' at All; Man's Job; I Wish I Were Blind; The Long Goodbye; Real Man; Pony Boy. CD Columbia CK 53000.

Lucky Town. 1992. Better Days; Lucky Town; Local Hero; If I Should Fall Behind; Leap of Faith; The Big Muddy; Living Proof; Book of Dreams; Soul of the Departed; My Beautiful Reward. CD Columbia CK 53001.

In Concert: MTV Plugged. 1992. Red Headed Woman; Better Days; Atlantic City; Darkness on the Edge of Town; Man's Job; Human Touch; Lucky Town; I Wish I Were Blind; Thunder Road; Light of Day; If I Should Fall Behind; Living Proof; My Beautiful Reward. CD Columbia CK 68730.

Greatest Hits. 1995. Born to Run; Thunder Road; Badlands; The River; Hungry Heart; Atlantic City; Dancing in the Dark; Born in the USA; My Hometown; Glory Days; Brilliant Disguise; Human Touch; Better Days; Streets of Philadelphia; Secret Garden; Murder Incorporated; Blood Brothers; This Hard Land. CD Columbia CK 67060.

The Ghost of Tom Joad. 1995. The Ghost of Tom Joad; Straight Time; Highway 25; Youngstown; Sinaloa Cowboys; The Line; Balboa Park; Dry Lightning; The New Timer; Across the Border; Galveston Bay; My Best Was Never Good Enough. CD Columbia CK 67484.

Notes

1. In an informal gleaning done in record stores around Boston in the summer of 1992, I located 42 different unofficial fanzines for music groups, which did not include the equal or greater number of publications I found focusing on music scenes or genres. In June 1993, something called the "Musical List of Lists" on the Internet listed 267 computer discussion groups about music.

2. The show first aired in October 1992 and featured female fans of Michael Bolton, Scott Baio, and Carl Weathers. Oprah Winfrey emphasized her incredulity: "I never had—I really don't get it because—is the fantasy that you're someday going to be with him or something? Is that part of it?"

3. Mark Chapman killed John Lennon after getting an autograph; John Hinckley Jr., a Jody Foster admirer, attempted to assassinate President Reagan.

4. For a history of the Frankfurt School, see Jay 1973. "Cultural Studies" is a notoriously vague label; my understanding of it comes from Hall and Jefferson 1976; Hebdige [1979] 1991; Fiske 1989; Grossberg 1992b; and Aronowitz 1993.

5. Sociologist D. M. Hayano (1979; 1982) has referred to this kind of research as "auto-ethnography."

6. Keil derived this term from Wilhelm Windelband's notion of the "idiographic sciences" (quoted in Bettelheim 1982).

7. Few people have used electronic mail to conduct ethnographic fieldwork; in fact, the "anthropology of cyberspace" is a practice only beginning to develop and gain recognition. See, for instance, Baym 1993; Stone 1991; and Tomas 1991.

8. To my knowledge, I have never been deceived by Springsteen fans on electronic mail, but the possibility exists. I made it a habit to obtain U.S. mail addresses from everyone to whom I spoke and to have them complete "e-mail consent" forms before using their words in my project.

1. Boston Garden has since been torn down and replaced with the Fleet Center, a large entertainment complex. I have left the description in the present tense—as it was written in 1993, soon after the concert—to avoid unnecessary confusion.

2. Dave Marsh (1987, p. 243) reports that these lines are an interpolation of lyrics from Chuck Berry and John Lennon.

3. The *We Are the World* album, including the title song and several other tracks do-

nated by artists, was released in 1985 as a way to raise funds for United Support of Artists for Africa, an organization started by several music stars including Michael Jackson, Harry Belafonte, and Quincy Jones, to help those starving on the African continent.

4. A winter storm blanketed Boston with snow and ice the day before.

5. Springsteen said, "And I'm pleased to introduce, ladies and gentlemen, my buddy, my pal, the man whose guitar licks are like honey, the man who goes to the record company to get me more money, a man that I met right here in this very town, a hometown boy—I'm talking about producer! seducer! wave reducer! the master of managerial disaster!—Jon Landau on guitar!" Before becoming Springsteen's manager, Landau was a rock critic for Boston's *Real Paper*.

6. Wolf, who hadn't toured since the J. Geils Band broke up in 1984, later recalled in the *Boston Globe* that he wasn't expecting to sing that night. "Bruce said, 'You belong out there. This is your town. It's your crowd. Get out there!'" Wolf explained. "Bruce was just so gracious. He said, 'Here's my band. Here's the stage. Just go for it.'" (Morse 1992, p. 62).

Chapter 2

1. The editors of the third edition of the *American Heritage Dictionary* (1992) classified "fan" as "informal," meaning that it is "acceptable in conversation with friends and colleagues [but] would be unsuitable in the formal prose of an article written for publication in the journal of a learned society, for example."

2. James actually borrowed the types from another psychologist of religion, E. D. Starbuck. See Starbuck's book, *Psychology of Religion* (1899).

3. David is referring to the refrains of two of Springsteen's hit songs, "Hungry Heart" (1980) and "Born to Run" (1975). He is implying that he knew only as much as any ordinary listener.

4. Springsteen's only previous video, of his song "Atlantic City," was released in 1982. It contained a series of black-and-white images of street scenes in the city, and he didn't appear in it.

5. During the 1984 presidential election campaign, Ronald Reagan created a minor brouhaha by mentioning Springsteen—who was clearly not a supporter of Reagan's social and economic policies—in a campaign speech in Hammonton, New Jersey. "America's future rests in a thousand dreams inside your hearts," he said. "It rests in the message of hope in songs by a man so many young Americans admire: New Jersey's own Bruce Springsteen. And helping you make those dreams come true is what this job of mine is all about" (Marsh 1987, pp. 260–266).

6. Jeff Titon (1988, p. 389) reported a similar occurrence in his work with Appalachian Baptists. The influences of researchers in the shaping of conversion narratives is a well-known problem in conversion research; see, for example, Beckford 1978 and Lofland and Skonovd 1981.

Chapter 3

1. Sony Music Entertainment, Inc., owns Springsteen's record label, Columbia Records.

2. Camille Bacon-Smith (1992, p. 282) raises the same analogy in reference to certain scholars of the media fanzine community.

3. A listing of all the probable songs, outtakes, and alternative tracks for Springsteen's recording sessions between 1966 and 1988 can be found in Cross et al. 1989, pp. 149–162. See also Humphries and Hunt 1985, pp. 119–130.

4. According to Heylin (1995, p. 8) pirates "copy official material but make no attempt to pass their product off as the original" while counterfeiters "try to replicate the official product, presumably with the intention of hoodwinking the public."

5. Given the controversial nature of concert tapes and bootlegs, I will not use specific names in this section in order to protect those to whom I spoke.

6. "Lost in the Flood" is the title of a song from Springsteen's 1973 Debut album, *Greetings from Asbury Park, N.J.*

7. Bruce Springsteen and his management have taken a similar view. When Bruce Springsteen was first becoming a star, he openly supported bootlegged recordings of his performances, did frequent radio broadcasts, and even once encouraged bootleggers from the stage, yelling, "Roll your tapes, bootleggers!" But then, after 1980, Springsteen and CBS sued a bootlegger, Vicki Vinyl, for copyright infringement, with Springsteen explaining: "When I first started out, a lot of the bootlegs were made by fans, and there was a lot more of a connection. But there came a point where there were just so many made by people who didn't care what the quality was" (Heylin 1995, p. 136).

8. Judi is referring to Springsteen's practice of moving random audience members in the rearmost rows into the front rows.

Chapter 4

1. "Spirit in the Night" (1973) is rarely played live by Springsteen anymore.

2. Richard Bauman (1977, 1986) first used the idea of performance along these lines to move folklore away from a focus on texts to a focus on "verbal behavior."

3. Victor Turner (1974) has defined this kind of framed feeling as "communitas," a sense of solidarity at a performance in which people who are ordinarily are divided by various social categories such as class, race, and gender come together through their adoption of various performance roles.

4. Erving Goffman (1974) has written much about "breaking the frame," focusing especially on instances in which one's involvement in a particular frame may be disrupted or influenced by certain intrusions ("slippage" or "flooding") of what might be considered out-of-frame behavior. However, in the case of Springsteen fans, I think it may be more appropriate to talk of breaking the frame in the opposite direction, of the ways in which daily life, out of frame, is shaped by intrusions of *framed* behavior.

5. Springsteen made an appearance at the taping of Melissa Etheridge's *MTV Unplugged* performance in 1995.

Chapter 5

1. During fieldwork, I became aware that my own role as an academic encouraged fans to represent themselves as intellectual. While I think that such representations were entirely genuine, I think it is important to point out that the relationships I developed with some fans, at least initially, were due to the academic context of the project.

2. "Highway Patrolman" (1982) is a serious song about a police sheriff who must in-

vestigate his brother; "Pink Cadillac," a b-side released in 1984, is a more superficial song about love for a car.

3. During the *Born in the USA* tour in the mideighties, Springsteen often covered Edwin Starr's anti-Vietnam song, "War" and, in a long spoken introduction, warned his audience against blindly following leaders.

4. Of course, both social and individual forces are at play in this process. Fans use music according to established social conventions, but they also do so in terms of highly idiosyncratic and personal experiences and associations. Instead of separating such processes, as I did the previous section, I have combined them here; while I introduce general conventions of fans' uses of their listening, I let fans' own accounts point to the different ways in which they work within those conventions.

5. The quotation is the third verse of "Factory."

6. The 1990 Christic Institute Benefit Show was one of two concerts for the Christic Institute, an interfaith, nonpartisan, nonprofit center for public policy and public interest law in Washington, D.C. They took place at Shrine Auditorium in Los Angeles and included sets by artists Jackson Browne and Bonnie Raitt, as well as Springsteen. Springsteen gave what some fans see as some of his most moving performances, playing solo guitar or piano and covering several new songs, which later appeared, in different form, on 1992's *Human Touch*.

Chapter 6

1. This notion of the collection standing in for the self has been echoed in a number of works from different disciplines and genres. See, for instance, Koestenbaum 1993, pp. 62–69; Modell 1993, pp. 88–95; Baudrillard [1968] 1994; Windsor 1994.

2. James's idea of "self-seeking" can be seen as in some ways similar to the theories of French psychoanalyst Jacques Lacan, in which a person also searches for an ideal self. However, while James's ideal is the "potential self" that is chosen and sometimes realized, Lacan's ideal is the feeling of "non-self" that people automatically lose as they enter social life and is never recovered.

3. Leonard Pitts is a writer for the *Miami Herald*; Mark McEwen is the co-anchor of *CBS Morning News*; Al Roker is the weatherman on NBC's *Today Show*; and J. J. Jackson was a VJ for MTV during Springsteen's height of fame in the mideighties.

4. The idea that the collection can help organize a history of the self has also been articulated by Benjamin 1968 and Rheims 1980, p. 211.

Chapter 7

1. Some fans also use the term "Bruce stories" to refer to stories about Springsteen and his career. While I do not dispute such a usage, to avoid confusion, I have chosen to use the term here to refer solely to stories about being a fan.

References

Interviews

Anderson, Kirk. April 27, 1993. Conversation over drinks at the bar in B. B. Binks Restaurant, Norton, Massachusetts.

Chyzowych, Gene. April 21, 1993. Meeting in Waggoner Room, at the Department of American Civilization, Brown University.

Curley, Russell. April 20, 1993. Meeting in the Blue Room, Faunce House, Brown University.

———. November 2, 1993. Meeting in kitchen of Department of American Civilization, Brown University.

Everson, Zachary. October 23, 1993. Meeting at his parents' home, Reading, Massachusetts.

Fischer, Paul. May 25, 1993. Telephone conversation.

Gabriel, Carrie. April 26, 1995. Meeting in an office at the Department of American Civilization, Brown University.

Gillis, Jacqueline. May 12 to June 16, 1993. Electronic mail dialogue.

Johnson, Judi. January 13, 1994. Telephone conversation.

Khorasani, Al. March 23, 1993. Telephone conversation.

———. October 28, 1993. Telephone conversation.

Krause, Mary, and Lynn Cavicchi. April 30, 1993. After-dinner conversation at the Cavicchi home in Norton, Massachusetts.

Laurence, Andrew. May 12 to November 2, 1993. Electronic mail dialogue.

Levine, Alan. April 2, 1993. Telephone conversation.

Lucullo, Louis. March 21 to August 23, 1993. Electronic mail dialogue.

McLain, Laurie. March 9 to March 16, 1993. Electronic mail dialogue.

———. March 28, 1993. Telephone conversation.

Merrill, David. March 9 to May 25, 1993. Electronic mail dialogue.

Mocko, David. May 11 to June 10, 1993. Electronic mail dialogue.

O'Brien, John. March 15, 1993. Meeting in the Waggoner Room, Department of American Civilization, Brown University.

Olderman, LeAnne. May 13, 1993. Telephone conversation.

Rummel, J. D. May 7 to June 7, 1993. Electronic mail dialogue.

Selden, Anna. January 12, 1994. Telephone conversation.

Sirk, Andrew. March 5, 1993. Telephone conversation.

Smith, Monty. March 15 to May 12, 1993. Electronic mail dialogue.

Stein, Alan. May 24, 1993. Conversation over lunch at the Lemon Grass Restaurant, Lexington, Massachusetts.

———. October 7, 1993. Conversation over lunch at the Lemon Grass Restaurant, Lexington, Massachusetts.

Thom, Amy. April 1, 1993. Telephone conversation.

Van Atten, Mark. March 11 to June 22, 1993. Electronic mail dialogue.

———. December 7 to December 14, 1993. Electronic mail dialogue.

West, Susan. March 9 to May 14, 1993. Electronic mail dialogue.

Warner, Linda. March 25, 1993. Telephone conversation.

Wilson, Mary Beth. January 17, 1994. Telephone conversation.

Internet Online Postings

Andrulis, Cathy. 1995. "Subject: Secret Garden." *Luckytown Digest* 2.125 (March 2).

Antonia. 1995. "Subject: Am I really a fan???" *Luckytown Digest* 2.169 (April 5).

Aristidis, Arvanitis. 1995. "Subject: Reflecting on the new songs, the tour, etc." *Luckytown Digest* 2.424 (December 12).

Beth. 1995. "Black Audience (?)." *Luckytown Digest* 2.181 (April 17).

Bulger, Mike. 1995. "Subject: BitUSA." *Luckytown Digest* 2.435 (December 18).

Burke, Tom. 1995. "Subject: Born in the U.S.A./Patriotism." *Luckytown Digest* 2.432 (December 16).

Carl. 1995. "Re Question for Foreign Fans." *Luckytown Digest* 2.183 (April 18).

Cavicchi, Daniel. 1993. "Subject: Reason to Believe." *Backstreets Digest* 2.314 (October 6).

Cecchini, Ron. 1995a. "Subject: Question for Foreign Fans." *Luckytown Digest* 2.181 (April 17).

———. 1995b. "Subject: Re Question for Foreign Fans." *Luckytown Digest* 2.184 (April 19).

Detweiler, Anne. 1995. "Subject: Women identifying with Bruce." *Luckytown Digest* 2.157 (March 25).

Dropdog. 1995. "Poll results? and some stuff." *Luckytown Digest* 2.173 (April 9).

Duerr, Linda. 1995. "Subject: SG." *Luckytown Digest* 2.129 (March 3).

Eric. 1993. "Subject: The Faded Glory of Asbury Park." *Backstreets Digest* 2.258 (August 18).

Goldspiel, Jules. 1993. "Subject: The casuals." *Backstreets Digest* 2.136 (May 8).

Joergensen, Jens Baek. 1992. "Subject: Boston Garden, 12/14, setlist." *Backstreets Digest* 1.276 (December 15).

Kieltyka, David. 1993a. "Subject: Atlantic City Q's." *Backstreets Digest* 2.312 (October 4).

———. 1993b. "Subject: Reason, Belief, Etc." *Backstreets Digest* 2.327 (October 18).

Kilmer, Jen. 1995. "Subject: Me and Melissa on Bruce." *Luckytown Digest* 2.155 (March 24).

Lewis, John. 1992. "Subject: Boston 12/14 setlist." *Backstreets Digest* 1.276 (December 15).

Lipsky, Steve. 1995. "Subject: Re BUSA." *Luckytown Digest* 2.437 (December 19).

Louis. 1993. "Subject: lyrics." *Backstreets Digest* 2.348 (November 2).

Marsh, Dave. 1995. "Subject: Peter Gabriel, James Taylor . . . ?" *Luckytown Digest* 2.183 (April 18).

Maynard, John. 1995. "Subject: Recent Debates." *Luckytown Digest* 2.188 (April 23).

Mc, Kevin. 1995. "I am a Patriot." *Luckytown Digest* 2.431 (December 16).

McCann, Barry. 1995. "Subject: Bruce, Race, and Universality." *Luckytown Digest* 2.189 (April 23).

McCrae, Gus. 1995. quoted in "Greatest Hits and Mass Appeal." *Luckytown Digest* 2.18 (January 15).

McDonald, Marc F. 1995. "Subject: One more thing." *Luckytown Digest* 2.24 (January 16).

McLean, Flynn. 1995a. "Subject: Secret Garden and 30 Days Out." *Luckytown Digest* 2.125 (March 2).

——. 1995b. "Subject: This Foreign Listeners Thing." *Luckytown Digest* 2.191 (April 23).

Mills, Daniel J. 1995. "Subject: Re Am I really a fan?" *Luckytown Digest* 2.172 (April 7).

Moolman, Riaan. 1995. "Subject: Bruce relevant to all." *Luckytown Digest* 2.186 (April 20).

Palasti, Gabor. 1993a. "Subject: Various Subjects." *Backstreets Digest* 2.324 (October 15).

——. 1995b. "[No Subject]." *Luckytown Digest* 2.185 (April 19).

Papleonardos, Chris T. 1993. "Subject: Casual Fans." *Backstreets Digest* 2.133 (May 5).

——. 1995. "Subject: Bruce and African-Americans." *Luckytown Digest* 2.185 (April 19).

Powell, Gareth. 1995. "Subject: Secret Garden." *Luckytown Digest* 2.124 (March 2).

Purlia, John. 1992. "Subject: Re Boston 12/13 setlist." *Backstreets Digest* 1.276 (December 15).

Sanders, Matt. 1995. "Subject: Greatest Hits and mass appeal." *Luckytown Digest* 2.18 (January 15).

Shareshian, Monica. 1993. "Subject: Another local Bruce bit." *Backstreets Digest* 2.92 (March 30).

Shaw, Steve. 1995. "Subject: Re Rock and Roll, and Race." *Luckytown Digest* 2.184 (April 19).

Shaw, Suzy. 1995. "Subject: GH—First Impressions." *Luckytown Digest* 2.134 (March 5).

Slovin, Jeff. 1992. "Subject: Boston 12/14 setlist." *Backstreets Digest* 1.276 (December 15).

Stagl, David. 1995. "Subject: Tickets and Tramps and a Festival." *Luckytown Digest* 2.147 (March 17).

Stinnett, Jason M. 1992. "Subject: Dallas 12/2." *Backstreets Digest* 1.271 (December 11).

Stockinger, Craig. 1996. "Subject: Poll Results." *Luckytown Digest* 3.231 (November 12).

Svoboda, Brian. 1995. "Subject: Brian to Digest: Mellow Out!" *Luckytown Digest* 2.26 (January 17).

West, Susan. 1994. "Subject: Oliver's Story." *Backstreets Digest* 2.371 (November 20).

Wilkie, Gloria. 1995. "Subject: Secret Garden." *Luckytown Digest* 2.130 (March 3).

Yamashita, Paul. 1995. "Subject: BitUSA/Patriotism." *Luckytown Digest* 2.429 (December 15).

Published Sources

Abrahams, Peter. 1995. *The Fan.* New York: Warner Books.

Adorno, Theodor. [1941] 1990. "On Popular Music," in *On Record: Rock, Pop, and the Written Word.* Simon Frith and Andrew Goodwin, eds. New York: Pantheon. 301–319.

American Heritage Dictionary. 1992. Boston: Houghton Mifflin Company.

Anderson, Benedict. 1991. *Imagined Communities: Reflections on the Origin and Spread of Nationalism.* Revised edition. London: Verso.

Ang, Ien. 1985. *Watching Dallas: Soap Opera and the Melodramatic Imagination.* London: Methuen.

Appadurai, Arjun. 1991. "Global Ethnoscapes," in *Recapturing Anthropology.* Richard Fox, ed. Sante Fe: School of American Research Press. 191–210.

Ardner, Edwin. 1986. "Remote Spaces: Some Theoretical Considerations," in *Anthropology at Home*. Anthony Jackson, ed. London: Tavistock Publications. 38–54.

Aronowitz, Stanley. 1993. *Roll Over Beethoven: The Return of Cultural Strife*. Middletown, Conn.: Wesleyan University Press.

Auster, Albert. 1984. *Actresses and Suffragists: Women in the American Theater, 1890-1920*. New York: Praeger.

Babcock, Barbara. 1980. "Signs about Signs: The Semiotics of Self-Reference," *Semiotica* 30, 1–2.

Bacon-Smith, Camille. 1992. *Enterprising Women: Television Fandom and the Creation of Popular Myth*. Philadelphia: University of Pennsylvania Press.

Baker, Bob. 1985. "A Plague on Nouveau Boss Fans." *The Buffalo News* (September 27): pages unknown.

Bakhtin, M. M. 1986. *Speech Genres and Other Late Essays*. Translated by V. W. McGee. Austin: University of Texas Press.

Barglow, Raymond. 1993. *The Crisis of Self in the Age of Information: Computers, Dolphins, and Dreams*. New York: Routledge Press.

Barnhart, Robert K., ed. 1988. *The Barnhart Dictionary of Etymology*. Bronx, N.Y.: H. W. Wilson Co.

Barnouw, Erik, and Catherine E. Kirkland. 1992. "Entertainment," in *Folklore, Cultural Performances and Popular Entertainments: A Communications Centered Handbook*. Richard Bauman, ed. New York: Oxford University Press. 50–52.

Bateson, Gregory. 1972. *Steps to an Ecology of Mind*. New York: Ballantine.

Battaglia, Debbora, ed. 1995a. *Rhetorics of Self-Making*. Berkeley: University of California Press.

———. 1995b. "Fear of Selfing in the American Cultural Imaginary or 'You Are Never Alone with a Clone.'" *American Anthropologist* 97, 672–678.

Baudrillard, Jean. [1968] 1994. "The System of Collecting," in *The Cultures of Collecting*. John Elsner and Roger Cardinal, eds. Cambridge: Harvard University Press. 7–24.

Bauman, Richard. 1977. *Verbal Art as Performance*. Prospect Heights, Ill.: Waveland Press.

———. 1986. *Story, Performance, and Event*. Cambridge: Cambridge University Press.

Baym, Nancy K. 1993. "Interpreting Soap Operas and Creating Community: Inside a Computer-Mediated Fan Culture." *Journal of Folklore Research* 30, 143–176.

Beckford, James A. 1978. "Accounting for Conversion." *British Journal for Sociology* 29, 249–262.

Beeman, William O. 1993. "The Anthropology of Theater and Spectacle." *Annual Reviews in Anthropology* 22, 369–393.

Benjamin, Walter. 1968. "Unpacking My Library," in *Illuminations*. Hanna Arendt, ed. New York: Schocken Books. 59–67.

"Best of Bruce Springsteen Readers' Poll." 1995. *Backstreets* 48, 22–25.

Bettelheim, Bruno. 1982. "Reflections." *The New Yorker* (March 1), 52–93.

Billings, Stephnie. 1987. Letter. *Backstreets* 19, 31.

Biolsi, Thomas. 1995. "The Birth of the Reservation: Making the Modern Individual among the Lakota." *American Ethnologist* 22, 28–53.

Bird, Elizabeth. 1994. "'Is That Me, Baby?': Image, Authenticity, and the Career of Bruce Springsteen." *American Studies* 35, 39–57.

Bloomfield, L. 1933. *Language*. New York: Henry Holt.

Boorstin, Daniel. 1972. *The Image: A Guide to Pseudo-events in America* . New York: Atheneum.

Braudy, Leo. 1986. *The Frenzy of Renown*. New York: Oxford University Press.

Buxton, David. [1983] 1990. "Rock Music, the Star System, and the Rise of Consumerism," in *On Record: Rock, Pop, and the Written Word*. Simon Frith and Andrew Goodwin, eds. New York: Pantheon. 427–440.

"Can You Testify?" 1993. *Backsteets* 42, 18–23.

Carbaugh, Donal. 1988. *Talking American: Cultural Discourse on Donahue*. Norwood, N.J.: Ablex.

Caughey, James. 1984. *Imaginary Social Relations*. Lincoln: University of Nebraska Press.

Cavicchi, Daniel. 1989. "The Critical Stance." Unpublished master's degree thesis, Department of American Studies, State University of New York at Buffalo, 1989.

Clifford, James. 1988. *The Predicament of Culture*. Cambridge: Harvard University Press.

Cosgrove, Jim. 1992. Letter. *Backstreets* 39, 4.

Crafts, Susan D., Daniel Cavicchi, Charles Keil, and the Music in Daily Life Project. 1993. *My Music*. Middletown, Conn.: Wesleyan University Press.

Cross, Charles. 1990. *50 Guaranteed Tips to Great Springsteen Tickets*. Seattle: Backstreets Publishing.

———. 1994. "Brilliant Disguise: An Investigation into Counterfeit Bruce Collectibles." *Backstreets* 12, 20–28.

Cross, Charles, and the editors of *Backstreets*. 1989. *Backstreets: Springsteen, the Man and his Music*. New York: Harmony Books.

Cullen, Jim. 1992. "Bruce Springsteen's Ambiguous Musical Politics in the Reagan Era." *Popular Music* 16, 1–22.

Darnton, Robert. 1984. "Readers Respond to Rousseau: The Fabrication of Romantic Sensitivity," in *The Great Cat Massacre and Other Episodes in French Cultural History*. New York: Vintage Books. 215–256.

———. 1989. "What Is the History of Books?" in *Reading in America: Literature and Social History*. Cathy N. Davidson, ed. Baltimore: Johns Hopkins University Press. 27–52.

DeCordova, Richard. 1991. "The Emergence of the Star System," in *Stardom: Industry of Desire*. Christine Gledhill, ed. New York: Routledge. 17–29.

DesBarres, Pamela. 1988. *I'm with the Band*. New York: Dell Books.

DiNatale, Sal. 1987. Letter. *Backstreets* 22, 30.

Douglas, Jack D., and John Johnson, eds. 1977. *Existential Sociology*. Cambridge: Cambridge University Press.

Dunlop, Charles, and Rob Kling. 1991. "Social Relationships in Electronic Communities," in *Computerization and Controversy*. Charles Dunlop and Rob Kling, eds. New York: Academic Press. 322–329.

Durkheim, Émile. 1964. *The Division of Labor in Society*. New York: Free Press.

Eddy, Chuck. 1988. "If It Feels Good, Do It!" *Creem*, (October). 10–11.

Ewen, Elizabeth. 1980. "City Lights: Immigrant Women and the Rise of the Movies," *Signs* 5 (supplement), S45–S66.

Feinberg, Erin. 1993. Letter. *Backstreets* 44, 5.

Feld, Steven. 1982. *Sound and Sentiment: Birds, Weeping, Poetics, and Song in Kaluli Expression*. Philadelphia: University of Pennsylvania Press.

———. [1984] 1994. "Communication, Music and Speech about Music," in Charles Keil and Steven Feld. *Music Grooves: Essays and Dialogues*. Chicago: University of Chicago Press. 77–95.

———. 1987. "Dialogic Editing: Interpreting How Kaluli Read Sound and Sentiment," *Cultural Anthropology* 2, 190–210.

Fernandez, James. 1986. *Persuasions and Performances*. Bloomington: Indiana University Press.

Finnegan, Ruth. 1989. *The Hidden Musicians: Music-Making in an English Town*. Cambridge: Cambridge University Press.

Fiske, John. 1989. *Understanding Popular Culture*. Boston: Unwin Hyman.

Flanagan, Bill. 1987. *Written in My Soul*. New York: Contemporary Books.

Flanagan, Erik. 1994. "The Shadow World," *Musician*, (September), 36–49, 94–95.

Foucault, Michel. 1986. "The Discourse on Language." Excerpted in *Critical Theory since 1965*. Hazard Adams and Leroy Searle, eds. Tallahassee: Florida State University Press. 148–162.

Fowles, Jib. 1992. *Starstruck: Celebrity Performers and the American Public*. Washington, D.C.: Smithsonian Institution Press.

Frith, Simon. 1981. *Sound Effects: Youth, Leisure, and the Politics of Rock'n'Roll*. New York: Pantheon Press.

———. 1988. "The Real Thing—Bruce Springsteen," in *Music for Pleasure*. New York: Routledge. 94–101.

Galatzer-Levy, Robert M., and Bertram J. Cohler. 1993. *The Essential Other: A Developmental Psychology of the Self*. New York: Basic Books.

Gay, Peter, ed. 1989. *The Freud Reader*. New York: W. W. Norton.

Geertz, Clifford. 1973. *The Interpretation of Cultures*. New York: Basic Books.

———. 1984. "'From the Natives' Point of View': On the Nature of Anthropological Understanding," in *Culture Theory: Essays on Mind, Self, and Emotion*. Richard Shweder and Robert Levine, eds. Cambridge: Cambridge University Press. 123–136.

Gergen, Kenneth. 1993. *The Saturated Self: Dilemmas of Identity in Contemporary Life*. New York: Basic Books.

Ginsberg, Merle. 1985. "The Fans: Springsteen's Followers Are Convinced He's Just Like Them," *Rolling Stone* (October 10), 31–33.

Glassie, Henry. 1982. *Passing the Time in Ballymenone*. Philadelphia: University of Pennsylvania Press.

Goffman, Erving. 1974. *Frame Analysis: An Essay on the Organization of Experience*. Cambridge: Harvard University Press.

Goodwin, Andrew. [1988] 1990. "Sample and Hold: Pop Music in the Digital Age of Reproduction," in *On Record: Rock, Pop, and the Written Word*. Simon Frith and Andrew Goodwin, eds. New York: Pantheon Press. 258–274.

Gorn, Elliot. 1986. *The Manly Art: Bare Knuckle Prize Fighting in America*. Ithaca,N.Y.: Cornell University Press.

Grossberg, Lawrence. 1992a. "The Affective Sensibility of Fandom," *The Adoring Audience: Fan Culture and Popular Media*. Lisa Lewis, ed. New York: Routledge. 50–65.

———. 1992b. *We Gotta Get Out of This Place*. New York: Routledge.

Gumperz, John J. 1971. *Language in Social Groups*. Stanford, Calif.: Stanford University Press.

Gumperz, John J., and Dell Hymes, eds. 1972. *Directions in Sociolinguistics*. New York: Holt, Rinehart & Winston.

Hall, Stuart, and Tony Jefferson, eds. 1976. *Resistance through Rituals.* London: Hutchinson.

Harrison, Ted. 1992. *Elvis People: The Cult of the King.* New York: Harper Collins.

Hastrup, Kirsten. 1986. "Fieldwork among Friends: Ethnographic Exchange within the Northern Civilization," in *Anthropology at Home.* Anthony Jackson, ed. London: Tavistock Publications. 94–108.

Hayano, D. M. 1979. "Auto-Ethnography," *Human Organization* 38, 99–104.

———. 1982. *Poker Faces.* Berkeley: University of California Press.

Hebdige, Dick. [1979] 1991. *Subculture: The Meaning of Style.* New York: Routledge Press.

Heylin, Clinton. 1995. *Bootleg: The Secret History of the Other Recording Industry.* New York: St. Martin's Press.

Hilburn, Robert. 1989. "Out in the Streets," in *Backstreets: Springsteen, the Man and His Music.* Charles Cross, ed. New York: Harmony Books. 77–81.

Holzhauer, Matt. 1993. Letter, *Backstreets* 44, 4.

Hume, David. [1739] 1961. *Treatise on Human Nature.* New York: Doubleday Press.

Humphries, Patrick, and Chris Hunt. 1985. *Blinded by the Light.* New York: Henry Holt.

Hymes, Dell. 1974. *Foundations in Sociolinguistics.* Philadelphia: University of Pennsylvania Press.

James, William. [1890] 1981. *Principles of Psychology, Vol. 1.* Cambridge: Harvard University Press.

———. [1902] 1925. *The Varieties of Religious Experience.* Toronto: Longmans, Green & Co.

Jameson, Frederic. 1979. "Reification and Utopia in Mass Culture," *Social Text* 1, 130–148.

Jay, Martin. 1973. *The Dialectical Imagination: A History of the Frankfurt School and the Institute of Social Research, 1923–1950.* Boston: Little, Brown and Co.

Jenkins, Henry. 1992. *Textual Poachers: Television Fandom and Participatory Culture.* New York: Routledge.

Jensen, Joli. 1990. *Redeeming Modernity.* New York: Sage Publications.

———. 1992. "Fandom as Pathology," in *The Adoring Audience.* Lisa Lewis, ed. New York: Routledge. 9–29.

Jones, Delmos J. 1982. "Toward a Native Anthropology," in *Anthropology for the Eighties.* Johnetta B. Cole, ed. New York: Free Press. 471–482.

Kalčik, Susan. 1975. "Like Ann's Gynecologist or the Time I Was Almost Raped: Personal Narratives in Women's Rap Groups," *Journal of American Folklore* 88, 3–11.

Kammen, Michael. 1991. *Mystic Chords of Memory: The Transformation of Tradition in American Culture.* New York: Knopf.

Keil, Charles. [1966] 1994. "Motion and Feeling through Music," in Charles Keil and Steven Feld. *Music Grooves: Essays and Dialogues.* Chicago, University of Chicago Press. 53–76.

———. [1985] 1994. "People's Music Comparatively," in Charles Keil and Steven Feld. *Music Grooves: Essays and Dialogues.* Chicago: University of Chicago Press. 197–217.

Keil, Charles, and Steven Feld. 1994. "Grooving on Participation," in *Music Grooves: Essays and Dialogues.* Chicago: Chicago University Press. 151–180.

Keith, Jennie. 1982. *Old People, New Lives: Community Creation in a Retirement Residence.* Chicago: University of Chicago Press.

Kiesler, Sara, Jane Siegel, and Timothy McGuire. 1991. "Social Psychological Aspects of Computer-Mediated Communication," in *Computerization and Controversy.* Charles Dunlop and Rob Kling, eds. New York: Academic Press. 330–349.

Koestenbaum, Wayne. 1993. *The Queen's Throat: Opera, Homosexuality, and the Mystery of Desire*. New York: Vintage Press.

Kondo, Dorinne. 1990. *Crafting Selves: Power, Gender, and Discourses of Identity in a Japanese Workplace*. Chicago: University of Chicago Press.

Kotarba, Joseph A., and Andrea Fontana. 1984. *The Existential Self in Society*. Chicago: University of Chicago Press.

Langer, Susan K. 1942. *Philosophy in a New Key*. Cambridge: Harvard University Press.

Lausch, Greg. 1992. Letter, *Backstreets* 40, 5.

Leary, James P. 1977. "White Guys' Stories of the Night Street," *Journal of Folklore Institute* 14, 59–71.

Levine, Lawrence. 1988. *Highbrow/Lowbrow: The Emergence of Cultural Hierarchy in America*. Cambridge: Harvard University Press.

Lifton, Robert Jay. 1993. *The Protean Self*. New York: Basic Books.

Limon, Jose E. 1991. "Representation, Ethnicity, and the Precursory Ethnography: Notes of a Native Anthropologist," in *Recapturing Anthropology*. Richard Fox, ed. Sante Fe, N.M.: School of American Research Press. 115–136.

Lofland, John. 1977. "Becoming a World Saver Revisited," *American Behavioral Scientist* 20, 805–818.

Lofland, John, and Norman Skonovd. 1981. "Conversion Motifs," *Journal for the Scientific Study of Religion* 20, 373–385.

Lofland, John, and Rodney Stark. 1965. "Becoming a World Saver," *American Sociological Review* 30, 862–874.

Lombardi, John. 1988. "St. Boss: The Sanctification of Bruce Springsteen and the Rise of Mass Hip," *Esquire* (December), 139–154.

MacAloon, John. 1984. "Olympic Games and the Theory of Spectacle in Modern Societies," in *Rite, Drama, Festival, Spectacle: Rehearsals toward a Theory of Cultural Performance*. John MacAloon, ed. Philadelphia: University of Pennsylvania Press. 241–280.

Marciano, Jennie. 1994. Letter, *Backstreets* 45, 4.

Marcus, George E., and Michael M. J. Fischer. 1986. *Anthropology as Cultural Critique*. Chicago: University of Chicago Press.

Marsella, Anthony, George DeVos, and Francis Hsu, eds. 1985. *Culture and Self: Asian and American Perspectives*. New York: Tavistock Publications.

Marsh, Dave. 1979. *Born to Run: The Bruce Springsteen Story*. New York: Dell Books.

———. 1987. *Glory Days*. New York: Pantheon Press.

Mascarenhas-Keyes, Stella. 1986. "The Native Anthropologist: Constraints and Strategies in Research," in *Anthropology at Home*. Anthony Jackson, ed. London: Tavistock Publications. 180–195.

McConachie, Bruce. 1990. "Pacifying Theatrical Audiences, 1820–1900," in *For Fun and Profit*. Richard Butsch, ed. Philadelphia: Temple University Press. 49–62.

Meyer, Leonard. 1956. *Emotion and Meaning in Music*. Chicago: Chicago University Press.

Modell, Arnold. 1993. *The Private Self*. Cambridge: Harvard University Press.

Moore, Sally Falk, and Barbara G. Myerhoff. 1975. *Symbol and Politics in Communal Ideology: Cases and Question*. Ithaca, N.Y.: Cornell University Press.

Morse, Steve. 1992. "Wolf, on Home Turf, Gets Boost from Boss," *Boston Globe* (December 18), 62.

Mukerji, Chandra, and Michael Schudson. 1991. "Introduction: Rethinking Popular Culture," in *Rethinking Popular Culture: Contemporary Perspectives in Cultural Studies*. Chandra Mukerji and Michael Schudson, eds. Berkeley: University of California Press. 1–61.

Munson, Ronald. 1993. *Fan Mail*. New York: Dutton.

Myers, Fred. 1991. "Representing Culture: The Production of Discourse(s) for Aboriginal Acrylic Paintings," *Cultural Anthropology* 6, 26–62.

Narayan, Kirin. 1993. "How Native Is a Native Anthropologist?" *American Anthropologist* 95, 671–686.

Nattiez, Jean-Jacques. 1990. *Music and Discourse: Toward a Semiology of Music*. Princeton, N.J.: Princeton University Press.

Oates, Wayne E. 1978. "Conversion: Sacred and Secular," in *Conversion: Perspectives on Personal and Social Transformation*. Walter Conn, ed. New York: Alba House. 149–168.

Ortner, Sherry. 1991. "Reading America: Preliminary Notes on Class and Culture," in *Recapturing Anthropology*. Richard Fox, ed. Sante Fe, N.M.: School of American Research Press. 163–189.

Oxford English Dictionary (2nd edition). 1989. London: Oxford University Press.

Partridge, Eric. 1956. *A Dictionary of Slang and Unconventional English*. London: Routledge and Kegan Paul, 1956.

Pearce, Susan. 1992. *Museums, Objects, and Collections: A Cultural Study*. Washington, D.C.: Smithsonian Institutions Press.

Peiss, Kathy. 1986. *Cheap Amusements: Working Women and Leisure in Turn-of-the-Century New York*. Philadelphia: Temple University Press.

Penley, Constance. 1992. "Feminism, Psychoanalysis, and the Study of Popular Culture," in *Cultural Studies*. Lawrence Grossberg et al., eds. New York: Routledge. 479–500.

Perrolle, Judith A. 1991. "Conversations and Trust in Computer Interfaces," in *Computerization and Controversy*. Charles Dunlop and Rob Kling, eds. New York: Academic Press. 350–363.

Pfiel, Fred. 1993. "Rock Incorporated: Plugging in to Axl and Bruce," *Michigan Quarterly Review* 32, 534–571.

Polkinghorne, Donald E. 1988. *Narrative Knowing and the Human Sciences*. Albany: SUNY Press, 1988.

Pratt, Ray. 1990. *Rhythm and Resistance: Explorations in the Political Uses of Popular Music*. New York: Praeger.

Rader, Benjamin G. 1983. *American Sports: From the Age of Folk Games to the Age of Spectators*. Englewood Cliffs, N.J.: Prentice-Hall.

Radway, Janice. 1984. *Reading the Romance: Women, Patriarchy, and Popular Literature*. Chapel Hill: University of North Carolina Press.

Random House Dictionary of American Slang, Vol. 1, A–G. 1994. New York: Random House.

Rheims, M. 1980. *The Glorious Obsession*. London: Souvenir Press.

Riesman, David. [1950] 1990. "Listening to Popular Music," in *On Record: Rock, Pop, and the Written Word*. Simon Frith and Andrew Goodwin, eds. New York: Pantheon. 5–13.

Riess, Steven A. 1980. *Touching Base: Professional Baseball and American Culture in the Progressive Era*. Westport, Conn.: Greenwood Press.

Rosaldo, Renato. 1989. *Culture and Truth*. Boston: Beacon Press.

Sapir, Edward. 1985. "Group," in *Selected Writings of Edward Sapir*. David G. Mandelbaum, ed. Berkeley: University of California Press. 357–364.

Sarbin, Theodore R. 1986. *Narrative Psychology: The Storied Nature of Human Conduct*. New York: Praeger.

Schechner, Richard. 1977. *Essays on Performance Theory, 1970-1976*. New York: Drama Book Specialists.

———. 1985. *Between Theater and Anthropology*. Philadelphia: University of Pennsylvania Press.

———. 1988. *Performance Theory*. New York: Routledge.

Schickel, Richard. 1985. *Intimate Strangers: The Culture of Celebrity*. Garden City, N.J.: Doubleday.

Schruers, Fred. [1981] 1987. "Bruce Springsteen and the Secret of the World," in *What a Long, Strange Trip It's Been*. New York: Friendly Press, 1987. 352–361.

Seely, Hart. 1985. "A Steenian Tells Why," *Syracuse Post-Standard* (January 25), D-1, D-12.

Shafer, Roy. 1992. *Retelling a Life*. New York: Basic Books.

Shank, Barry. 1994. *Dissonant Identities: The Rock'n'Roll Scene in Austin, Texas*. Middletown, Conn.: Wesleyan University Press.

Shepherd, John. 1977. "Media, Social Process, and Music," in *Whose Music? A Sociology of Musical Languages*. John Shepherd et al., eds. New Brunswick, N.J.: Transactions. 7–51.

———. 1991. *Music as Social Text*. Cambridge, U.K.: Polity Press.

Skeen, Paul. 1993. Letter, *Backstreets* 44, 5.

Smith, Patricia. 1992. "Surfing with Springsteen: The Boss' Music Marathon at the Garden Sends Fans into a Frenzy," *Boston Globe* (December 15th), 67, 70.

Spence, Donald. 1982. *Narrative Truth and Historical Truth*. New York: Norton.

Stahl, Sandra K. 1989. *Literary Folkloristics and the Personal Narrative*. Bloomington: Indiana University Press.

Staiger, Janet. 1991. "Seeing Stars," in *Stardom: Industry of Desire*. Christine Gledhill, ed. New York: Routledge. 3–15.

Starbuck, E. D. 1899. *Psychology of Religion*. New York: Charles Scribner's Sons.

Stark, Rodney, and William Bainbridge. 1980. "Networks of Faith: Interpersonal Bonds and Recruitment to Cults and Sects," *American Journal of Sociology* 85, 1376–1395.

Stewart, Susan. 1993. *On Longing: Narratives of the Miniature, the Gigantic, the Souvenir, the Collection*. Durham, N.C.: Duke University Press.

Stone, Allucquere Rosanne. 1991. "Will the Real Body Please Stand Up? Boundary Stories about Virtual Cultures," in *Cyberspace: First Steps*. Michael Benedikt, ed. Cambridge: MIT Press.

Taylor, Helen. 1989. *Scarlett's Women: Gone with the Wind and Its Female Fans*. New Brunswick, N.J.: Rutgers University Press.

Taylor, Paul. 1985. *Popular Music since 1955: A Critical Guide to the Literature*. Boston: G. K. Hall & Company.

Tedlock, Dennis. 1983. *The Spoken Word and the Work of Interpretation*. Philadelphia: University of Pennsylvania Press.

Thornton, Richard H. 1962. *An American Glossary*. New York: Frederick Ungar.

Titon, Jeff. 1988. *Powerhouse for God: Speech, Chant, and Song in an Appalachian Baptist Church*. Austin: University of Texas Press.

Tomas, David. 1991. "Old Rituals for New Space: Rites de Passage and William Gibson's Cultural Model of Cyberspace," in *Cyberspace: First Steps*. Michael Benedikt, ed. Cambridge: MIT Press.

Tönnies, Ferdinand. 1973. *Community and Society*. New York: Harper & Row.

Trinajstick, Blanche, ed. 1993. *The Fan Club Directory*. Pueblo, Colo.: National Association of Fan Clubs.

Turner, Victor. 1974. *Dramas, Fields, and Metaphors*. Ithaca, N.Y.: Cornell University Press.

————. 1988. *The Anthropology of Performance*. New York: PAJ Publications.

Turner, Victor W., and Edward M. Bruner, eds. 1986. *The Anthropology of Experience*. Urbana: University of Illinois Press.

Tyler, Steven. 1987. *The Unspeakable*. Chicago: University of Chicago Press.

Ullman, Chana. 1989. *The Transformed Self: The Psychology of Religious Conversion*. New York: Plenum Press.

Van Gelder, Lindsy. 1985. "The Strange Case of the Electronic Lover," *MS* (October), 94+.

Van Maanen, John. 1988. *Tales of the Field*. Chicago: University of Chicago Press.

Little Steven Van Zandt. 1984. *Voice of America*. LP. EMI America Records ST-17120.

Vermorel, Judy, and Fred Vermorel. 1985. *Starlust: The Secret Life of Fans*. London: W. H. Allen & Co.

————. 1989. *Fandemonium! The Book of Fan Cults and Dance Crazes*. London: Omnibus Press.

Wallace, Irving. 1974. *The Fan Club*. New York: Simon & Schuster.

Wallerstein, Immanuel. 1991. *Unthinking Social Science*. Cambridge, U.K.: Polity Press.

Walser, Robert. 1994. *Running with the Devil: Power, Gender, and Madness in Heavy Metal Music*. Middletown, Conn.: Wesleyan University Press.

Watson, Graham. 1991. "Rewriting Culture," in *Recapturing Anthropology*. Richard Fox, ed. Sante Fe, N.M.: School for American Research Press. 73–92.

We Are the World. 1985. LP. Columbia USA 40043.

Weber, Heidi, and Karsten Andersen. 1992. Letter, *Backstreets* 41, 5.

Weber, Max. 1968. *Economy and Society, Vol. 1*. New York: Bedminster Press.

White, Geoffrey, and John Kirkpatrick, eds. 1985. *Person, Self, and Experience*. Berkeley: University of California Press.

Wikan, Unni. 1990. *Managing Turbulent Hearts*. Chicago: University of Chicago.

————. 1991. "Toward an Experience-Near Anthropology," *Cultural Anthropology* 6, 285–305.

Windsor, John. 1994. "Identity Parades," in *The Cultures of Collecting*. John Elsner and Roger Cardinal, eds. Cambridge: Harvard University Press. 49–67.

Index